# SPANISH LAND GRANTS in FLORIDA

*- Volume #4 -*

( Confirmed Claims: K-R )


By:
Works Progress Administration

Southern Historical Press, Inc.
Greenville, South Carolina

This volume was reproduced from
An 1941 edition located in the
Publisher's private library,
Greenville, South Carolina

All rights reserved. No part of this publication may be reproduced,
stored in a retrieval system, transmitted in any form, posted
on to the web in any form or by any means without
the prior written permission of the publisher.

Please direct all correspondence and orders to:

www.southernhistoricalpress.com
or
SOUTHERN HISTORICAL PRESS, Inc.
PO BOX 1267
375 West Broad Street
Greenville, SC   29601
southernhistoricalpress@gmail.com

Originally published: Jacksonville, FL. 1941
Reprinted by: Southern Historical Press, Inc.
Greenville, SC
ISBN # 978-1-63914-003-9
All rights Reserved.
*Printed in the United States of America*

PREFACE

The Historical Records Survey program operates as a series of state-wide projects in the several states under the Research and Records Section, Division of Professional and Service Projects, Work Projects Administration. The program was organized in Florida in 1936 under the national direction of Dr. Luther H. Evans. On March 1, 1940, Dr. Evans left to become Director of the Legislative Reference Section of the Library of Congress and was succeeded by Sargent B. Child.

The survey program includes an inventory of state, county, municipal and church archives, of American imprints and of manuscript depositories and collections. In keeping with its object to make hitherto inaccessible material available to students, the survey program in Florida undertook the project of translating and transcribing the archives in Florida known as the Spanish Land Grants, which required practically three years to complete. The work was edited and the Introduction written in our office by Dr. Louise Biles Hill, Manuscripts Editor. The Unconfirmed Claims appear in Volume I, the Confirmed Claims in the four succeeding volumes.

Our appreciation is due to the professional historians of our State Advisory Committee and to students of Spanish-American history outside the state, who from its inception have been interested in the Spanish Land Grants project and have given freely of their advice and counsel. Our thanks are due also to the Honorable Nathan Mayo, Commissioner of Agriculture, through whose courtesy our translators were given desk room in the Field Note Division, Tallahassee, during the time in which they were engaged in the task of translating the Spanish land grants.

Publications of the Florida Historical Records Survey, a list of which will be found at the end of this volume, are issued for free distribution to public and institutional libraries. Requests for information concerning the publications or the work of the Survey in Florida should be addressed to the State Supervisor, Historical Records Survey, 49 West Duval St., Jacksonville, Florida.

                                        Sue A. Mahorner
                                        State Supervisor
                                        Florida Historical Records Survey

Jacksonville, Florida
March 1941

CONTENTS

| | Page |
|---|---|
| Preface | |
| Introduction | i |
| Governors of Florida from 1763 to 1821 | lxi |
| Surveyors of Florida from 1763 to 1821 | lxiii |
| Land claims K | 1 |
| Land claims L | 41 |
| Land claims M | 75 |
| Land claims N | 135 |
| Land claims O | 147 |
| Land claims P | 159 |
| Land claims Q | 229 |
| Land claims R | 231 |
| Index--Personal Names | 259 |
| Index--Place Names | 273 |
| Errata P | 228 |

## INTRODUCTION

The Unconfirmed Claims which form Volume I of <u>Spanish Land Grants in Florida</u> are the records of those claims which after the cession of Florida the United States authorities found invalid. Confirmed Claims make up the remaining volumes of the series.

The work of translation and transcription of the Spanish land grants was done under the supervision of Professor E. V. Gage, former head of the Department of Modern Languages at Florida State College for Women, who was assisted by two workers of Spanish descent.

The original documents of foolscap size comprise a linear footage of eleven feet and five inches. The work of translation and transcription required about three years. Every scrap of writing was examined and included and every name mentioned--whether governor, grantee, attorney, witness, register, notary, surveyor, or chain bearer. The spelling in the original manuscripts has been preserved. The form in which the claims appear in the present volume is that adopted by the translator and follows somewhat closely the form in which the manuscripts are now filed. Each separate document is numbered and is followed by S or E to indicate whether the language is Spanish or English. Notations of governors, registers, and notaries on margins are indicated, and the decrees of the United States Boards of Commissioners who examined and passed upon the validity of the claims are included whenever the decrees were found in the original documents. Missing decrees may be found in <u>American State Papers, Public Lands</u>, references to which are given in all but a very few instances.[1]

While practically every claim appears in some form in the above mentioned publication, the great majority are shown as mere abstracts in tabular form, without the supporting evidence which gives to the present volume its interest and value. For example, James Darley[2] applies for a land grant, promising to import 50 slaves from Africa. He sends a schooner and sloop for them. The sloop is caught in a storm off the coast of Santo Domingo, the slaves revolt, murder some of the crew, and flee into the interior. Darley is under the necessity of going after them, retrieving his property, and proving it before the courts, which requires two years. Such stories appear in print for the first time in this series.

Whenever a full transcription of a claim is given in American State Papers, the translator has made that claim correspondingly brief that there may be no undue repetition.

The value of the translation of the Spanish land grants and their supporting documents is also enhanced by the inclusion of geographical data such as the names and locations of creeks, roads, and Indian trails, as well as basic information on the size, location and basis of each claim, all of which, it is hoped, will be found to be important social and economic data on both the English occupation of Florida (1763-83)

---

1. In those cases which do not appear in American State Papers the claims were substantiated neither by documents nor by witnesses.
2. See Vol. I, D 4.

and the second Spanish occupation (1783-1821).

For convenience the Gales & Seaton and the Duff Green editions of American State Papers, Public Lands, are indicated by the initials G&S and DG respectively. A list of the governors of East and West Florida from 1763 to 1821 and the names of the surveyors and their deputies for the same period are included.

## THE SPANISH ARCHIVES

Archives in Tallahassee consist of dossiers containing the papers filed in evidence before the United States Boards of Commissioners; books or record containing the minutes of the Boards; transcripts of original papers and translations of some of the transcripts; maps, plats, and surveys; and a large file of untranslated Spanish documents of a miscellaneous character labeled "Spanish Protocols, 1804-19", consisting of wills, deeds, titles, testimony, and bills of sale. Many documents for claims in West Florida are unaccountably missing; the translator often found dossiers which contained only a survey and a certificate from the Tallahassee land office for a patent.

Each separate land claim with its supporting documents is encased in a manila jacket on the outside of which appear the name of the claimant, his number within the letter of the alphabet in which his name belongs, the number of acres claimed, disposition of the claim, and page reference to American State Papers.[1]

---

1. This systematic arrangement was made ca.1900 by Dr. S. B. Chapin, chief clerk of the surveyor-general's office, in R. L. Scarlett's administration.--Vol. II, C 27.

1

Documents within a jacket form a dossier of 1 piece to as many as 81 pieces. Especially is the number of documents large if the claim has been through the superior court of East or West Florida, to the Supreme Court of the United States and by it remanded to the court of origin. A dossier may, therefore, contain: (1) a petition, or memorial to a governor for land; (2) the governor's order for information concerning the petitioner; (3) a list of members of the family and slaves, with their ages; (4) a certificate of service from the petitioner's former captain; (5) a grant by a governor, by the intendant of the army, or by the captain-general of Cuba and the Two Floridas, or, if an English grant, by a governor of East or West Florida or the British Privy Council; (6) attest of the government secretary or of the Havana College of Notaries, or, if an English grant, the attest of the recorder in West Florida or of David Yeats (recorder) in East Florida; (7) attest by the United States Trade Commissioner in Havana of copies of documents in Cuban archives required by the United States Boards of Commissioners if the grant was made by a Spanish official in Cuba, or attest by the United States Minister to Great Britain if the grant was made by the Council during the British occupation; (8) fiat of the English governor and attorney general in Florida; (9) warrant or precept or order of survey; (10) signed plats or unfinished plats, unsigned and without date; (11) testimony that conditions of the grant were or were not fulfilled; (12) lease and release,

---

1. The term dossier rather than its Spanish equivalent, *expediente*, having been employed by the translator is continued in the published volumes

under the English law, by which property was sometimes leased one day for so many shillings a year and sold to the same party the following day for so many pounds sterling "and one peppercorn when legally demanded"; (13) instructions to notaries at a distance for taking testimony of witnesses; (14) affidavit of character and tenure; (15) deeds of sale, gifts, wills, bequests, exchanges; (16) reports on auctions of land; (17) formal applications to the United States Boards of Commissioners for recognition of the claim and the decree of the commissioners, or proceedings of United States courts; (18) translations and copies of documents from Spanish archives in the United States or in Cuba.[1]

American court papers within a dossier are bound together with tape, a clip, narrow ribbon, or pins. The pieces in a large Spanish dossier are usually stitched with linen thread; in the smaller ones they are pasted together or attached by seals.

The documents described are filed in steel cabinets in the vault of the Field Note Division of the Florida Department of Agriculture in the capitol at Tallahassee where they are well protected from dust, vermin and fire. They have not always been so protected. Due to the ravages of vermin, highly acid ink, much handling and undesirable methods of filing in the past, they are exceedingly fragile and some are undecipherable.

The path of the Spanish land grant archives in reaching a permanent home in Tallahassee was a devious one. The second article of the

---

1. See Vol. I, A 9.

treaty of February 22, 1819, providing for the annexation of Florida to the United States required that the archives and documents relating directly to the property and sovereignty of that territory be left in possession of officials of the United States. Two years prior to Spain's relinquishment of the Floridas a large number of such records were removed to Havana. Even after the transfer Spanish officials continued to remove documents contrary to the provisions of the treaty until prohibited from doing so by officials of the United States. A determined effort was made by the United States Department of State to have these papers returned. Six agents--Colonel James Grant Forbes, Captain James Riddle, Judge Thomas Randall, Honorable Daniel P. Cook, General R. K. Call, and Jeremy Robinson--were sent to Havana over a period extending from 1821 to 1834 in special missions for this purpose. But each agent was prevented from achieving results by delays and corrupt practices on the part of Spanish officials and American land interests. Finally a total of 45 documents were returned, but they proved to be almost worthless.[1]

The following account of the early history of the documents in East Florida[2] was given by Antonio Alvarez in testimony in a suit in the superior court of East Florida in 1833: The archives were forcibly taken from the Spanish secretary's office in St. Augustine by American authority at the time of the cession and were stored at the old customs house. A

---

1. A. J. Hanna, "Diplomatic Missions of the United States to Cuba to Secure the Spanish Archives of Florida", in manuscript.
2. The provinces of East and West Florida were established and the dividing line fixed as the Apalachicola River by the King of England in the Proclamation of Oct. 7, 1763.

commission of five, appointed to examine them and select those claimed by the United States under the treaty, made a list of the bundles but did not inventory the papers. Three of the members of the commission were (Patrick?) Lynch, William Reynolds, and Anthelm Gay. They stored the papers in an office "in the lower part of a building now occupied as a court house," where they were cared for by (Edmund?) Law, (Lawyer and Notary). The papers next went to (James S.?) Tingle, (later Clerk of the Circuit Court?), and in 1823 to William Reynolds, who the previous year, was appointed Keeper of the Public Archives by the Governor and the legislature meeting in Pensacola. Some of the papers while in the possession of Reynolds were delivered to Dr. (Edward R.) Gibson and Dr. (W. H.) Simmons. From Reynolds the papers passed to (Thomas?) Murphy, and were delivered to Alvarez himself in 1829 (as Keeper of the Public Archives), in boxes, by the U. S. marshal. Alvarez also received an inventory made by Reynolds himself.[1] Alvarez seems to have been mistaken with reference to the role of the state in the appointment of keepers. In 1822 the Territorial Council passed an Act creating the offices of Keepers of the Public Archives, appointments to be made by the governor. On July 3, 1823, the Act was amended. On January 1, 1825, when there was a blanket repeal of a number of territorial laws, the Act of 1822 was continued in force, but on November 23, 1828, it was repealed.[2] On the

---

1. G&S, VIII, 271-273. For sketch of Alvarez' services to the Spanish government, see Vol. II, A 7.
2. Territorial Acts, 1822, pp. 64-67; Ibid., 1823, pp. 117-118; Ibid., 1825, p. 303; Ibid., 1828, p. 208.

other hand, the records show that on April 5, 1823, William Reynolds was notified by the U. S. Secretary of State of his appointment as commissioner to have charge of the archives of East Florida, with Antonio Alvarez as assistant. By presidential appointment these two were superseded the next year by Edward R. Gibson and W. H. Simmons, also appointed by the President.[1]

On March 3, 1825, Congress created the offices of Keepers of the Public Archives, to be located in St. Augustine and Pensacola.[2] To the East Florida office William Reynolds was restored by presidential appointment, with Antonio Alvarez again as his assistant.[3] In 1826 Alvarez was appointed Keeper and held the office until it was abolished in 1848.[4]

Those archives for West Florida which had not been sent to Havana were taken in charge by General Andrew Jackson at the time of the exchange of flags and were for some time handled in much the same way as the East Florida documents. Whether or not Joseph E. Caro filled the office in Pensacola from the beginning, he was Keeper of the Public Archives in 1827[5] and seems to have held the office as a Federal appointee until it was abolished. He was then appointed by the state.

---

1. DG, III, 772; Minutes of the U. S. Board of Coms. for E. Fla.--*Ibid.*, IV, 290. The appointment of new commissioners may have been the result of the charges which Alexander Hamilton made against Reynolds and Alvarez in 1824.--*Infra.*, pp. 44, 45.
2. U. S. Stat. at Large, IV, 126-127.
3. Minutes of the U. S. Board of Coms. for E. Fla.--DG, IV, 280.
4. A photograph of Alvarez' commission, signed by John Quincy Adams as President and Henry Clay as Secretary of State, hangs on the wall of the "Oldest House" in St. Augustine. The original is owned by Mrs. Reyes of St. Augustine, who had it from a relative, Geronimo Llambias, who was the son of a sister of Alvarez.--Information supplied by Miss Emily Wil- of St. Augustine.
5. See Vol. II, B 41, par. 1.

Certified copies of the Spanish documents and sometimes the originals were used by the Boards of Commissioners and with other papers were by law turned over to the respective Keepers when the Boards and their successors, the Registers and Receivers, had completed the work of adjudicating land claims.[1]

In 1844 Congress raised the question of dispensing with the offices of Keepers of the Public Archives in Florida and transferring the records to the office of the Commissioner of the General Land Office or to some public office in the Territory of Florida. The committee on public lands reported adversely and the resolution was tabled.[2] Four years later, however, in a deficiency appropriation, the offices were abolished,[3] and on October 16, 1848, the Secretary of the Treasury through the Commissioner of the General Land Office instructed Antonio Alvarez and Joseph E. Caro, Keepers for East and West Florida respectively, to make schedules in duplicate of the archives in their possession and deliver, each, one of the schedules and the archives to Robert Butler, United States Surveyor-General for Florida, whose office was in St. Augustine, retaining one schedule signed by the Surveyor-General as a receipt.[4]

Neither of the late Keepers complied and on May 7, 1849, Commissioner Young of the General Land Office instructed Benjamin A. Putnam, who had

---

1. U. S. Stat. at Large, IV, 126, 202-203, 204, 285, 406.
2. Report No. 140, H. of R., 28th Cong., 1 sess.
3. U. S. Stat. at Large, IX, 215.
4. Richard M. Young, Com. of Gen. Land Off., to Robert Butler.--"Letters from Commissioner," Vol. V, 1847-1849, p. 505, in Field Note Div., Dept. of Ag., Tallahassee.

succeeded Butler,[1] to demand the archives for East Florida from Alvarez.[2] As for the West Florida archives, the Commissioner stated that he would instruct the clerk of the United States district court at Pensacola to demand and receive them from Caro and hold them at Pensacola until either the surveyor-general should be ordered by the Department of the Interior, which now had charge of the matter, to take possession of them or until some other disposition should be made under the fifth section of the Act of Congress of March 3, 1849. This Act, making appropriations for the civil and diplomatic expenses of the government, directed, "That whenever it shall be shown to the President of the United States that the State of Florida has by law provided for the safe custody of the public archives, which were formerly kept at St. Augustine and Pensacola, it shall be lawful for him to cause to be delivered to duly authorized officers of the state, such of the archives as do not relate to grants of land which remain unconfirmed or unsurveyed, provided that the President of the United States may suspend the execution of this provision, if in his judgment the public interest requires it."[3]

The difference in the disposition proposed at this time by the Commissioner for the East Florida archives and those in West Florida was probably due in part to the fact that the former were in a "safe building, the property of the government," as stated by the Commissioner in his

---

1. Ibid., p. 557.
2. Ibid., pp. 583-587.
3. Ibid.; U. S. Stat. at Large, IX, 370.

letter of October 16, 1848, which building in all probability was Government House, where the Board of Commissioners had held its sessions. The Commissioner authorized that the office of the archives should, after the delivery, be considered a part of the surveyor-general's office.

Another and probably a stronger reason for not insisting upon bringing the West Florida archives to St. Augustine as at first proposed was the evident opposition of state authorities to the plan. On January 11, 1849, the Florida legislature provided by law for offices for the Spanish Archives at St. Augustine and Pensacola, the Governor and Senate to appoint the Keepers for a term of two years. As soon as Congress should provide for transferring to the state the Spanish records and documents "which are now, or which have been, in the office of the Keepers of the public archives in the said cities of St. Augustine and Pensacola," the Keepers to be appointed under state law were "to ask for, demand and receive from the United States the records . . . which now are or have been in the office" in East and West Florida.[1]

On January 15, 1849, Joseph E. Caro was commissioned Keeper of the West Florida Spanish Archives by the state for a term of two years.[2] An act of the legislature in 1861 authorized Filo E. de la Rua, Clerk of the Circuit Court of Escambia County, "to hold, exercise and perform the duties of the office of Keeper of the Spanish Archives at the City of

---

1. Florida Acts, 1849, Ch. 281.
2. "Commission Record," Book D, p. 362, in office of Sec. of State, Tallahassee.

Pensacola, to which said office he has heretofore been appointed by the Governor and General Assembly of this State."[1]

In Ordinance Number 20 the Sesession Convention on January 1, 1861, abolished certain Federal offices and ordained "that the Surveyor-General of the late Federal Government be instructed to deliver over to the register of Public Lands at St. Augustine all the papers and property appertaining to said office, . . . "[2] After the war the Constitutional Convention, on October 28, 1865, repealed the ordinances of the Secession Convention, including the one mentioned above.[3]

According to instructions of Federal authority, the archives for East Florida were delivered by Alvarez to the surveyor-general in St. Augustine on June 5, 1849, and on June 7, 1849, the surveyor-general reported the matter to Commissioner Young, stating that in accord with instructions he had had the files and furniture which belonged to Alvarez appraised. A requisition for $122 was issued in favor of Alvarez by the Commissioner.[4]

On June 22, 1869, Joseph S. Wilson, Commissioner for the General Land Office, Washington, instructed M. L. Stearns of Quincy, Florida, newly appointed surveyor-general for the state, to remove to Tallahassee

---

1. Florida Acts, 1861, Ch. 1296, sec. 1.
2. Journal of the Proceedings of the Convention of the People of Florida. . . . 1861 (Tallahassee, 1861), reprinted (Jacksonville, 1928), p. 119.
3. Harry B. Skillman, Comp., The Compiled General Laws of Florida, 1927 (Atlanta, 1929), p. 163.
4. B. A. Putnam to Commissioner Young.--"Letters of Surveyor-General," 1849-1853, Vol. VIII, p. 10. Reply of Commissioner, "Letters from Commissioner," Vol. V, p. 641.

the surveyor-general's office then at St. Augustine, "the location of the office prior to the commencement of our late domestic difficulties in 1861." Seven days later the surveyor-general reported that he had arrived in Tallahassee on the 27th in his official capacity. Instructed to obtain from U. S. District Attorney H. Bisbee, Jr., the Spanish archives stored in St. Augustine, Stearns leanred that H. Bisbee had never had them in his possession and had no knowledge of them. Stearns found them in the custody of J. H. Goss, Collector of customs, Port of St. Augustine, who turned them over to him. There were seven large boxes but no invoice.[1]

When in 1907 the Federal government made known its intention to abolish the office of surveyor-general, a state law directed the Commissioner of Agriculture to take charge of all field notes, surveys, maps, plats, papers and records, a part of which were those pertaining to Spanish land grants, and created the Field Note Division as a depository.[2]

## BRITISH LAND GRANTS IN FLORIDA

By the Treaty of Paris which in 1763 ended the Seven Years War Spain ceded to Great Britain the province of Florida. In the war with Spain during the American Revolution, Great Britain lost West Florida to Spain and in 1783 ceded to her both Floridas. In the twenty years

---

1. "Letters from Commissioner", 1869-1873, Vol. IX, pp. 3-4; "Letters of Sur.-Gen.", 1869-1881, Vol. XI, p. 3; Stearns to Wilson, Ibid., p. 9.
2. Florida Acts, Ch. 5611, No. 16, Acts of 1907, approved May 22; Twenty-fifth Biennial Report of the Department of Agriculture of the State of Florida: Land and Field Note Division. . . . 1936-1938. Tallahassee, July 1, 1938.

of British occupation the government made rapid progress in colonization, granting thousands of acres of land. The treaty of 1763 and instructions to British governors promised to Spanish subjects recognition of all authentic titles to immovable property. To those who wished to remain in Florida the British government offered liberty in their Catholic religion. Those who preferred to emigrate were given eighteen months in which to dispose of their property, provided they sold to British subjects. There was no difficulty over private property in St. Augustine, but when Jesse Fish and John Gordon acquired ten million acres of land to dispose of for Spanish citizens, in addition to the property in St. Augustine, the British government disallowed the sale. The British government felt that the Spanish civilian population had been too small to have acquired authentic titles to that amount of land.[1] These lands were later granted to British subjects.

In line with their usual policy toward the Indians the British in 1765 made a treaty with them in which a definite boundary was fixed. By the terms of the treaty the area south of St. Marys River and east of the St. Johns River, together with the entire coast line, was opened

---

1. Charles L. Mowat, *East Florida as a British Province, 1763-1764*, Ph. D. thesis in University of Minnesota Library, 1939, pp. 6, 336. Emigration was encouraged by the Spanish government which provided settlements for its subjects in Cuba and sent a commissary to Florida to make valuation of property favorable to the owners, the government making up the difference between the valuation and the price receoved.--*Ibid.*, p. 24.

to colonization.[1]

Land in Florida was offered to settlers by the British government under the so-called "family right", to be granted by the councils of East and West Florida. The head of a family could obtain 100 acres and for each member of the family, whether white or black, 50 acres. If a family could cultivate more, a patent for an additional amount up to 1,000 acres would be issued, with other grants if conditions were fulfilled. The number of acres to be cleared or drained each year and the number of livestock to be maintained were specified. Grants were laid out in parallelograms, the front measuring one-third of the length. That the choicest locations might not be monopolized by the few, the length extended inland rather than along a highway, river, or creek.[2] Quit rents of one half-penny per acre were required after the first two years of grace.

Grants of 20,000 acres or more were made only by Orders of the King in Council and to those who petitioned the Board of Trade promising to settle a specified number of families upon the land within a given time.

---

1. Spain never made formal treaties with the Indians, although the Law of the Indies recognized the right of Indians to the land they occupied and used. When a village site or other Indian land was taken, they were compensated with lands elsewhere, or individual grantees purchased the Indian titles.--Eighteenth Annual Report of the Bureau of Ethnology, 1896-1897. Part 2. "Indian Land Cessions in the United States." Compiled by Charles C. Royce, pp. 539-542. See also a discussion of the subject in G&S, VIII, 259, and R. K. Call's caustic criticism of the decision of the Supreme Court in the case of Mitchell et al. vs. U. S. Ibid., pp. 256-260.

2. G&S, V, 757.

On such grants quit rent was payable on half the acreage after five years, on the whole after ten years.[1]

In the decade following 1765 the Council of East Florida made 576 grants based on "family right" totaling more than 210,000 acres; the King in Council made 114 which amounted to 1,443,000 acres. After the American Revolution began Florida became a mecca for loyalists from the southern colonies, who were offered land free of quit rents for ten years.[2] Among those receiving large grants from the British government were Denys Rolle[3] and Dr. Andrew Turnbull. The latter established at New Smyrna 1,400 Minorcans, Greeks, and Italians, the largest initial American colony in the history of what was later the United States.[4]

Six steps were necessary in making an English grant under "family right": (1) application to the register and council in which the applicant stated the size of his family and the number of slaves he possessed, if any; (2) a warrant of survey signed by the governor and addressed to the surveyor-general empowering that official to make a survey in proportion to the size of the petitioner's family; (3) a precept signed by the surveyor-general authorizing a deputy surveyor to measure the tract, which was later returned to the surveyor-general with plat of survey; (4) a

---

1. Charles L. Mowat, "The Land Policy in British East Florida", *Agricultural History*, Vol. XIV (Apr., 1940), p. 75.
2. Ibid., p. 77; Wilbur H. Siebert, *Loyalists in East Florida, 1774-1785*, 2 vols., DeLand, Fla., 1929, cited hereafter as Siebert, Loyalists.
3. Carita Doggett Corse, "Denys Rolle and Rollestown, A Pioneer for Utopia", *Florida Historical Quarterly*, Vol. VII (Oct., 1928), pp. 115-22
4. Carita Doggett (Corse), *Dr. Andrew Turnbull and the New Smyrna Colony of Florida* (Jacksonville, Fla., 1919), passim.

fiat signed by the attorney-general authorizing a grant to be made; (5) a grant signed by the governor and embodying the conditions; and (6) registration of the grant in the register's and auditor's offices, with copies of entries supplied to the treasury and commissioners for trade and plantation in London.[1]

The Spanish population in East and West Florida in 1763 numbered about 7,000 practically all of whom left when the English took possession.[2] In 1783, when Spain regained the province, the population of East Florida alone numbered 17,000; of those only 450 whites[3] and 200 negroes remained.

The definitive treaty between Great Britain and Spain in 1783, following in principle that of 1763, provided that subjects of the former should have eighteen months in which to sell their property, recover their debts, and transport themselves and effects from East Florida.[4] The time was later extended but in 1786 the period of grace ended. A royal order of the King of Spain decreed that those who had been inhabitants of Florida under English authority might remain and be protected

---

1. G&S, V, 757.
2. Three men who were out searching for their horses when the last boat sailed were left behind.--Wilbur H. Siebert, "Slavery and White Servitude in East Florida, 1726 to 1776", Florida Historical Quarterly, Vol. X (July, 1931), pp. 3-23. See also "How the Spanish Evacuated Pensacola in 1763", and "The Departure of the Spaniards and Other Groups from East Florida, 1763-1764", by the same author, Ibid., Vol. XI, pp. 48-57, and Vol. XIX, pp. 145-154.
3. The majority were Minorcans whom Dr. Turnbull had brought over for his colony at New Smyrna; they were Roman Catholics and had been subjects of Spain before Great Britain acquired the Island of Minorca.--Siebert, Loyalists, I, 208, 209.
4. The Definitive Treaty of Peace and Friendship Between His Britannick Majesty, and the King of Spain Signed at Versailles, the 3d of September, 1783 (London, 1783), Art. V, p. 10.

in their possessions on condition that they take the oath of fidelity, which meant also embracing Catholicism, and not attempt to augment their land holdings or leave the province, but that all who did not accept these conditions were to depart within thirty days.[1] The conditions were accepted by some and their land titles were confirmed by the Spanish authorities and later by the United States Boards of Commissioners. Those who refused the terms left the province, in many instances abandoning their property, as many had done three years earlier, because of their inability to sell it advantageously in the time allowed them.

## SPAIN'S LAND POLICY

The land policy of Spain's first regime in Florida was based on the Law of the Indies, which was a codification in 1680 of the royal cedulas --the orders, provisions, ordinances and instructions under which Spain's colonies had previously been governed. At the same time the Council of the Indies was established at the Spanish court with absolute authority under the King dealing with colonial matters.

Land was granted to individuals in peonias and caballerias, according to rank, a distinction being made between laborers and gentlemen. Originally a peonia was a grant made to a peon (foot soldier); a caballeria, a grant to an escudero (squire) who was generally a mounted trooper. With the exception of the lot on which the residence was built, a caballeria was five times that of a peonia. The term caballeria came to mean, in Mexico, a piece of land granted for the purpose of raising

---

1. G&S, V, 761-762.

horses or cattle, and measured 1,104 varas long by 552 varas wide, or 609,408 square varas.

In Florida a peonia was a lot of fifty feet in breadth and one hundred in depth; sufficient arable land to produce 100 fanegas[1] of wheat and barley and 10 of Indian corn; two huebras[2] for a garden and eight huebras of woodland; pasture land for ten breeding sows, twenty cows, five breeding mares, one hundred ewes and twenty goats. A caballeria consisted of a lot one hundred by two hundred feet and five times as much arable land, pasture, etc., as in a peonia.[3] Houses were to be built and lands cultivated within a given time under penalties provided by law.[4] If possession was not taken within three months the land was forfeited to the crown.[5]

No stranger (alien) was permitted to trade with the Indies except those who had been licensed by the King, and they were under surveillance and forbidden to reside in port towns. Naturalization required residence in the Kingdom or in the Indies twenty consecutive years, the ownership of a house and real property to the value of 4,000 ducats, and marriage

---

1. A fanega was 1.6 bu.
2. As much land as a yoke of oxen can plow in a day.
3. Matthew St. Clair Clarke, comp., Laws of the United States . . . Spanish Regulations . . . Respecting the Public Lands (Washington, 1828), p. 994, henceforth cited as Clarke, Land Laws; G&S, V, 649. The last mentioned reference is to "Spanish and French Ordinances Affecting Land Titles in Florida and Other Territories of France and Spain" which Joseph M. White compiled for the use of the Boards of Commissioners in which he served as secretary and commissioner and which was published in G&S, V, 631-674.
4. Ibid., p. 653.
5. Ibid., p. 650.

with a native, or daughter of a stranger, born in the Kingdom or in the
Indies. Even with these conditions satisfied the naturalized citizen
could not trade or contract without the sanction of the Council of the
Indies, and if licensed he could trade only with his own funds and after
filing with the court under oath an inventory of his possessions.[1]

Although the Law of the Indies was useful to the United States
Boards of Commissioners in interpreting claims, no grant was presented to
them under its provisions. The earliest grant brought before them was of
English origin, dated 1765.

After the retrocession of the Floridas, Spain adopted in part the
policy the English had followed in granting lands. Under the royal order
of 1786 Spain permitted British subjects to remain in Florida and retain
possession of their lands provided they would take the oath of allegiance.[2]
Efforts to attract Irish Catholics as settlers having in large part failed,
the King issued the royal order of 1790 inviting aliens to Florida regardless of their religious affiliations. Grants under this order were popularly known as "head rights." Under the regulations issued by Governor
Quesada immigrants who would take the oath of allegiance and could furnish transportation for themselves, their families and goods, and who
could be self-supporting until they were established, were invited to
come in and receive free land. They were promised freedom in matters of
religion, although only the Catholic worship was to be permitted in public. The head of a family was offered 100 acres of land with 50 acres for

---

1. Ibid., pp. 654-655.
2. Ibid., p. 762.

each white or colored person in the family, whatever their ages. An additional grant up to 1,000 acres could be obtained if there was probability of its being cultivated. During his probation the grantee could not alienate the land without the consent of the government but must hold and cultivate it continuously for a term of ten years. He was required to build a house with a suitable chimney as prescribed by the regulations, to build fences, and to keep a certain number of livestock. When his tenure and improvements were proved by the testimony of witnesses under oath, a title in absolute property would be issued.[1]

Captain Pedro Marrot of the 3d Battalion of Infantry, garrisoned at St. Augustine, was chosen to supervise the surveys and was given minute instructions. He was to take with him the public surveyor and to see that measurements were made according to the general regulations and the terms of any particular grant. He was to ascertain that applicants had taken the oath of allegiance, make a list of the white and black members of each family, noting their sex and ages, and take the oath of the applicant on those points. Surveys were to be so made that the length would extend inland and be two-thirds more than the width, or frontage. Owners of adjacent lands were to be cited to appear and exhibit their titles and the lines were to be run accordingly, the matter to be reviewed later by the government. Even the physical equipment and the size of the surveying party were specified: in addition to the public surveyor, Marrot was to take four sailors and two laborers, a canoe, two tents, and two

---

1. *Ibid.*, p. 749; DG, III, 728; Clarke, <u>Land Laws</u>, p. 997.

tarpaulins. He was to record "in a large book" all the pertinent facts of each survey.[1]

Although the royal order of 1790 had been issued with the expectation of attracting aliens, Spanish subjects claimed head rights under its terms and accepted the longer tenure because of the more generous allotments it offered over those prescribed in the Law of the Indies.

In the following thirteen years the intent of the law was often disregarded by new settlers and to prevent the abuses which had come to be customary Governor White in 1803 issued new regualtions. Only 50 acres were to be allotted to heads of families and none for children under eight years of age. For children and slaves between eight and sixteen years, 15 acres were allowed; 25 acres for those who were sixteen or over. To those who sold or conveyed their lands before they had acquired title, other grants were denied and all conveyances were illegal unless sanctioned by the government. When no other date was specified, grantees were required to take possession within six months. On grants made to those residing in towns cultivation must begin within one month. To prevent fraud and avoid disputes, each petitioner was required to designate a point from which measurement was to begin, and he was to give up his improvements for the benefit of the royal treasury in the event a change of location should later be desired. Those who abandoned their lands or discontinued cultivation for a period of two years were to lose their rights and the lands might be receded by the governor to the persons making such

---

1. Ibid., p. 998.

proof.[1]

In the absence in 1811 of the public surveyor,[2] Juan Purcell, Jorge J. F. Clarke, acting surveyor, was appointed to the office.[3] Clarke's instructions like those of Marrot, were specific:

Article 1. He was to consider possessors of land under three classes--proprietors, those holding lands by title not obtained from the government; grantees, those who after compliance with conditions will receive titles; grantees and proprietors, those who have already fulfilled conditions and acquired titles.

Article 2. He was to demand title or grant before acceding to any request to measure or bound lands.

Article 3. He must cite owners of adjacent lands to appear with their titles and satisfy himself that there was no conflict between claims.

Article 4. He was to lay out grants in rectangular parallelograms, the narrower portion, fronting rivers, creeks, and roads, to be one-third the depth which was to extend inland. If necessary to prevent empty spaces, however, he was to increase the frontage and correspondingly decrease the depth.

Article 5. He was to give each grantee a plat, signed and dated, made on a certain scale, with perimeters, distances in chains and links, corners, magnetic directions and the number of acres, marked in ink.

Article 6. He was to retain a copy of each plat in a book the index of which would show the page of each plat, its number, and the name of the grantee. At the back of the book the surveys, each bearing the proper number, were to be drawn to a given scale.

Article 7. The book described in the foregoing article being designed to serve the purpose of showing the government what lands were unmeasured and exhibit the surveyor's operations so as to satisfy grantees as to their boundaries, must be accurate.

Articles 8, 9, and 10 gave instructions for making corners for

---

1. Ibid., pp. 1001, 1002, 1003; G&S, V, 730-731, 749-750.
2. Presumably the office was the same as that of surveyor-general.
3. Clarke, Land Laws, pp. 1003, 1004.

tracts and a list of the fees the surveyor might charge.[1]

In view of these explicit regulations and the tradition for meticulous care which Marrot had given to the office of surveyor-general and which had been continued by John Tate and Juan Purcell, Clarke's testimony before the United States Boards of Commissioners denying that he had been bound by rules[2] is surprising.

Despite generous land grants colonization lagged. Juan Estrada, appointed governor upon the death of Governor White in 1811, felt that the difficulty lay in requiring a ten-year tenure before title was granted. He accordingly proposed that the West Florida plan be adopted of selling the land and giving title in fee simple, which he thought would attract settlers from the United States. The captain-general of Cuba called his attention to the fact that by royal order of 1804 and 1806 the admission of citizens of the United States was prohibited.[3]

The royal order of 1815 permitting grants for patriotic serivces was supposed to have been made in response to Governor Kindelan's recommendation two years earlier. The "Patriot War"[4] had just ended and the Governor suggested to Juan Ruiz de Apadoca, Captain-General of Cuba, rewards for the three white militia companies and for the 3d Battalion

---

1. Ibid., p. 1004.
2. G&S, VI, 57.
3. Ibid., V, p. 734.
4. The defense by the Spanish authorities against the attempt of the U. S. government in 1811-1812 to acquire East Florida by fomenting a revolution on the plea of preventing Great Britain using it as a naval base. The defense of East Florida in the Gregor McGregor invasion a few years later was also the basis of service grants.

of Cuba: (1) to each of the militia officers, a royal commission for each grade possible to him as a provincial; and (2) to all soldiers of the milita and to the married officers and soldiers of the 3d Battalion of Cuba, lands in proportion to the size of their families. He admitted that his plan would not in reality give them anything which was not already open to them, but he thought that "public approbation would content the men and stimulate their patriotism."[1]

The authenticity of the copies of Kindelan's letter and of the royal order of 1815 was called into question by Alexander Hamilton, member in 1823 of the United States Board of Commissioners for East Florida. He sent to Secretary of the Treasury Crawford "a translation of what is commonly called the Royal Order of 1815, together with a copy and translation of a letter supposed to have been written by Governor Kindelan, the apparent inducement to the order", under which he said "the most numerous and extensive grants have been made." He asserted that there had been an erasure in Kindelan's letter and the word "extensively" substituted for "exclusively", making a sentence read, " . . . which gifts can also be _extensively_ made to the married officers and soldiers of the said third battalion of Cuba."[2]

No other authority being available, the Board adjudicated service grants on the basis of the order and letter in question. No conditions were attached to such grants, but in the main their size was based upon

---

1. G&S, V, 750.
2. Clarke, Land Laws, pp. 1009, 1010, 1034.

head rights. The recital of services rendered often makes the memorials humorus reading.

Spanish land grants may thus be said to have been based upon three royal orders: that of 1786 for the English in Florida; that of 1790 for strangers, of which Spanish subjects also availed themselves; and that of 1815 for patriotic service. In addition there were two other types of grants which may be said to have contemplated future services to the province: saw or grist mill grants and cow pen grants or cattle ranges. There was controversy between Alexander Hamilton and his colleagues as to the extent of discretion premitted to Spanish governors in the matter of land grants, and certainly no royal orders covered these types, but the Council of the Indies evidently did not disapprove of the action of the governor in making such grants.

Memorials for sawmill grants usually asked for five leagues square, or 16,000 acres, and urged the value to the province of mills such as the petitioners proposed to establish. The first was granted in 1793 and later they were readily granted, but in every instance the governor made the establishment of the mill a condition precedent to the license to cut timber. In no instance save one was a perfect title to this type of grant conferred by Spanish authorities, since none fulfilled the conditions before the cession. The exception was the grant of 26,000 acres to George (Jorge) J. F. Clarke who claimed to have invented a sawmill to be propelled by animal power, and who in addition had served the government in various capacities and especially in the Patriot War when the rebels put a price upon his head and upon the heads of members of his family.

The United States Boards of Commissioners and later the Registers and Receivers of the land offices who took over the duties of the commissioners took the position that only a mill site and the right to cut timber over an area of 16,000 acres were granted. As Richard Keith Call, Receiver, put it, the grants were not intended to convey land but "a mere usufruct for the enjoyment of the timber." Call pointed out in his report to the Secretary of the Treasury in 1835 that the land claimed under these twenty odd grants amounted to 312,600 acres, whereas the whole amount confirmed to grantees for habitation and cultivation--the paramount object of the laws and ordinances of Spain--from October, 1790, until the cession was only about 129,000 acres.[1] A few of the mill site grantees fulfilled the conditions after the cession as permitted in the treaty and the Supreme Court confirmed their claims.

The concession to Clarke referred to above was made December 17, 1817, and Governor Coppinger at the same time gave complete title to 22,000 of the 26,000 acres granted. When Clarke had established the sawmill the Supreme Court confirmed his claim to 22,000 acres, but denied the validity of the title to 4,000 acres which had been completed after January 24, 1818, the date specified in the treaty as the last on which grants made by Spain would be recognized.[2] Call was critical of the court's action in confirming the concession and plainly intimated that Governor Coppinger's object in making the grant was to defraud the United

---

1. G&S, VIII, 251 et seq.
2. The U. S. vs. Clarke, 8 Peters, 436.

States.[1]

Cow pen grants, or cattle ranges, gave less trouble than did mill grants. In most instances conditions were fulfilled, including tenure of ten years, after which titles were granted. Pablo Sabate's grant[2] of 2,500 acres for such a purpose was an exception. He received a royal title without seemingly being called upon to meet any conditions whatever. This extraordinary title having been granted on April 2, 1818, the Board of of Commissioners disallowed the claim as being contrary to the treaty.[3]

In West Florida the terms for granting lands were somewhat different from those which obtained in East Florida. Governors there had changed frequently and lands were granted not only by the governors, but also by acting governors and intendants. In the main, the United States Board of Commissioners for West Florida followed the general regualtions made on July 17, 1799, by Juan Ventura Morales, who was principal comptroller of the army and finances of the provinces of Louisiana and West Florida, intendant *par interim* and subdelegate of the superintendence, general of the same, judge of admiralty and of lands, etc., of the King, etc. These regualtions provided for three types of grants: gratuities, lands sold, and compromise grants.

Gratuities, or conditional grants to colonists (a chaque famille nouvelle), were based upon the size of the family and were not in any case

---

1. G&S, V, 428-430; VIII, 251 et seq. A list of mill grants may be found in Ibid., V, 427.
2. See Vol. I, S 1.
3. G&S, VI, 72.

to exceed 800 _arpens_.[1] These settlers were under the necessity of clearing and putting into cultivation a certain amount of land within the three-year tenure required. If the grant bordered the Mississippi River, the owner was in addition required during the first year to build levees, canals, a highway, and bridges. Failure to comply with the conditions would prevent the sale of the land which would revert to the crown.[2]

The policy of selling land outright was preferred by the authorities of West Florida. The tax price (quit rent) was set by the King's agent and the lands were sold at auction. When purchasers did not have ready money with which to pay for their lands, they were permitted to buy them at redeemable quit rent during the continuance of which they paid 5% yearly. However, they were expected to pay down the right of media _annala_, or "half year's rent", to be remitted to Spain, and they had to pay the fees of the surveyor and notary.[3]

Compromise grants were made to "squatters" who had cultivated and improved the land for ten years and who after investigation and assessment by the treasury paid "a just and moderate retribution, calculated according to the lands, their situation, and other circumstances", and the cost of making the estimate.[4]

Whether lands were sold or donated, the King reserved the right of taking from them any timber he might need, particularly cypress for the

---

1. A French measure varying with the locality, being about 84/100 of an acre in West Florida.
2. G&S, V, 732, Arts. 1-6.
3. _Ibid._, 733-734, Arts. 24-26.
4. _Ibid._, p. 733, Art. 20.

navy.[1]

There were usually seven steps in acquiring land under Spanish authority:

1. A memorial or petition, to the governor setting forth the claimant's right to a service grant or to head rights, or a proposal to render a service to the province by erecting a mill or establishing a cow pen, and usually specifying the tract desired.

2. A review of the petition by the governor's office; if favorable, it was referred to the commandant of engineers to ascertain whether there were any objections from the standpoint of defense. The commandant frequently stipulated that the grantee should have no claim for damages if ordered to retire to the interior or if his buildings should be burned in case of military necessity. Particularly was this so if the grant lay within the mil y quinientas--the land within a radius of 1,500 varas from the flagstaff, outside the walls of fortified towns such as St. Augustine and Fernandina, which the King had placed at the disposal of the commandant for purposes of defense. The grant in the mil y quinientas was usually an acre, on which the commandant allowed the cultivation of low-growing crops, usually vegetables which the grower peddled in the town, and the building of a palm shack ten or eleven feet square and ten feet high. He forbade the digging of ditches and the building of picket fences, only rail fences being allowed.[2]

3. A grant made by the governor, usually noted on the margin of the petition, giving the authority under which the concession was made and stating the conditions of settlement, cultivation, the bringing in of a certain number of slaves, etc., together with instructions to the surveyor-general. The grant, however, did not mean, as in the United States, a perfect title, but an incipient right which required confirmation by the governor at a later date. The petition was filed in the office of the escribano.

4. Verification of the petitioner's statements by the governor's office or by the surveyor-general through the examination of witnesses. If the grant was for head rights, the number in the family, white and black, was ascertained, regarding which the petitioner made oath. The surveyor-general also ascertained whether there was a prior claim to the land in question. Having satisfied himself on these points he made the survey, entered it on his records, and issued a certificate. The

---

1. Ibid., p. 732, Art. 9
2. After the cession the U. S. Board of Commissioners recommended that the mil y quinientas be relinquished to the several claimants.

petitioner was now at liberty to take possession and begin the fulfillment of conditions.

5. A memorial by grantee for absolute title.

6. Decree of the governor for taking testimony to prove whether conditions had been fulfilled.

7. Decree of the governor for absolute title, after which the owner could dispose of the land in any way he saw fit.

Frequently a grantee became dissatisfied with his land and petitioned the governor for an exchange. If the reasons were good it was usually granted.

Titles issued by the Spanish government were therefore of two kinds: those in "absolute property" and those which were "conditional." Conditional titles were represented by certificates of survey reciting the conditions to be fulfilled. Titles in absolute property were given when all conditions had been fulfilled or when grants were made for services already performed. Under the Law of the Indies the term required for a perfect, or complete, title was four years of inhabitation and cultivation ; under the royal order of 1790 and Governor Quesada's regulations, ten years; under Governor Kindelan, whenever improvements had been made, regardless of the number of years. Kindelan's regulation, issued in 1815, was made necessary by the conditions following the Indian wars and the revolutions which drove many people from their lands and prevented the fulfillment of conditions within the time specified in the grants. Once a title in absolute property was obtained, the possessor of land, his heirs, and assigns, had the power to discontinue cultivation, to sell, cede, exchange, transfer, and alienate at will, all conditions having been fulfilled.[1]

## BOARD OF COMMISSIONERS--WEST FLORIDA

By Article VIII of the treaty of February 22, 1819, whereby Spain ceded the Floridas to the United States, all Spanish grants of land made prior to January 24, 1818, the date on which the King of Spain definitely expressed his willingness to negotiate, were to be "ratified and confirmed to the persons in possession of the lands, to the same extent that the said grants would be valid if the territories had remained under the domain of his Catholic Majesty." Owners in possession of such lands, who by reason of the recent circumstances of the Spanish nation and the revolutions had been prevented from fulfilling all the conditions of their grants, were to be permitted an equal time to complete them after the date of the treaty. Grants subsequent to January 24, 1818, were to be considered null and void.[2] The treaty was not ratified and proclaimed until February 22, 1821[3] and yet another year passed before a permanent territorial government was established in Florida by the Act of March 30, 1822.[4]

On May 8, 1822, Congress passed what proved to be the first of a series of Acts designed to carry out the provisions of Article VIII of the treaty of cession. The Act provided for the appointment by the

---

1. G&S, V, 742, 751-754.
2. F. N. Thorpe, Constitutions, Colonial Charters, and Other Organic Laws. . . . (Washington, 1908-1909), II, 652.
3. Ibid., II, 649 f.n.
4. U. S. Stat. at Large, II, 654-659.

President of three commissioners who on or before the first Monday in July, 1822, should open an office at Pensacola for the adjudication of land claims in West Florida. They were to hold sessions also at St. Augustine, for the purpose of passing on similar claims in East Florida. The sessions were to terminate on June 30, 1823, when the commissioners should forward to the Secretary of the Treasury to be submitted to Congress a record of all they had done and deliver over to the surveyor all archives, documents, and papers in their possession.

The commissioners were authorized to appoint a suitable and well qualified secretary who was acquainted with the Spanish language and who should record in a well-bound book their acts and proceedings, including claims admitted and rejected, with the reason for their admission or rejection.

Persons claiming titles to lands under any patent, grant, concession, or order of survey, dated prior to January 24, 1818, which were valid under the Spanish government, or by the law of nations, and which were not rejected by the treaty ceding the Floridas to the United States,[1] were instructed to file their claims before the commissioners, with supporting evidence, and, where claimants were not the original grantees, with deraignment of title. Claims not filed before May 31, 1823, were to be null and void.

With reference to titles derived from British grants the commissioners

---

1. The reference was in particular to the three large grants which the King of Spain made in 1820.--See G&S, V, 722-726.

were to consider only such as were claimed by citizens of the United States and which were valid under the Spanish government and had never been compensated for by the British government.[1]

To facilitate their inquiries the commissioners were authorized to administer oaths and to compel the attendance of witnesses, and were granted access to and the right to make transcripts of all public records relative to land titles. They were empowered to confirm all valid claims under 1,000 acres, but were directed to report to the Secretary of the treasury for the action of Congress all testimony concerning claims in excess of that amount or of undefined quantity with their opinion thereon, and the testimony concerning conflicting claims emanating from both the British and Spanish governments.[2]

The first meeting of the commissioners was held in Pensacola on July 15, 1822, with Samuel R. Overton and Nathaniel A. Ware present. Business transacted was the appointment of Joseph M. White as secretary to whom written instructions were given concerning his duties, and the adoption of rules to be observed by all claimants.[3] Claimants were requested to file a written petition or notice setting forth the boundaries

---

1. The British government compensated its subjects in part for losses in Florida in consequence of the American Revolution and the cession of the province to Spain.
2. U. S. Stat. at Large, III, 709-18.
3. "Record Book A. Proceedings of the Board of Commissioners Showing Claims Presented and what papers were filed in Support of Same, West Florida, July 17, 1822 to July 24, 1824", pp. 1-2, cited hereafter as "Record Bk. A, W. Fla."

of the land claimed, evidence in support of their claims, and deraignment of title, together with a brief reference to the laws and ordinances under which the grants were made.[1]

The secretary was instructed (1) to keep in the minutes "a record of the meetings and adjournments of the commissioners, with a statement of their proceedings and decisions, accompanied by the evidence on which the decisions were made"; (2) "to record <u>in their original</u> language, all the papers necessary to the establishment of the title, with the reason of their admission or rejection", in the following order: notice or petition, notarial certificate of sales and transfers, mesne conveyances so abbreviated as to show the claim of title and date of transfer, the patent, grant, or concession, report of the surveyor as to whether the land was vacant, report of the fisc.[2] stating whether there were any objections to the petition, order and certificate of survey and the plat (if the survey was executed prior to January 24, 1818); and (3) to file in his office for the inspection of the commissioners when considering claims all papers not recorded. The secretary was further instructed that translations would be confined to recorded papers and such other documents as the commissioners might from time to time require.[3]

Having organized and adopted rules of procedure the commissioners were ready to receive claims. Few were forthcoming. Only four meetings

---

1. Ibid.
2. Fiscal, or King's Solicitor
3. "Record Bk. A, W. Fla.," p. 2.

including the first were held in July. A fifth session was held on August 16. Four days later the minutes record: "In consequence of the appearance of a malignant fever in the City of Pensacola, and the impracticability of either remaining in safety or of doing business, Ordered that the Court be adjourned until further appointment."[1] It reconvened on October 4, only to adjourn until December 12.

Congress had not supplied the commissioners with published copies of Spain's land laws, nor indeed were copies easily obtained in this country. Throughout what came to be a three-year term the commissioners were handicapped in this particular. As late as November 12, 1824, they complained that they had been unable to obtain a copy of the ordinance of 1754 issued by Ferdinand VI and that very few settlers would answer questions concerning land laws and practices.[2] Not until Joseph M. White[3] compiled from his experience as secretary and commissioner of the Board for West Florida and from published works, which he finally obtained from Spain, his "Spanish and French Ordinances Affecting Land Titles in Florida and Other Territories of France and Spain"[4] was there an adequate guide for the adjudication of Spanish land claims in Florida.

On December 12, 1822, the Board issued an order "to summon the most

---

1. Ibid., p. 17; Niles Register, Vol. XXIII, Oct. 19, 1822.
2. DG, IV, 84.
3. Joseph M. White was a delegate to Congress from Florida, 1825-1837. He served as secretary to the Board of Commissioners during 1822 and as commissioner during 1823-1824. He was born in Kentucky, studied law and moved to Pensacola in 1821.
4. Published in G&S, V, 631-774.

respectable Spanish Inhabitants to give evidence in relation to the customs and practice of the Spanish Officers of the provincial Government" with reference to land grants, and four days later these citizens appeared before the Board.[1]

In all, nine sessions were held between July 15 and December 16, 1822.[2] It was evident that the date limits set forth in the Act of May 8, 1822, had not given sufficient time for the business in hand, and the commissioners apparently made no effort to comply with its provisions for holding sessions in St. Augustine.

On March 3, 1823, Congress provided for two Boards of Commissioners, who were to hold sessions in East and West Florida, at St. Augustine and Pesnacola respectively, until the second Monday in February, 1824. Claimants were no longer required to produce in evidence deraignment of titles, and the commissioners were authorized to confirm claims up to 3,500 acres instead of 1,000, as provided in the law of 1822. District attorneys when required to do so were to attend sessions of the Boards for the purpose of arguing and explaining points of law. Claims not filed before December 1, 1823, were to be considered null and void.[3]

---

1. "Record Bk. A, W. Fla.," p. 18.
2. Ibid., passim.
3. U. S. Stat. at Large, IV, 6-7; Tipton B. Harrison, dist. atty. for W. Fla. in 1822, died and was succeeded in 1823 by Wm. F. Steele. In E. Fla. Edgar Macon in 1823 succeeded Alexander Hamilton in that office, Hamilton having veen appointed the previous year.--Niles Register, Vol. XXII, May 18, 1822, p. 180. .(Of great convenience to students of Fla. history is the "Digest of Florida Material in Niles Register", 1939, in manuscript, made by T. Frederick Davis in Jacksonville, to whom the editor is indebted for references to that journal appearing herein.)

It required six weeks for the Act of March 3, 1823, to reach West Florida. A session of the Board was called for April 19, but only Samuel R. Overton was in the territory and present.[1] No further meeting was held for four months. On September 2 the Board was reorganized, Joseph M. White being sworn in to replace James P. Preston, resigned. Morris Hunter of Pensacola was appointed secretary to succeed White.[2]

The Board set itself the task of hearing claims for three town lots or two tracts of land each day[3] and met regularly until February 9, 1824, when, the time limit set for its sessions having expired, it adjourned "until further order" with its business still unfinished.[4] Its life was extended to January 1, 1825, by the Act of February 28, 1824,[5] and the commission reconvened with the same personnel on April 5, 1824.[6] On May 4 Craven P. Luckett succeeded Ware[7] and Overton failed to sit at any session recorded after May 20,[8] although he signed the reports of the Board to the Secretary of the Treasury on November 12, 1824, and January 12, 1825.[9]

There is no record in the minutes of a session after July 19, 1824, but White and Luckett evidently continued to transact business during the remainder of the year and even subsequent to January 1, 1825, for

---

1. "Record Bk. A, W. Fla.," p. 18.
2. Ibid., p. 30
3. Ibid.
4. Ibid., p. 226.
5. U. S. Stat. at Large, IV, 6-7.
6. "Record Bk. A, W. Fla.," p. 267
7. Ibid., p. 337.
8. Ibid., passim.
9. DG, IV, 83-117, 118-157.

an Act of Congress of April 22, 1826, legalized their activities after that date.[1] Afterwards the Register and Receiver for the Land Office of West Florida[2] completed the work in which the commissioners for that district had for three years been engaged.

## BOARD OF COMMISSIONERS--EAST FLORIDA

The three commissioners appointed for East Florida were Davis Floyd, William F. Blair, and Alexander Hamilton. At the first meeting of the Board on August 4, 1823, Floyd was elected chairman and Francisco Jose Fatio was appointed secretary. John Lowe was appointed messenger; Joseph Lancaster was sworn in as deputy to the secretary.[3] William Reynolds was at this time in charge of the public archives, with Antonio Alvarez as assistant. Edgar Macon was district attorney.

The Board adopted unanimously the following regulations:

"All persons claiming title to Lands under any patent, grant, concession, or order of survey, will make a brief statement, by Memorial, setting forth the situation, boundaries, and if possible, the deraignment of title, to the Lands claimed, and by whom granted, and by what authority, and whether the same be the whole or part of the original grant.

"All cases where grants have been made on conditions it will be necessary to show the nature of the conditions, whether they have been performed and if not the reasons why they have not been complied with.

"Where lands are claimed by actual settlers, without grants, concessions, patents, or orders of survey, the same must be declared, occupancy stated distinctly, together with the nature of the evidence, in

---

1. U. S. Stat. at Large, IV, 156.
2. Samuel R. Overton, Register for 1825, G. W. Ward for 1826, and Richard Keith Call, Receiver.
3. "Record Bk. No. 8. Minutes of the Board of Land Commissioners for East Florida, Aug. 4, 1823, to Nov. 30, 1827", pp. 1, 3, cited hereafter as "Record Bk. 8, E. Fla."

support of the claim; and whether the said possession ever was and in what manner acknowledged or sanctioned by the Spanish government.

"In all instances where claims are made in virtue of British Patents, grants, etc., the claimants must describe in what manner they claim, whether as original patentees or Grantees or by assignment, also whether they are in actual possession, and if out of possession that they claim 'bona fide' as American Citizens.

"All original documents if in possession of the claimants must be exhibited and in other cases certified copies including the Memorial, Order of Survey, Survey and confirmation, together with translations of the same.

"Claimants must shew whether they were actual residents at the time of the cession and where they now reside."[1]

Rules adopted by the Board for its guidance included, among others:

"Resolved that claimants be not required to produce their title papers translated into the English Language, but in all cases be permitted to file the original documents--the Honble. Alexander Hamilton dissenting.

"Resolved, that the District Attorney, the Keeper of the Public Archives, nor the Secretary of this Board are not authorise (sic) to represent as Attorney or Agent any claims before the commissioners,-- Honble. Davis. Floyd dissenting.[2]

"Resolved, that hereafter whenever a claimant of Land shall present his evidence of title to the Secretary of this Board desiring to bring the same before the commissioners, it shall be the duty of said Secretary without any fee therefor, to put the same in the form of a Memorial, containing in substance what has already been required by the resolution of this Board. And that the said Secretary be authorized to obtain from the Printer of this city One thousand blank copies of said form & authorize said Printer to present his account therefor, before this Board who will direct the said account to be paid out of any monies which may come into their hands for appropriation--or in case of none such will certify said account to the Treasurer of the United States.

"And be it further ordered that the Secretary be required to deliver one of these printed forms to any person or persons applying for

---

1. Ibid., pp. 1-2.
2. Ibid., p. 3.

the same.[1]

On three occasions the following resolution was offered before it was adopted on November 28:

"Resolved that claimants desiring to obtain the Testimony of any witness residing without the Territory of Florida shall file with the Secretary their Interrogatories; and that the District Attorney under the direction of the Board shall if required, annex Cross Interrogatories, on behalf of the United States--and that in all cases where the Witnesses are residents within the Territory, the claimant may file depositions taken 'Ex parte' as the said witnesses are subject to the jurisdiction of the Commissioners: leaving it optional with the Claimants to procure by filing interrogatories, And that a Commission with the interrogatories so annexed shall be directed to any person authorized to administer oaths, sealed by the Secretary and delivered to the party so making application and it shall be the duty of said person to take the answers of said Witness to all such interrogatories and none other, and to certify the same, and whether the said Commission was sealed when delivered.[2]

On December 9 it was ordered that "the Rules of evidence governing Courts of Law, govern the Board for the future--viz., that the party calling the Witness, first examine him, & then turn him over to the District Attorney, and when he has finished the Board can ask him any pertinent question which they conceive to have been omitted; but the party examining the witness, cannot be interrupted without he is putting an improper question--Mr. Hamilton dissented as to any restraint on the Board in its examination.[3] The Board adjourned sine die on February 9, 1824.[4]

The difficulties with which the commissioners had to contend were

---

1. Ibid., p. 6.
2. Ibid., p. 19.
3. Ibid., p. 160.
4. Ibid., p. 189.

enumerated in their report at the end of the year. The law required that all Spanish documents be translated and recorded, but allowed only one secretary. No means of collecting fees for translating papers for claimants having been provided by Congress and the fees being too small to justify collection by the orderly process of law, no funds from that source were available for employing additional clerks. To meet the situation the commissioners required the secretary to hire an assistant, Joseph B. Lancaster, and pay him from his own salary. Lancaster resigned on December 8, and Lewis Huguon was appointed in his place. After adjudication began the services of the secretary were necessary to record the evidence of titles and the commissioners were compelled to pay the salary of a second assistant, John H. Lawrence, to take the minutes.[1] The number of claims was too great for the commissioners to dispose of of them in the time allowed under the conditions stipulated in the law there being something like 600 by February 21, 1824. Property owners in St. Augustine and Fernandina were disgruntled because they were required to exhibit their titles, Section II of the treaty seeming to imply that all private claims in those towns were accepted as valid, only the public property being transferred to the United States.[2] They accordingly held mass meetings and petitioned Congress to exemp them from the necessity of exhibiting their titles, and the Board agreed to submit the question to the Secretary of the Treasury. No reply had been received at the end

---

1. Ibid., pp. 158-159.
2. DG, III, 759-760.

of the year and the claims had not been considered.[1]

The Board had other troubles which prevented its functioning smoothly. It moved its offices twice--from Government House to a house belonging to Joseph Sanchez then back to Government House.[2] It was unable to obtain certain documents from the Public Archives and was compelled to issue a <u>subpoena duces tecum</u> to William Reynolds.[3] The same procedure was necessary even after the Secretary of State instructed him to deliver the documents.[4] And finally there was such a divergence of opinion between Hamilton and the other commissioners as to procedure[5] that Hamilton refused to participate in the sessions and bombarded President Monroe, Secretary of Treasury Crawford, Secretary of State Adams, and the chairman of the house committee on public lands with serious charges against his colleagues and those in charge of Public Archives.[6] After Hamilton ceased to participate[7] the two commissioners adopted the rule that in cases of disagreement between them the claims with all the facts should be reported to Congress for disposition.[8]

As former United States district attorney for East Florida Hamilton was on the ground when he was appointed to the Board, and on June 7, before the other commissioners arrived, he had appointed a secretary, Patrick Lynch, to receive land claims. When the Board organized on

---

1. Ibid.
2. Ibid., pp. 770, 777, 788.
3. "Record Bk. 8, E. Fla.," p. 8.
4. DG, III, p. 788.
5. "Record Bk. 8, E. Fla.," pp. 159, 160, 162, 165, 170, 173, 176.
6. DG, III, 725 et seq., 762 et seq., 892, et seq.
7. He continued to attend the meetings of the Board
8. "Record Bk. 8, E. Fla.," p. 185.

August 4 it dispensed with Hamilton's appointee, chose Fatio secretary and ordered all papers that had been filed returned to claimants "to be presented in proper order."[1]

Whether or not friction was first caused by Hamilton's officiousness in beginning the work before the Board had organized and inserted in the newspapers the necessary instructions to claimants, the minutes show that there was seldom agreement between Hamilton and his colleagues. He complained of "the important and procrastinated situation of the business of the commission", of the failure of the Board, as he saw it, to adopt certain principles to govern their decisions, and of the "illegal and improper manner in which the Minutes were kept on loose sheets." On December 9 the Board ordered the secretary to record the minutes in a "well-bound book", as the law required.[2]

The Act creating the Board for East Florida had not defined "actual settlers." The majority of the Board defined the term as meaning persons actually settled within the province at the time of the exchange of flags but not necessarily on the land claimed. Hamilton did not agree with the definition[3] and neither did Congress, for the following year in an Act to extend the time for the settlement of private land claims in Florida it defined actual settlers as those who were in the cultivation or occupation of the land at or before the date of cession.[4]

---

1. Ibid., pp. 2, 5.
2. Ibid., p. 159.
3. Ibid., p. 170
4. U. S. Stat. at Large, IV, 7.

The more serious charges made by Hamilton were in regard to (1) the careless and haphazard manner in which he said the public archives were kept, which had resulted in one or more documents being altered, one stolen and another substituted, and the dependence of the Board on such an office for transcripts or certified copies instead of insisting upon the original documents; and (2) fraud in connection with the favorable action of the Board on the McIntosh, Segui, and Arredondo claims.[1] Hamilton was skeptical of the testimony of George J. F. Clarke, surveyor-general under the Spanish government, and of his "pretended deputy, Burgevin", the latter of whom he characterized as "comtemptible." He commented on Clarke's "extravagant pretensions and inconsistent representations, with a memory on some subjects singularly tenacious, and on others peculiarly forgetful."[2] Hamilton resigned on March 31, 1824, but a month later withdrew his resignation until the end of the session of Congress that his communications might in the meantime have official

---

1. Hamilton stated to the Secretary of the Treasury that he would go from St. Augustine to Charleston and there hold himself in readiness should his presence be required in Washington in connection with his charges. An aftermath of Hamilton's sojourn in Florida was three court cases. Two of the cases, filed Feb. 9, 1824, were for libel in the sums of $10,000 and $20,000 in connection with his alleged candidacy for territorial delegate to Congress and a petition to the president signed by a number of persons for his removal as a member of the Board of Land Commissioners.--Alexander Hamilton vs. Eusebio Gomez, and Alexander Hamilton vs. Eusebio Gomez and Joseph M. Hernandez, File H 3, Superior Court, St. Johns County, Fla. In the third case Hamilton brought suit for damages in the sum of $1,600 against the master and commander of the sloop "Rapid" for loss of his trunk and law books when the sloop burned at Charleston wharf on July 6, 1824.--Alexander Hamilton vs. Alexander G. Swasey, File H 10, Superior Court, St. Johns County, Fla.

2. DG, III, 764 et seq., 892, et seq.

importance.[1] The committee on public lands did not sustain Hamilton, but recommended that the President give the Board instructions as to its powers and duties and adopt such measures as were necessary for the safe-keeping of the archives.[2]

At the end of the year the Board reported to Congress the principles upon which it had based its decisions: (1) the Law of the Indies; (2) royal orders; (3) decrees and regulations made and published by the local governors; and (4) customs and usages which prevailed in the various offices of the territorial government.[3] Another principle upon which they acted was acceptance of royal titles granted without conditions and of those allowed after January 24, 1818, provided conditions specified in grants of the latter had been fulfilled before that date.[4]

Early the following year Congress increased the work of the commissioners by adding another class of claimants. There was in the Territory of Florida a large number of settlers who had no titles to show for the lands they occupied--renters, squatters, or purchasers of lands with doubtful titles. The majority of these were probably citizens of the United States. To retain and do justice to these settlers Congress by the "Donation Act" of May 26, 1824, authorized the commissioners "to receive and examine all claims founded on habitation and cultivation of any tract of land, town or city lot or outlot by any person being head

---

1. *Ibid.*, 766, 866. Hamilton's charges and law suits have been included as a possible assistance in interpreting certain claims.
2. *Ibid.*, p. 863.
3. *Ibid.*, p. 725.
4. *Ibid.*, pp. 1-10, 725, V, 394.

of a family and 21 years of age", who on February 22, 1819, the date of the signing of the treaty, "actually inhabited and cultivated such tract of land, or actually cultivated and improved such lot, or who, on that day, cultivated any tract of land in the vicinity or any town or city having a permanent residence in such town or city." To such persons they were to grant certificates of confirmation not to exceed 640 acres.

The Act provided also that the commissioners were to receive claims to land founded on habitation and cultivation commenced between February 22, 1819, and July 17, 1821, the date of the exchange of flags, with evidence in support of same, and report an abstract of all such claims to the Secretary of the Treasury. Claims merely reported upon were to be laid before Congress "with the evidence of the time, nature and extent of such inhabitation and cultivation . . . and extent of the claim," but no claim was to be received, confirmed, or reported in favor of any person who claimed any tract by virtue of any written evidence of title from either the British or Spanish governments.[1]

Davis Floyd and William W. Blair, commissioners for East Florida, met on March 29, 1824, pursuant to the law of February 19 which extended the time limits for the settlement of private land claims in East Florida to January 1, 1825.[2] Congress having failed to make an appropriation for employing assistant clerks, the services of the minuting secretary and the messenger were discontinued.[3] Through April to August the

---

1. U. S. Stat. at Large, IV, 47.
2. Ibid., pp. 6-7.
3. "Record Bk. 8, E. Fla.," p. 191.

Board had often to adjourn for lack of a quorum, due to Blair's illness.[1] On August 24 George Murray, who had been appointed "vice for William W. Blair", was present for the first time,[2] and on September 29 William Henry Allen, who had been appointed on August 12 as the third member of the Board, was in attendance.[3]

On December 28 the Board adjourned sine die.[4] In its report, dated January 1, 1825, the Board stated that it had found it impossible to complete the work within the time specified by law. The commissioners explained that property had often been conveyed one, two, three, or even four times and petitioners had frequently received grants at certain places, changed their minds, and had surveys made elsewhere, which made the examination of claims exceedingly tedious. They had employed an additional clerk (probably Thomas Murphy) for the past three months who so far had received no pay, and he had been able within that time to record only 34 claims, since they averaged 21 pages each. There were 1,104 claims filed during the year, of which 80 were still under advisement.[5]

On March 3, 1825, an Act of Congress extended the time of the commissioners for East Florida to the first Monday in January, 1826, and made appropriations for two additional clerks.

---

1. Ibid., p. 223.
2. Ibid., p. 226.
3. Ibid., p. 258.
4. Ibid., p. 287.
5. DC, IV, 157-158.

The Board in West Florida having in large part completed its work, the Act directed the commissioners there to deliver all records and evidence relative to land claims to the Register and Receiver of the Land Office in West Florida, who should examine and decide the remaining claims subject to the rules which had governed the commissioners.[1]

On March 28 the Board for East Florida met with Davis Floyd, George Murray, and William H. Allen, commissioners, and Francisco Jose Fatio, secretary, present. Thomas Murphy and Lewis Huguon were appointed assistant clerks.[2] Sessions were held in Jacksonville on May 16 and several times thereafter for the convenience of claimants.[3] It adjourned sine die on December 20, 1825.[4] Its reports of January 1 and 31, 1826, showed more than 500 claims yet undetermined.[5] The Board was criticized in the press, being charged with allowing counsel to appear for claimants and for itself with the object of killing time and prolonging its life. Floyd made a spirited defense to the Secretary of the Treasury and related the difficulties under which the commissioners had labored. He charged charged that doubtful claims had been held back by their owners and criticisms against the Board made in the hope that "the business might fall into more favorable hands."[6]

There is no doubt that the commissioners for East Florida had a far

---

1. U. S. Stat. at Large, IV, 125-126.
2. "Record Bk. 8, E. Fla.," p. 228.
3. Ibid., pp. 303-305.
4. Ibid. p. 355.
5. DG, IV, 275-277, 400-501.
6. Ibid., p. 507; Floyd's charges in 1826 seem to have been confirmed by the fact reported by R. K. Call nearly ten years later.--Infra, pp. liii-liv.

greater task than did those for West Florida. The number of claims in East Florida was greater, the claims were more complicated, and it may have been that the commissioners were less systematic in handling them. It would seem also that friction among themselves retarded the work. The remaining claims were disposed of by the Register and Receiver of the Land Office for East Florida,[1] Charles Downing and William H. Allen.

## FINAL DISPOSITION OF LAND CLAIMS

By Act of Congress on February 8, 1827, the "secretary of the late commissioners" for East Florida was directed to deliver all land papers in his possession to the Register and Receiver of the Land Office for East Florida who should examine and decide the remaining claims subject to the several laws of Congress. Claimants were directed to file their claims before November 1 and the Register and Receiver to report on January 1, 1828. Conflicting claims were to be subject to court decision. Holders of claims of more than 3,500 acres and other claims not yet reported by commissioners, or by Register and Receiver, were to furnish to the surveyor within one year information concerning their claims so that he might connect them with the township plats then under survey.[2]

On May 23 of the following year Congress enacted a law limiting to one league square the amount of land which might be confirmed in any one claim.[3] The Register and Receiver were directed to continue

---

1. "Record Bk. 8, E. Fla.," p. 387 et seq.
2. U. S. Stat. at Large, IV, 202-204.
3. This amount had been fixed upon in Louisiana as the maximum.-- G&S, V, 474. Several claimants in Florida accepted one league square in lieu of the whole grant.

to examine and decide the remaining claims in East Florida until the first Monday in December, 1828, after which it would be unlawful for any claimant to exhibit any evidence in support of a claim.

Spanish claims not settled before that date, containing a greater amount of land than the commissioners were authorized to decide, and which had not been reported as antedated by the commissioners or the Registers and Receivers, were to be adjudicated by the judge of the superior court of the district within which the land lay, upon petition of the claimant, under restrictions prescribed to the district judge. The judge was not to take cognizance of any claim annulled by the treaty nor any claim presented to the commissioners or to Registers Receivers. Claimants were to be permitted to take an appeal form the superior court to the United States Supreme Court within four months after the decision. Claims which exceeded one league square and all other cases in which the United States district attorney thought the superior court had erred were to be appealed. Claims were to be brought before the court by petition within one year and prosecuted to a final decision within two years or be forever barred both by law and equity, but decrees so rendered were to be conclusive between the United States and claimant only and were not to affect the interest of third persons.[1]

The question of certain claims which the Spanish government had confirmed subsequent to January 24, 1818, and which the commissioners had reported favorably to Congress had not been passed upon by that body.

---

1. U. S. Stat. at Large, IV, 284-286.

On May 26, 1830, a law was passed providing that these claims should be re-examined and reported by the Register and Receiver before the next session of Congress. The Act further provided that all remaining claims which had been presented according to law and not finally acted upon were to be adjudicated as prescribed in the Act of May 23, 1828. All confirmations of land titles were to operate only as a relinquishment of the right of the United States and were not to be construed either as a guarantee of such titles or in any manner affect the rights of other persons to the same lands. Those who availed themselves of the opportunity to takw one league square in lieu of the whole grant were allowed one year in which to execute their relinquishment.[1]

Legislation respecting the settlement of Spanish land claims was now ended. Henceforth cases were settled in the courts. When Florida attained statehood in 1845 it abolished the superior court and transferred its former territorial jurisdiction to the state circuit courts. By the Act of February 22, 1847, Congress transferred the Federal jurisdiction which the superior court had exercised to the newly created district court of the United States for the District of Florida, and land cases pending in the superior courts were transferred to it.[2]

In February, 1835, the House of Representatives asked for a detailed report on claims pending in the courts under the Act of 1828 and on those confirmed by the United States Supreme Court, together with an opinion as to whether the pending cases come within the provisions

---

1. Ibid., pp. 405-406.
2. Ibid., IX, 128-130.

of those already decided by the court. The report, made in the following December by Richard Keith Call, Receiver at Tallhassee and counsel for the United States in the settlement of claims, shows:

    No. 1--Abstract of mill grants . . . . . . . . . . . . 20 in number
    No. 2--Abstract of grants "alleged to have been made
        for services rendered the Spanish government" 19 " "
    No. 3--Abstract for claims under grants made on con-
        dition of habitation and cultivation . . . . . 4 " "
    No. 4--Abstract of miscellaneous cases . . . . . . . 16 " "

    Pending in Superior Court of East Florida, at
        St. Augustine . . . . . . . . . . . . . . . . . . 60 " "
    Petitions filed but not yet placed on docket . . . . . 18 " "
    Pending in Superior Court of East Florida, at
        Jacksonville . . . . . . . . . . . . . . . . . . 14 " "
    Appeals to be made to the U. S. Supreme Court
        from decisions against the government ren-
        dered in the Southern Judicial District . . . . 2 " "
    Pending in Western and Middle Districts (involving
        title to island in the Apalachicola River, on t
        the line between the two districts) . . . . . . 1 " "

Call was of the opinion that three of the mill grants might be confirmed in line with the case of Francisco Richard (U. S. vs. Richard, 8 Peters, 470) who had built a mill and so fulfilled the condition. In his discussion of group No. 2, Call said that under the careful scrutiny of the commissioners these claims had been abandoned, but under the law of 1828 they again "sprang up", and while the Register and Receiver did not positively declare them forgeries and so exclude them from the courts under the law of 1828, it was evident that they regarded the claims as fraudulent. He was critical of the Supreme Court's favorable decision in the case of Mitchell et al vs. United States (9 Peters, 711), in which he said the court accepted as authentic documents which were "copies of copies", none of which were executed by a notary public and authenticated under his official seal. He thought the "badges of fraud" were as strongly developed in that case as in any of the pending cases, and if the latter were to be decided according to the principles laid down in the Mitchell case, then all the pending cases against the government would be confirmed.[1]

## REASONS FOR NON-CONFIRMATION OF LAND GRANTS

There were numerous reasons why certain land grants in Florida were not confirmed; some of the less obvious reasons are given below.

Often claimants had not filed within the prescribed time, which expired November 1, 1827. One such person was Antonio Pania (Pancia?),[2] who the Board remarks had according to witnesses fulfilled every requirement for a donation grant and had cultivated the place for 12 or 15 years, but filed his claim in September, 1828.[3] The same was true of John Hall,[4] of whom the commissioners' decree said: " . . . if his claim had been filed in time we would confirm it; but it was presented to this board in September, 1828."[5]

Sometimes there was a suspicion of fraud. Of one such claim the commissioners said: " . . . This paper is not filed in the office of the archives, where it certainly should have been, if the claim is genuine. The paper presented to us is claimed to be the original, and proof of the signature of Kindelan was tendered to this Board, but not

---

1. G&S, VIII, 247-260.
2. See Unc. P 1, Vol. I.
3. DG, V, 410.
4. See Unc. H 16, Vol. I.
5. DG, V, 410.

received." The Board noted also that the land lay within the Indian boundary in which grants were almost never made by Spanish governors, but "above all, the grant is dated on the 15th May, 1815, by authority of a royal order of 29th of March preceding, which was transmitted from Madrid by way of Havana, and communicated to the governor of this place by the captain-general, Apadoca, by a letter bearing date of 7th July, 1815, nearly two months after the date of the grant. . . ."[1]

The grants of Governor Coppinger and the surveys of George J. F. Clarke shortly before the cession were looked at askance. Although instructions to the surveyor-general directed him "when called on by any person to measure and bound lands . . . to require his title of property or grant from the government . . ." and to keep regular books in which his surveys were to be recorded, he testified before the commissioners that he possessed authority to survey without a special order, that he located wherever the claimant pointed out, that he kept no regular books of survey after the summer of 1817, and that he did not consider the governor's order obligatory.[2] On October 20, 1817, he issued a number of certificates of survey, alleging "disposition of S. S." (Su Senoria, His Excellency) for which no authorization from the governor could be found.[3]

Often conditions had not been fulfilled. Both British and Spanish grants as a rule carried conditions with respect to occupation and

---

1. Ibid., p. 397.
2. G&S, VI, 57.
3. See Unc. S 29; T 27; W 13, 21, 24, 25, Vol. I.

cultivation, the number of acres which should be cleared or drained within a given period, the number of cattle that should be pastured, or the establishment of a saw or grist mill, and the treaty permitted the same length of time for such conditions to be fulfilled in the event circumstances had previously prevented their fulfillment.[1] Many who presented claims had made no effort either under the Spanish government or under that of the United States to fulfill the conditions of their grants.

Sometimes royal titles were granted after January 24, 1818, when there was no evidence or occupation of even a conditional grant previous to that date. For example, Joseph M. Hernandez[2] received a grant on April 6, 1818, and two days later a title in absolute property.[3]

Often the surveys were not in agreement with the terms of the grants. The Supreme Court held that surveys to have validity must have been in conformity with the grants on which they were founded.[4]

Certificates issued by Thomas Aguilar as Spanish government secretary were questioned by the Board, particularly by Alexander Hamilton, and later by government counsel in cases before the courts. Here the Board was not sustained, the Supreme Court deciding in several cases

---

1. On this point the court said that the eighth article of the treaty was intended to apply to claims to land whose validity depended on the performance of conditions in consideration of which the concessions had been made and which must have been performed before Spain was bound to perfect the titles; and that the United States was bound after the cession to the same extent that Spain had been bound before ratification to perfect them by legislation and adjudication.--U. S. vs. Wiggins, 14 Peters, 334.
2. See Unc. H 21, Vol. I.
3. DG, V, 397.
4. U. S. vs. Forbes, 15 Peters, 173.

that Aguilar's certificates were valid evidence.[1]

Sometimes surveys had been made and certified only by private surveyors, the claimant offering no other evidence. The Supreme Court held that the certificate of a private surveyor purporting to show that he had permission from the governor to make a survey was no evidence of the fact, but that plats and certificates of the surveyor-general, because of his official capacity, should be given the credence that would have been accorded them by the Spanish government.[2]

There remain to be mentioned those British claims for lands which British subjects were unable to dispose of at the time of the retrocession of the province to Spain in 1783. They were brought forward after the cession of Florida to the United States, but were not confirmed by the Boards of Commissioners or by Congress. Even William Drayton's claims[3] failed of confirmation, although his difficulties with Governor Tonyn, which resulted among other things in the loss of his position as chief justice of East Florida, were in large part due to his sympathy for the patriot cause in the American Revolution. The law of Congress under which the Board was organized in 1822 instructed the commissioners (1) to ascertain how far the British claims were valid under the law of nations and (2) how far they had been considered valid under the Spanish government. If satisfied of their validity, the claims were to be

---

1. U. S. vs. Wiggins, 14 Peters, 325; U. S. vs. Delespine, 15 Peters, 226; U. S. vs. Acosta, 17 Peters, 16.
2. U. S. vs. Hanson, 16 Peters, 196.
3. See Unc. D 23½-38, Vol. I.

confirmed.[1]

English claimants did not pretend that their claims were valid under the Spanish government, but endeavored to avail themselves of the jus postliminium as laid down in Vattel and other writers on international law by means of which persons and things taken by the enemy might be restored. In their report of January 20, 1825, on the British claims, Overton and White went into the subject thoroughly, showing that according to Vattel the principle which the British invoked could only be made to operate in favor of British claimants had Florida been restored to England rather than sold to the United States which was not a party to the war between Great Britain and Spain. In addition, the treaty of 1783 between Great Britain and Spain recognized the claims by providing that subjects of the former should have eighteen months in which to dispose of them.

Furthermore, the commissioners expressed the opinion that had these claims been presented to the Spanish government before the cession of Florida to the United States, Spain would have pronounced them null and void. That the claims were not presented was evidence in their judgment that the English themselves thought so.

The commissioners pointed out also that the conditions of the English grants were not fulfilled under the Spanish government and quoted Blackstone as authority for this fact alone as being evidence that the claims were at least voidable. They expressed the opinion that even under English law the claims would not be recognized. Spain regranted

---

1. U. S. Stat. at Large, III, 709-718.

the lands claimed by those British subjects who left their lands in Florida after 1783, and "if Spain could regrant them and sell them at public auction, the United States, as the successor of Spain, are entitled to all the advantages resulting from a similar disposition of the property." They concluded that the British grants which were not confirmed by Spain are "forfeited, void, and of none effect."[1]

---

1. G&S, IV, 250-253. For a list of English claims, see Ibid., p. 250, and Unc. T 28-43, Vol. I.

Louise Biles Hill<br>Manuscripts Editor

## GOVERNORS OF FLORIDA FROM 1763 TO 1821

### BRITISH OCCUPATION 1763-1783

East Florida[1]

| | |
|---|---|
| James Grant | 1763-1771 |
| James Moultrie (lieutenant governor) | 1771-1774 |
| Patrick Tonyn | 1774-1785 |

West Florida[2]

| | |
|---|---|
| George Johnstone | 1763-1767 |
| Montfort Browne (lieutenant governor) | 1767-1769 |
| John Eliot | 1769 |
| Montfort Brown (lieutenant governor) | 1769 |
| Elias Durnford (lieutenant governor) | 1769-1770 |
| Peter Chester | 1770-1781 |

---

1. Grant left the province in 1771 on leave of absence; he did not resign until 1773. Tonyn remained in East Florida until Nov. 1785 although the Spanish governor had arrived and taken up his duties in the preceding June. Tonyn received his salary as governor up to June 1786.

2. Johnstone, appointed in 1763, arrived in the province in the autumn of 1764 and presided at council meetings as late as Jan. 10, 1767. He was dismissed from office for his policy in commencing hostilities against the Creek Indians. Montfort Browne was in charge of the province, by virtue of his commission as lieutenant governor, from Jan. 1767 until Apr. 3, 1769, when at the council meeting on that date John Eliot's commission as governor was published. Eliot died on May 2, according to the announcement made by Lieutenant Governor Browne at the council meeting on May 3. Historians have made conflicting statements with reference to Eliot,

Governors continued.

## SECOND SPANISH OCCUPATION 1783-1821

East Florida

| | |
|---|---|
| Vicente Manuel de Zespedes (Cespedes) | 1783-1790 |
| Juan Nepomuceno de Quesada y Arrocha | 1790-1795 |
| Bartolome Morales[1] (acting governor) | 1796 |
| Jose de Ortega | 1796 |
| Enrique White | 1796-1811 |
| Juan Jose de Estrada y Torro (provisional gov.) | 1811-1812 |
| Sebastian Kindelan y Oregon | 1812-1815 |
| Juan Jose de Estrada y Torro (provisional gov.) | 1815-1816 |
| Jose Coppinger | 1816-1821 |

---

some claiming that although appointed governor, he never left England; others, that he died at sea; and still others hint that he was a suicide or was killed in a duel. Recent research in the British Public Records Office shows that Eliot arrived in the province on Apr. 2, 1769, took up his duties and in all presided at seven council meetings. The cause of his death is not revealed in the minutes of the council meeting on May 3, nor in other Public Records Office manuscripts consulted. Browne as lieutenant governor was in charge of the province from the time of Eliot's death until his removal from office in the latter part of 1769, when Elias Durnford, former surveyor general for the province, was appointed lieutenant governor. Peter Chester presided over the council on Aug. 11, 1770, at which time his commission as governor was published. He served until the capitulation to Spain on May 10, 1781. (Letter from Prof. C. N. Howard, University of California in Los Angeles, dated 2/15/41, addressed to the editor, and a series of articles by Prof. Howard on "Colonial Pensacola", in the Florida Historical Quarterly, 1940-41, and the Journal of Southern History, May 1940. See also John Walton Caughey, Bernardo de Galvez in Louisiana 1776-1783, University of California Press, 1934, p. 211.)

1. Morales served as acting governor for short periods in 1900 and on other occasions.

Governors continued.

West Florida[1]

| | |
|---|---|
| Arturo O'Neill | 1783-1793 |
| Enrique White | 1793-1795 |
| Francisco de Paula Gelabert (ad interim) | 1795-1793 |
| Juan Vicente y Folch | 1796-1811 |
| Francisco Maximilian de St. Maxent (ad interim) | 1809, 1810 |
| Francisco Collel (ad interim) | 1810, 1811 |
| Francisco Maxmilian de St. Maxent | 1811, 1812 |
| Mauricio Zuniga | 1812-1813 |
| Mateo Gonzales Maurique | 1813-1815 |
| Jose de Soto (ad interim) | 1815-1816 |
| Francisco Maximilian de St. Mexent (ad interim) | 1816 |
| Jose Masot | 1816-1818 |
| Jose Maria Callava | 1819-1921 |

---

1. Grants of land were made also by Juan Ventura Morales and Alexander Ramirez, who at different times held the office of Intendant of the Army, Superintendent and General and Subdelegate of the Royal Treasure of the Island of Cuba and the Two Floridas, and sometimes by Don Juan Ruiz de Apadoca, Captain-General of Cuba.

SURVEYORS OF FLORIDA FROM 1763 TO 1821
(Surveyor-General and Public Surveyor are indicated by initials)

## BRITISH OCCUPATION 1763-1783

| | |
|---|---|
| Jonathan Davis | Frederick George Mulcaster, S.G. |
| William Gerard DeBrahm, S.G. | William Randall |
| James DeLaire | George Rolfe |
| Elias Durnford, S.G. | Bernard Romans |
| Jonathan Funk | Seton Wedderburn Row |
| Benjamin Lord, S.G. | Andrew Way |

## SECOND SPANISH OCCUPATION 1783-1821

| | |
|---|---|
| Antonio Balderas | Pedro Marrot, S.G. |
| Daniel Blue | Robert McHardy |
| Louis de Burdecat | D. S. H. Miller |
| Andres Burgevin | Juan N. Perchet |
| George J. F. Clarke, P.S. | Vicente Sebastian Pintado, S.G. |
| Josiah Dupont | John Purcell/Porcel, P.S. |
| Samuel Eastlake | Pedro Reggio |
| Dr. Eslick | John Tate |
| William/Guillermo Lawrence | Thomas T. Woods |

Kehr, John D., Heirs of          Con. K 1; DG V 413

1 [E] petitions for permit to build a house on one of the vacant lots near the Battery in Fernandina, 1/26/1811.

Justo Lopez, referred to, says, 2/10/1811, there is plenty of land on which John Kehr may build. Governor White agrees, 2/15/1811.

[The above is a Thomas Murphy translation attested by William Reynolds, 10/8/1828.]

[Jacket refers to descriptive list, No. 574.]

Kelker, Jacob          Con. K 2; DG IV 117

1 [E] Benjamin Clements certifies plat of 640 acres, a donation grant on the eastern margin of Escambia Bay, confirmed to Jacob Kelker by U. S. Commissioners and Congress, being Sec. 31, T. 1, R. 29 N&W. Countersigned by Robert Butler. Chainmen: C. I. [?] Drake and Joseph Brady.

The plat shows the bay on the southwest, I. [John?] Innerarity's land on the west, other sides vacant.

Kershaw, John          Con. K 3; DG V 57, 60
of Camden, S. C.

1 [E] claims, through John Rodman, 10/25/1823, as trustee of the children of John and Margaret DuBoso of St. Augustine, 100 acres at Governor Grand on North River, bounded on the north by lands of Lazaro Ortega, on the south by a ditch between North River and Guana Creek; a service grant, 12/20/1815, of Governor Estrada and to Jose and Miguel Andreu who sold to Capt. James

Hesell [?], agent for Hugh P. Davis of Charleston, guardian of Thomas M. Hesell [?], a minor, 7/16/1821, and soon after sold to Fileon Ripley and S. Fairbanks who sold to John Kershaw, 10/2[?]/1823.

[Stitched together 2-5 in Spanish:]

2 - Title page: A. No. 4, Florida, year 1815. Jose and Miguel Andreu asking title of 100 acres in place known as the Chimnies.

3 - Jose and Miguel Andreu, legitimate brothers and natives of this province, who live with their father at his plantation on North River and who at the first call to arms, 3/19/1812, enlisted and were assigned to Urban Artillery where they served during the invasion, have just heard of service grants, and there being 300 acres on the west of North River, bounded on the east by Guana Creek, north by lands that belonged to Lazaro Ortega, and south by Alligator Point [Punta del Cayman], property of Juana Paredes, petition for 100 acres farther north of a place called Governor Grand. St. Augustine, 7/22/1815.

Jose de Zavalia signs at the request of supplicants, "who do not write." On the margin Governor Estrada notes that he has never heard of service grants. No action taken.

4 - Jose and Miguel Andreu, both over 25, wish to help their minor brothers and their aged parents who have not enough to support their numerous family and petition as head rights gratis for 50 acres each, or 100 acres in common, in the above place. Governor Estrada grants, Tomas Aguilar attests, 11/24/1815.

5 - Jose and Miguel Andreu, since order for service grants must be in the secretary's office by now, petition for the above land, 7/29/1815.

Jose de Zavalia again signs for memorialists. Governor Estrada refers the above to the auditor of war, Juan de Arredondo y San Felices, who replies, 12/7/1815, that this petition accords with the royal order of 3/29/1813. Governor Estrada agrees and orders the petition granted.

6 [S] Jose and Miguel Andreu, in the absence of the surveyor general, petition for Burgevin to be authorized to survey and give them a plat of the land granted. Jose Bernardo Reyes signs for Jose and Miguel Andreu "who can't write", 1/29/1819.

7 [S] Andres Burgevin certifies plat of 2/1/1819.

8 [S] Governor Estrada's royal title to Jose and Miguel Andreu, 12/20/1815. William Reynolds attests copy.

9 [E] U. S. Commissioners confirm to John Kershaw.

10 [E] Henry Washington's certified plat of 103.80 acres, confirmed to John Kershaw by Congress according to Report A, claim 8, being Sec. 43, T. 5, R. 29 S&E. Surveyor General Butler countersigns. John W. Townsend and Isaac Varnes are chainmen.

[Dossier has duplicate of 6, copies of 4, 5, 6, all by William Reynolds, and a Francisco Jose Fatio translation of 8. Descriptive list No. 567, no deed of sale.]

Keyser, Joseph C.            Con. K 4; DG IV 102

1 [E] Benjamin Clements certifies plat, 2/18/1828, of 680.70 acres confirmed to Joseph C. Kiser by Congress according to Report No. 36 of the Commissioners of West Florida, being Sec. 19, T. 3, R. 30 N&W. No details.

[Jacket notes 800 arpens claimed by Maria A. Artacho, Escambia River.]

Keyser, Joseph C.            Con. K 5; DG IV 102

1 [E] Benjamin Clements certifies plat of 7/18/1828 for 576.93 acres confirmed to J. C. Kiser by the Commissioners of West Florida and by Congress, being Sec. 20, T. 3, R. 30 N&W.

[No details and no confirmation.]

Jacket notes Escambia River, 800 arpens claimed by Joseph [?] E. Caro.

Keyser, J. C.            Con. K 6; DG IV 105

1 [E] James W. Exum certifies a plat of 2.59 acres confirmed to Jose C. Keyser by the Commissioners of West Florida and by Congress, being Sec. 24, T. 2, R. 30 S&W, where landmarks are four mounds of earth.

Chainmen: Frederic Ming and Wesley Inglish. Surveyor General Robert Butler countersigns and writes on the plat in pencil: "To be returned to this office by Col. Exum."

Plat on paper 10¼" x 16½" is a tiny yellow square of 5/16".

Paul Rivas' land is shown on the southwest side, the other sides are vacant.

King, Thomas            Con. K 7; DG V 69

1 [E] Thomas J. Prevatt deposes before James Green, J. P. of Nassau County, that he is acquainted with Thomas King, who before, on, and after 2/22/1819, did inhabit and cultivate betwixt 10 and 15 acres of a tract of land on St. Marys River, and that he is head of a family of ten, 9 whites and 1 black.

2 [E] Antonio Alvarez certifies abstract from descriptive

list, No. 573, 640 acres, a donation grant confirmed to Thomas King.

Decree slip missing, 640 acres confirmed on abstract, Report B, No. 17, 1827.

[Dossier has duplicate of 1, identical except that the word "before" in line 2 is omitted.]

King, Thomas                    Con. K 8; DG IV 281

1 [E] claims, through George J. F. Clarke, 350 acres of which 257 acres are at Live Oak Landing, St. Marys River and 100 acres in Walker's Swamp, St. Marys River; Governor Coppinger's grant as head rights according to Clarke plats and certificates presented herewith.

2 [S] Clarke certifies plat of 1/27/1821, 100 acres in Walker's Swamp alleging "disposition of S. S. of 10/20/1817".*

3 [S] Clarke certifies plat of 11/26/1818, 257 acres at Live Oak Landing, surveyed to Thomas King, alleging "Disposition of H. E. of 10/20/1817".

4 [E] Thomas Theopolus Woods certifies plat, same as 3, on which Jesse Newton's land is shown on the bank up stream.

5 [E] E. Stafforde, sworn, deposes that he knows Thomas King who has been residing at Walker's Swamp for 5 or 6 years, having removed from White Oak Landing where he lived for a number of years previously.

6 [E] On the back of 1, the Board of Land Commissioners confirms the 257 acres as a donation grant, but not the 100 acres.

---

* See p. lv.

7 [E] Antonio Alvarez attests abstract from descriptive list, No. 203, and translation of 3.

[Dossier has duplicate of 3, and translation of 2 and 3.]

Kingsley, Anna M.  Con. K 9; DG IV 279

1 [S] claims, through George Gibbs, 350 acres on the east side of River St. John [illegible] and [?] 250 acres between the lands of John Creighton and Henry Wright, on a peninsula, and 100 acres on Dunn's Lake opposite lands of the late Robert Cowan, a grant of Governor Coppinger, 1/12/1816, according to document in the archives.

2 [E] Another memorial not identical:] Anna M. Kingsley claims, through George J. F. Clarke, 350 acres on the east side of Dunn's Lake, and 125 acres on St. Johns River. [The survey quoted mentions that the first line is bounded by John Faulk and the second by John Creighton.] The grant is based on head rights and made by Governor Coppinger on the same date.

3 [S] Ana Madgigine Kingsley, 12/4/1815, free mulatto, inhabitant of St. Johns, says that on 9/13/1813, the governor's predecessor granted her 5 acres in one piece between the lands of John Creighton and Henry Wright where she built her dwelling and some smaller houses for her six slaves and considered herself safe from the insults and annoyances of the insurgents; but towards the end of that same year a party of those highwaymen from Georgia under the orders of a leader named Alexander came with the intention of robbing the inhabitants already tranquilized. Those on the small gun-boats saw from the river that her buildings might serve as a shelter for the robbers and their

commander arranged to raze and burn all this new establishment contained. The flames devoured grain and other things to the value of $1,500, all in the service of His Majesty. And now Anna M. Kingsley has increased her family to more than 3 children, 6 slaves and 20 head of livestock, which slaves, having no land of her own, share the land of Zephaniah Kingsley. Consequently she petitions for 350 acres, 250 acres to be used for pasturage in the vacant land between Creighton and Wrigh [sic], and 100 acres on the east side of Dunn's Lake in a place known as a peninsula, or tongue of land, on which the late Juan Forrester was given the right to cut cedar opposite the land of Robert Cowin. Governor Estrada, on the margin, refers the above to the military commander of St. Johns, 12/19/1815.

Thomas Llorente [on the bottom of 3rd page] says that Ana M. Kingsley deserves any favor the governor can grant her. Rather than afford shelter and provisions to the enemies of His Majesty, it would have been better if she, instead of trying to save a little food and clothes, had burned it all up and remained unsheltered from the weather; the royal order provides rewards for such services, 12/24/1815.

[On the 4th page] Governor Coppinger grants, 1/12/1816, and orders certificate sent and petition archived.

4 [S] Aguilar certified that copy of document in archives differs slightly from 3. In it Anne M. Kingsley writes from Kingsley's house; Governor Kindelan is named as grantor; Llorente writes from San Nicolas, 10/4/1813, crediting remarks about burning the property to Anna M. Kingsley when she arrived bringing 3

children and 4 slaves of age. It appeared later that she had 2 other slaves.

5 [S] Clarke's certified plat of 225 acres, part of 350 acres granted.

6 [E] Slip 8" x 2½" on which the Board confirms the claim.

7 [E] Antonio Alvarez' certified extract from descriptive list, No. 193. Attached are copies, [2pp.] of all but the survey. Signed by Antonio Alvarez, 12/20/1844.

[On the back of this sheet, labeled in ink:] No. 193, from descriptive list. [Below in pencil is added:] "The 100 a. surveyed by Randolph, 1849, near . . . not surveyed."

[Dossier has translation of all Spanish documents.]

Kingsley, Zephaniah          Con. K 10; DG IV 282

1 [E] claims, through George Gibbs, 2,611 acres more or less, on the west side of St. Johns River and the south side of Doctor's Lake, on a creek called Laurel Grove, bounded on the north by lands now or late of John Arnold; head rights granted by Governor Estrada to William Pengree, whose widow, Rebecca, with the consent of the Spanish governor, sold to Zephaniah Kingsley.

[Stitched together 2-9, in Spanish:]
2 - Title Page, in ink: P. No. 1, Florida, year 1803. Rebecca Pengree seeking permit to sell 78 caballerias and one third granted to her late husband, William Pengree. [In blue pencil:] 2,600 acres.

[On jacket below names are added:]

```
1753    "Laurel Grove"
 626    "Laurel Spring"
 100    "Cook Plantation"
 121    "Good Fortune"
-----
2,600
```

3 - [4½ pp. of foolscap MS:] Rebecca Pengree says that according to accompanying papers, Marrot and Eastlake surveyed and delivered to her late husband, William Pengree:

- 52 caballerias and 20 acres in the plantation called "Laurel Grove"
- 18 caballerias and 26 acres in the place called "Laurel Springs"
- 3 caballerias in another place called "Cooke"
- 3 caballerias and 21 acres in the place known as "Good Fortune"

All of which amounts to 78 1/3 caballerias, corresponding to the number in the family, 51 persons, consisting of husband, wife, one child and 48 slaves, according to the law of head rights in 1787 when they returned to the Province of Florida in which they had been old inhabitants under Great Britain. They remained on the plantation until 1794 when by government orders they withdrew to this side of the river, abandoning their property. All their improvements, houses, fences and crops, were destroyed to the value, according to experts, of $7,000 for which they have received no compensation.

This abandonment and loss was the immediate cause of the ruin of the considerable property they had introduced into the Province. Her husband had died and to start again and to keep so large a family in food and clothes required very high costs. They were unable to make a crop adequate to support themselves, since the rebels kept the country stirred up in 1795 and the Indians later. So that Rebecca Pengree was obliged to sell a number of slaves. She stated further that the Tribunal knows the large sums she paid to the house of Panton-Leslie Co., one of her heaviest creditors. She lost a crop for lack of hands; then came a division of the property in which a share of land and slaves went to her daughter, Isavel Leslie, who had married Juan Leslie. Again she lost a crop for lack of hands when much to her disadvantage she was forced to stay in the city to no avail. She is now driven to a fatal alternative: to fall into indigence or to sell. [There are two and one-half pages more of the memorial, in which she asks title to her property, permission to sell, and appraisement of its value, 11/10/1803.] Governor White refers the above to the Assessor General, as Zubizarreta attests.

4 - Josef de Ortega writes, 11/16/1803, that the troubles of the inhabitants are well known. Rebecca Pengree was compelled, through no fault of her own, to leave her land uncultivated and could not comply with orders of the government for continuous possession. He recommends that she be permitted to sell. Governor White agreed and Zubizarreta authorized deed of sale to Zephaniah Kingsley.

5 - Rebecca Pengree, 10/12/1803, petitions for copy of Marrot-Eastlake plats in the archives, which Governor White grants.

6 - On the back of the page and on the next is the Marrot-Eastlake plat labeled in pencil on 12/7/1791, "Laurel-Grove 1735".

7 - Marrot's certified plat of 2/16/1793 signed by Josiah Dupont and labeled in pencil "Laurel Spring, 626".

8 - Marrot's certified plat of 2/18/1793, signed by Josiah Dupont. Labeled in pencil, "Cooke-100".

9 - Another plat of 2/19/1793 labeled "Good Luck-121".

10 [S] Rebecca Pengree sells the above mentioned tracts of land to Zephaniah Kingsley for $5,300, 11/26/1803. After approval of contents by Bernadino Sanchez, public interpreter, Rebecca Pengree, Isabel Leslie, only co-heir [who signs herself "Eliza"] and Zephaniah Kingsley all sign in the presence of Bernardo Jose Segui and Juan de Entralgo before Jose de Zubizarreta. William Reynolds attests copy.

11 [E. Pasted together:] Antonio Alvarez' certified extract, No. 202 in confirmed descriptive list, of 2,611 acres confirmed to Zephaniah Kingsley. Names with dates are listed as above and survey plats follow.

12 [E. Pasted together:] Another, like 11, with Marrot certificate and 5 tracts of land confirmed to Zephaniah Kingsley. Four, contiguous, lie along the north side of Doctor's Lake. On the west and one-half mile beyond Cooke lies Fuente del Alamo, 300 acres, claim No. 198, descriptive list. [The land of A. Hull, claim No. 541, lies to the east of Buen Suceso.]

13 [E] Three surveys, neither signed nor approved: Laurel Spring, 440.50 acres in T. 4, R. 25 S&E; Laurel Grove, 1,880 acres in T. 4, R. 25 S&E. [J. M. McIntosh, marked on each of these]; and Cooke, 110.40 acres in T. 4, R. 25 S&E.

[Dossier has Thomas Murphy translation with Fatio's approval of all Spanish.]

Kingsley, Zephaniah          Con. K 11; DG IV 282

1 [E] claims, through George Gibbs, 2,000 acres at Twelve Mile Swamp, bounded on the south by lands of George J. F. Clarke, north by lands of Philip R. Yonge; a grant by Governor Coppinger based on head rights, 1/18/1816.

[Stitched together 2-10 in Spanish:]

2 - Title page: K. No. 4, Florida, year 1816. Zephaniah Kingsley asking title of 2,300 acres in 12 Mile Swamp and in two swales [Ensenadas] situated in Saw Mill Creek.

3 - Clarke's certified plat of 10/20/1815. [No details are shown except 2 houses on the east side in a small patch of cultivated ground.]

4 - Another Clarke plat of 11/1/1815 showing two swales connected by a tongue of land. The larger, on the north, showing house and cultivated land, is marked "250 a.". The other is marked "50 a.". A creek crosses the neck and runs along the northwest side of the latter.

5 - Zephaniah Kingsley refers to the "characteristic justice" of the governor who in his decree of yesterday said that Zephaniah Kingsley had a right to a concession of 3,300 acres, by virtue of which he asks anew that land be granted him from the following vacant land:

> 1,000 acres on the point formed by the main river of Santa Maria and the little one known by the name of Little St. Marys on the upper part or the west of said river which forms a swamp with a pine forest on the upper end or west.
>
> 300 acres at the district distinguished by the name of Swamp at the head of the Creek of the Saw Mill, its entrance on the west side being marked by a cross on a gum tree. This Swamp is situated 3 miles from, and on the west side of, a place known as Twelve Mile Swamp.

2,000 acres in Twelve Mile Swamp which begins with an oak [encina] marked with a cross on the west side of this Swamp and runs as far as the opposite, or east, side where it continues on the east side until it measures 110 chains, which is sufficient to complete the said number of acres.

[A half page more of the above with date, 1/29/1814.] Governor Kindelan grants, 1/31/1814, 3,300 acres attested by Entralgo. Aguilar attests copy, 2/1/1815.

6 - Zephaniah Kingsley having complied with conditions set by Governor Kindelan of keeping 12 slaves busy clearing and fencing his 2,300 acres and building warehouses, dwellings, etc., petitions, 1/16/1816, for permission to prove the above and receive title, as has already been granted for his other 1,000 acres on River Santa Maria. Governor Coppinger asks to see the documents [plats] and hear witnesses, 1/17/1816.

7 - Jose Mariano Hernandez, native, married, merchant, 27, swears to 11 or 12 slaves, etc., before Entralgo, same date.

8 - Moses Bowden, married, neighbor, 25, deposes that he has seen some of the slaves and H. [Z?] Kingsley himself building houses and he seemed to have all the farming tools necessary.

9 - John Ashton, single, native, has seen negro shacks, slaves laboring, etc.

10 - Z. Kingsley deposes that prior to 1803, Governor Kindelan told him he could have title as soon as his land was ready to farm.

[Entralgo signs all these documents, 1/18/1816. Z. Kingsley does not sign and Bowden and Ashton cannot write.] Governor Coppinger grants.

11 [S] Governor Coppinger's royal title to Zephaniah

Kingsley, 1/18/1816. Entralgo attested copy.

12 [E] Antonio Alvarez certified extract from descriptive list, No. 196.

13 [E. Pasted to 12] Copy of Clarke's plat, 5/15/1845.

14 [S] Plat marked in the northeast corner, "Copy given to the interested party, 10/20/1815." Plat, a rhombus, 110 x 199 chains, is crossed at the southern end by the "Old Cedar Road" and a mile farther to the north by the "New Road" which leads to houses and cultivated land on the eastern margin. At the northern extreme the plat is crossed by "Cedar Road of Roco."

15 [S] A smiliar plat, but unsigned by Clarke shows, better than does #14, 2,000 acres of Philip Robert Yonge just to the north with 1,000 acres of Hibbertson and Yonge just to the west in Trout Creek Swamp. The lands of Clarke are shown to the south of Zephaniah Kingsley.

[Dossier has Thomas Murphy translation of title. One paper in this case is to be found in No. 9, as penciled on jacket.]

Kingsley, Zephaniah          Con. K 12; DG IV 282, 289

1 [E. The right hand side of the document is blurred and broken off.] claims, through George Gibbs, 1,000 acres on Drayton, at the entrance to [La]ke George; bounded on all sides by St. Johns River, it being an island as attested by Entralgo, 7/27/1821; royal title based on head rights for 1,500 acres by George Sibbald who sold . . . all right, and rest and residence . . . was granted to H. [Z.?] Kingsley by the governor.

[Stitched together 2-13 in Spanish:]

2 - Title page: Florida, year 1814. Zephaniah Kingsley asking title to 2,000 acres on Drayton Island.

3 - Pierra certifies that Governor White granted to George Sibbald 1,500 acres, etc., where he will raise coffee with 10 negroes, which number will be increased as the coffee trees grow. This grant shall be considered null if the Indians oppose, in order to avoid trouble with them, 10/6/1804.

4 - Aguilar certifies that Zephaniah Kingsley petitioned for the 1,500 acres now vacant and claimed by the heirs of George Sibbald, and that Governor Estrada granted by right of sale and by Kingsley's paying the price and the costs, 9/5/1811.

5 - The heirs and goods of George Sibbald for improvements on Drayton Island, Debtor:

|  | Pesos |
|---|---|
| For the rent of negroes at various times between the years 1805 and 1811 for improving and cultivating said island | 2,517.4 |
| 4 sacks of seed coffee at various times | 47.2 |
| Pay of Mr. Manton as overseer | 96.4 |
| Idem for Samuel Toms, idem | 220. |
|  | 2,881.2 |
| Month's provisions (rum, coffee, sugar) and various attentions | 500. |
|  | 3,381.2 |

Errors excepted, San Augustine, 4/26/1811

Zephaniah Kingsley.

6 - Zephaniah Kingsley is creditor to the goods and heirs of the late George Sibbald for the amount of 3,381 pesos loaned at various times for the aid of a plantation, etc. He petitions the governor to kindly order the widow, Jane Sibbald, to satisfy him.

[On bottom:] Estrada passes this petition on to Jane Sibbald

On the back Zubizaretta attests Juan Jose de Estrada,

Governor ad interim after the death of Enrique White, that "The proprietor" made the above arrangement at the dictamen of the Auditor of War, and also pro tem, 4/30/1811. Signed by Jose Gregorio Quintana.

7 - Jane Sibbald admits the justice of Zephaniah Kingsley's claim but cannot satisfy it except by installments from profits on Drayton's Island, or by Zephaniah Kingsley's taking her rights in the island as complete payment. She begs the governor to consider as answered Zephaniah Kingsley's demand and to take any steps in justice, since she does not act from malice but from necessity. On the bottom and back, Governor Estrada initials [with an "E"] this letter with the dictamen of the Auditor of War, 5/31/1811. At the bottom and on the next page he orders it referred to Zephaniah Kingsley, signing only with his cypher. Zubizarreta attests the above, 6/1/1811.

8 - Z. Kingsley's power of attorney to Entralgo to act for him before the government court against George Sibbald, defunct. Witnesses: Segui, Arredondo, Castro y Ferrer, all neighbors. Before Zubizarréta, 7/16/1811, who attests that it conforms to the original in the archives.

9 - Entralgo does not wish to press Jane Sibbald in her indigence. She cannot sell; she has complied with all conditions except tenure. He asks the governor, who has shown a desire to promote agriculture in the Province, to order the government notary to authorize a writing from his office accepting the improvements, which Zephaniah Kingsley can continue with his numerous (and if needed, increased number of) slaves and overlook the incompleted

time. Governor Estrada initials, with his cypher, the above with the dictamen of the auditor of war *pro tem*, as Zubizarreta attests, 7/7/1813, and notifies Entralgo.

10 - Jose Gregorio Quintana agrees, subsequent to consent of archives and on condition of payment of fees (28 *reales*) which may be post-poned until Jane Sibbald's fortune improves. Zubizarreta, on back, badly inked through and nearly illegible, attests Governor's signature, 7/18, and states that Entralgo was notified. Governor Estrada initials documents.

11 - Fees, set by secretary in default of a regular public assessor, and by arrangement with treasurer's office:

```
Due: The governor for 5 signatures . . . . . .  10 rr.
     auditor of war, 2 assessments  . . . . . .  38  "
     Secretary (notary) . . . . . . . . . . . .  72  "
                                                120 rr. or 15
                                                        pesos
```

12 - Zephaniah Kingsley has held possession of Drayton Island, conceded to George Sibbald in October, 1804, since the decision of the tribunal, 7/18/1811. The Island, through lack of a surveyor, was thought to contain only 1,500 acres, but now, 1/3/1815, proves to contain 2,000. There being no other occupant or petitioner, Zephaniah Kingsley now petitions for the whole island which he has cleared and improved. Governor Kindelan refers the above to the auditor of war. Entralgo attests.

Arredondo, auditor of war, demands a statement of the conditions of the grant. Entralgo gives same and refers back to Zephaniah Kingsley with order for witnesses.

13 - Zephaniah Kingsley presents the following witnesses: Isaac Wickes, from New York, widower, 73, who swears to George Sibbald's

raising coffee, etc.; Juan Gayger [signs John Geiger], of the U.S.A., married, 34, who swears to work done by George Sibbald; Juan Andreu, married, merchant, 41, who cannot sign, but swears to the value of improvements on Drayton Island. Arredondo and Governor Kindelan approve Zephaniah Kingsley's request and order title sent. Entralgo complies.

[In No. 12 the order of the court with the cession of the land by Jane Sibbald was approved by both parties, but the document was not signed and made valid because of the neglect and delay of Zubizarreta who died shortly after.]

14 - Title, Governor Coppinger to Zephaniah Kingsley, 7/7/1821. Entralgo and Reynolds attest.

15 - The U. S. Land Commissioners find this British grant valid.

[Dossier has Thomas Murphy translation of title.]

Kingsley, Zephaniah          Con. K 13; DG IV 279

1 [E] claims through George Gibbs, 1,000 acres south of St. Marys River, bounded east and south by Little St. Marys River, west by the plantation of Higginbottom. Governor Estrada's royal title of 12/22/1815.

[Stitched together 2-12 in Spanish:]

2 - Title page: Florida, year 1815. Zephaniah Kingsley asking title of 1,000 acres of land on the banks of St. Marys and Little St. Marys.

3 - Zephaniah Kingsley says the governor has declared him deserving of 3,300 acres and petitions for the land in the following vacant places:

1,000 acres on point of land formed by St. Marys River and Little St. Marys River where on the upper, or west, side of said river it makes a swamp.

300 acres in a place known as the head of Saw Mill Creek, the place being marked with a tree called a gum, on the west side, 3 miles from a place called Twelve Mile Swamp.

2,000 acres in Twelve Mile Swamp beginning with a marked oak, etc., 1/29/1814.

Governor Kindelan grants, and orders certificate sent by Aguilar, who attests.

4 - George J. F. Clarke certifies plat of 1,000 acres. The land runs west 130 chains along White Oak Creek and embraces the southern end of Plantage de Higginbottom.

5 - Zephaniah Kingsley asks the Gobernador and the commandante politico y militar, to order Nathanial Wildes and Juan Ashton, both inhabitants, to appear and tell what they know about his improvements. Fernandina, 12/2/1815.

6 - Bernardo Segui, notary public ad interim, names Goerge J. F. Clarke interpreter, subject to his acceptance. Pangua also signs. [Same date and place.]

7 - George J. F. Clarke accepts and signs, as do Benita de Pangua and Bernardo Segui.

8 - Zephaniah Kingsley presents Nathaniel Wildes, native of Georgia, 36, who swears to buildings and improvements by Zephaniah Kingsley. Signed by Nathaniel Wildes, Clarke, Pangua and Segui.

9 - Zephaniah Kingsley presents Juan Aston [Ashton], native, unmarried, 24, who swears to house, etc., built by Zephaniah Kingsley but does not sign. Deposition signed by George J. F. Clarke,

Benita de Pangua, and Bernardo Segui.

10 - Zephaniah Kingsley petitions for absolute title, 12/19/1815. Governor Estrada passes the request to the auditor of war, Juan Arredondo. Governor Estrada and Arredondo refer back to Zephaniah Kingsley for further information. Entralgo so notifies Zephaniah Kingsley.

11 - Zephaniah Kingsley presents Enrique Yonge, married, merchant from Georgia, 39, who knows of the progress Zephaniah Kingsley has made with his negroes, etc.

12 - Zephaniah Kingsley [18 pp.] tells the governor that he has brought 74 negroes to devote to agriculture and not to the importation of edibles, as many have done, etc., 1/25/1814.

The governor orders the secretary to summarize the orders received by Governor White for the admission of settlers with slaves, and compare with the number introduced by Zephaniah Kingsley. Governor White signs and Entralgo, secretary pro tem, countersigns a document showing that Governor Juan de Quesada in the last mail received from the Captain General, 11/29, had the following royal order: that land will be granted only to those who take the oath of fealty, without bothering about their religion, as long as they make no public display of any religion except Catholic; that land granted shall be 1/3 x 2/3 and the long dimensions shall not be laid out on water front of rivers and creeks but towards the interior. [Copy certified by Domingo Rodriquez de Leon, 11/20/1790, government notary.]

Also Governor Enrique White, ordered by his Majesty to vary

partly the rules established for concessions and distribution of lands, submitted the following:

1st, that new settlers shall state the number and sex of their children and those under 8 shall receive nothing.

2nd, to each head of family 50 acres and same to unmarried or single of both sexes. To children and slaves between 8 and 16, 25 acres.

3rd, those employed in the city shall be given land to be farmed by self or slaves.

4th, these concessions shall die as if not made if the parties do not appear to take possession and cultivate inside of 6 months.

5th, no one can transfer or sell land without a government permit.

6th, if anyone wants to move, he can arrange with the government.

7th, wood or pasture land shall be conceded and trespassers forbidden.

8th, land granted shall be surveyed to avoid disputes.

9th, anyone who does not cultivate for 2 years may have his land assigned to another after it has been publicly announced.

Signed by Governor White, 10/12/1803, and by order of His Honor, Jose de Zubizarreta, notary of government. "Conforms to original in archives, Entralgo, notary ad interim."

Certified and sworn that Zephaniah Kingsley introduced into the province, 64 slaves; 21 of them in the sloop "Laurel" from the port of San Tomas, 5/5/1804; 10 on 6/25 of the same year in the schooner "Laurel", alias the "Juanita", proceeding from Havana; 16 in the sloop "El Jefe", coming from Charleston, 7/15/1806; 3 in the schooner "Esther", coming from Havana, on 10/21/1806; and 10 in the schooner "Industria", coming from Georgia, 3/9/1808.

Signed: Entralgo, St. Augustine, 1/27/1814.

Decree: That Zephaniah Kingsley introduced slaves before the new plan was introduced by the Captain General, 11/29/1790, and adopted by this government in 1803. Signed by Governor Kindelan and by Entralgo who certified copy from his archives, St. Augustine, 12/22/1815. Auditor of War Arredondo and Governor Estrada sign grant to Zephaniah Kingsley.

13 [S] Zephaniah Kingsley petitions for the land described in No. 3, 1/29/1814, and Governor Kindelan grants, 1/29/1814.

14 [S] Royal title for 1,000 acres on Little St. Marys granted to Zephaniah Kingsley, 12/20/1815, by Governor Estrada y Toro, written at the request of Zephaniah Kingsley by Entralgo, 7/7/1821.

15 [E] Antonio Alvarez attests extract from descriptive list No. 197, royal grant of 1,000 acres to Zephaniah Kingsley. Date of this certificate, 2/24/1845.

16 [E. Pasted to 15.] Antonio Alvarez' copy of Clarke survey of junction of two rivers.

17 [S] Clarke's certified plat of same junction showing 500 acres of Dona Ysabela Higginbottom and, just north of it, the land of Roberto Hutchison. Labeled on back, in pencil, 11/26/1815.

18 [S] Another Clarke certified plat of the same area, labeled on the back, "2nd Survey includes Jayme Martinely's 300 A." [Not shown on plat.]

[Dossier contains Murphy translation of title and Clarke plat.]

Kingsley, Zephaniah                Con. K 14; DG V 59, 68

1 [E] claims, through George Gibbs, an Island called Fort

George, 720 acres more or less, on the northeast side of St. Johns River, bounded by St. Johns River, which separates it from the mainland, by another creek and inlet which separates it from Talbot Island, and by the ocean to the south.

Title: Sale by George J. F. Clarke as attorney of John H. McIntosh who had title from John McQueen who had grant from the governor.

2 [S] Governor White's royal title based on head rights to John McQueen, of Island of San Jorge, 21 caballerias and 21 acres according to the Marrot-Eastlake survey, 2/27/1804. William Reynolds attests copy.

[Stitched together 3-7 in Spanish:]

3 - Zephaniah Kingsley points out that on 1/23 of last year Clarke was given power of attorney to act for John H. McIntosh in the matter of the Island of Fort Jorge which McIntosh owned, and petitions that these documents be united in a notebook of writings and be archived so as to be available, since he (Zephaniah Kingsley) is about ready to satisfy his rights . . ., 4/1/1818. Governor Coppinger refers this request to the Auditor of War, pro tem.

There are two rubrics. Entralgo signs and notifies Zephaniah Kingsley.

4 - Clarke's power of attorney from John McIntosh is in English and needs to be translated into Spanish. He begs the governor to pass it to the notary public for this purpose, 1/10/1817. Domingo Acosta will translate. Signed: Bartolome Morales.

5 - State of Georgia, Candeu [Camden] County, John H. McIntosh

power to George J. F. Clarke, signed in the presence of Roberto Holcombe, Archibald Clarke, notary public, Diego F. Coit.

Georgia: Know that 11/30/1816 appeared before me, Archibald Clarke, notary public of Santa Maria, Juan McIntosh, above named, and confessed that it was his own act, etc. Signed Archibald Clarke.

The translation is faithfully made according to above decree, 1/10/1817, Domingo Acosta.

Don Francisco Morales, knight of the royal military order of San Hermenegildo, Captain of the Regiment of Cuba Line Infantry and Military and Political Commander ad interim and subdelegate of the Royal Estates in the town of Fernandina and Island of Amalia, signs with two witnesses in the absence of the notary, who is in the capital, that the above agrees with the original in their archives: Morales, Domingo Estacholy, Juan Rosello.

6 - [Here follows a document in English:]

George Clarke, etc., has received from John McIntosh the enclosed letter, empowering him to execute a deed to Zephaniah Kingsley of the Island called Fort George, and petitions that this paper be translated and archived, 3/31/1818.

Governor Coppinger orders Jose Bousquet to translate in default of a public interpreter.

Translation: River, 1/19/1817.

Dear Sir: I believe that previously I advised you that I had agreed with Zephaniah Kingsley on the sale of Fort George. Now I would esteem it that as my agent you grant him full and sufficient title. As for Major Clarke, ask him to conclude this, business as quickly as possible. Enclosed is my paper for Fort George, but it also includes other lands, so please return as soon as the title is complete. Of the money that Mr. Kingsley will pay, i.e., $3,500, you will retain $250.

Kindly tell Mr. Kingsley that I have a claim against him for the rent of the Island before the sale, when he made a beautiful crop and offered to pay rent. There is no doubt he will pay a liberal rent, since he bought for a song. John H. McIntosh to George J. F. Clarke; Jose Maria Bosquet attests translation. Governor Coppinger approves sale if fees are paid. Entralgo notifies George J. F. Clarke.

7 - Clarke, with power from John H. McIntosh, sells to Zephaniah Kingsley, 21 caballerias and 21 acres, which is all of Fort George Island, surrounded by the marshes of San Juan, of the creek of Barra Chica and some others, which the government granted to John McQueen who sold to Juan Houston McIntosh who sells through Clarke to Zephaniah Kingsley for $7,000.

And in absence of a notary pro tem, Bernardo Segui acted in the presence of Francisco Morales, Juan de Rusello and Domingo Estacholy. Entralgo attests copy of original in the archives.

8 [E] Henry Washington certifies plat which Robert Butler countersigns, Johns W. Townsend and Amos Lee, chainmen, of 1,059.75 acres surveyed for Zephaniah Kingsley, being in Sec. 39, T. 1, R. 28, S&E and in Sec. 37, T. 1, R. 29.

Confirmed 6/20/1836.

[Dossier has Murphy translation of 15 pp. bound together and Fatio summary of case. Jacket shows 720 acres.]

Kingsley, Zephaniah        Con. K 15; DG V 59, 68

1 [E] claims, through George Gibbs, 565 acres on the east side of St. Johns River, being one-half of 1,135 acres bounded on the north by lands belonging to John M. Sanchez, owner of the other half, south by lands of Francis Miles, east by King's Road, west by St. Johns River, according to Andrew Burgevin plat.

Title, deed of sale by Francis Roman Sanchez, who inherited said lands from his father, Francis X. Sanchez, and his mother, Maria del Carmen Hill, according to division and partition of same as will appear in archives in deed of 3/6/1819 and certified by Entralgo.

2 [S] Governor White's grant of head rights to Francis X. Sanchez of 33 caballerias and 30 acres at a plantation known as San Jose, conceded to sons and heirs of the defunct Francis X. Sanchez, 1/29/1811. Jose de Zubizarreta attests and William Reynolds certifies copy.

3 [S] Francisco Roman Sanchez sells to Zephaniah Kingsley 575 acres, half of 33 caballerias and 30 acres that composed the plantation called San Jose, granted to the former's late father, Francis X. Sanchez, and after his death to his mother, Maria del Carmen Hill, and after her death to his brother, Juan Manuel and himself in common. The 575 acres belonging to Francisco Roman Sanchez, which is bounded on the north by the other half belonging to Juan Manuel Sanchez, on the south by land belonging to Francisco Miller, on the east by the Camino Real and on the west by the St. Johns River, according to Burgevin's plat, Francisco Roman Sanchez sells for $2,600 cash paid.

Witnesses: F. P. Sanchez, Jose Bernardo Reyes, Pedro Miranda. Copy attested by Entralgo.

4 [E] Antonio Alvarez attests extract from descriptive list, No. 572, 865 acres, to Zephaniah Kingsley.

5 [E. Pasted to No. 4:] Copy of Burgevin plat of 3/6/1819.

6 [E] Fatio's summary of grant and sale, confirmed to present purchaser.

7 [E] Unsigned and unattested plat of land surveyed to Zephaniah Kingsley, being in T. 3, R. 27 S&E. Plat shows to the north the claim of J. M. Sanchez, 280.50 acres in Sec. 42; to the northeast claim of F. Richard, Sec. 56; and to the southeast the claim, Sec. 44 of J. M. Hanson.

[Dossier has Thomas Murphy translation of signing of deed of sale with Fatio's attestation and complete Murphy translation of 4 pp. of deed of sale without attestation.]

Kingsley, Zephaniah        Con. K 16; DG V 57, 61

1 [E] claims, through George Gibbs, 500 acres on the south side of St. Marys River, bounded on the east by other lands of Zephaniah Kingsley and G. Hobkirk; royal title granted by Governor Coppinger as head rights to Burrows Higginbottom, whose widow, Isabella, and whose heirs sold, 1/30/1822, according to Clarke survey of 1/10/1816.

2 [S] Governor Coppinger's royal title to Isabel Higginbottom of 700 acres in two tracts, as surveyed by George J. F. Clarke at Higginbottom's Bluff of which 200 acres are now claimed by other parties and title is given to 500 acres.

3 [S] Clarke certifies plat of 500 acres as part of 700 acres conceded to Burrows Higginbottom, 9/24/1803, at the plantation of Reding Blunt, which turned out to be claimed by another, in consequence of which Isabel Higginbottom took possession of the 500 acres which she has cultivated since and conforms to plat below. The 200 acres remain in the district called Sandag's [?] Bluff. Fernandina, 10/10/1816.

4 [E] Antonio Alvarez certifies extract from descriptive list, No. 570, 500 acres to Zephaniah Kingsley. [Attached to 4 is copy of Clarke's plat.]

5 [E] Memo slip of U. S. Commissioners mentions conveyance by Isabel Higginbottom to Zephaniah Kingsley.

[Dossier contains duplicate of Clarke survey, and Murphy translation of same and of Higginbottom's petition for grant.]

Kingsley, Zephaniah          Con. K 17; DG IV 279

1 [E] claims, through George Gibbs, for 300 acres at the head of Saw Mill Creek, Governor Coppinger's grant for head rights, 1/18/1816.

2 [S] Governor Coppinger's royal title for 300 acres conceded as head rights to Zephaniah Kingsley in two little swales at the head of Saw Mill Creek. Entralgo attests act and copy of document.

3 [S] Clarke certifies plat marked "copy given to interested party 1 of Nov. of 1815". [This is same plat in K 11, No. 4.]

4 [E] Antonio Alvarez attests extract from descriptive list, No. 194, 300 acres to Zephaniah Kingsley.

5 [E. Pasted to 4:] Copy of Clarke plat, two swales, each labeled "Bay".

6 [E] Unsigned plat, 261.60 acres surveyed for Zephaniah Kingsley in Sec. 43, and 376.80 acres in Sec. 44, all being in T. 6, R. 28 S&E.

[Dossier has Thomas Murphy translation of title and duplicate of 3.]

[Jacket has penciled on it in blue:] "See No. 7 for 1 paper connected with this case." "See No. 9 for 1 paper connected with this case (?)."

Kingsley, Zephaniah          Con. K 18; DG IV 279

1 [E] claims, through George Gibbs, 300 acres on Doctor's Creek on St. Johns River, called Fuente del Alamo, title: Governor White's grant for head rights to William Kane, 8/19/1809, whose heirs sold to Zephaniah Kingsley, 9/1/1809.

[Stitched together 2-8 in Spanish:]

2 - Title page: Florida, year 1809. Ysavel Kane, widow of Guillermo Kane, asking to be sent title to plantation called Fuet [Fuente] del Alamo.

3 - Marrot-Eastlake certified plat to Guillermo Kane, 11/3/1791.

4 - Elizabeth Kane, widow of Guillermo Kane, says that 10 years of possession of 9 caballerias have passed, and petitions to present witnesses and receive title. Governor White grants; Zubizarreta attests, 3/21/1809, and notifies Elizabeth Kane.

5 - Zubizarreta lists conditions of grant.

6 - T. Hollingsworth, 54 [rest of page missing], deposes through Bernard Sanchez as to conditions fulfilled, 4/22/1809. Zephaniah Kingsley deposes, 8/11/1809, that he has been on Elizabeth Kane's plantation at various times and can swear to conditions.

7. - Elizabeth Kane presents Guillermo Lawrence, native of Scotland, married, farmer, 34, who swears as to cattle, etc.

8 - Governor White and Auditor of War Quintano sign grant, 8/19/1809. Fees:

          Governor for 2 signatures . . . . . . . .   4 rr.
          Auditor of War . . . . . . . . . . . . .   24 "
          Public Interpreter . . . . . . . . . . .   11 "
          Secretary [Zubizarreta] . . . . . . . . .  84 "
                                                    123 rr. or 15 pesos
                                                                  3 rr.

9 [E] Governor White's title [6 pp.], 8/19/1809.

10 [E] T. Hollingsworth with witnesses, William and John Hollingsworth, 1/18/1807, acknowledges receipt of $50 and one-half pipe of rum in exchange for his right to Mrs. Kane's property next to Zephaniah Kingsley's and by all means to make the purchaser, Zephaniah Kingsley, stand on the same footing he does now.

11 [S] Elizabeth, Margaret and Anne Cain [Kane] give their mother, Elizabeth Kane, the right to act for them in the sale of the plantation, Fuente del Alamo. All 3 make their mark, 9/1/1809, in the presence of witnesses, Juan E. Pate and Zephaniah Kingsley.

12 [E. This certifies that:] Elizabeth Cain [Kane] binds herself to give full right and title to a tract of land at the head of Doctor's Lake, granted to William Cain, and have the land surveyed to Captain Timothy Hollingsworth on demand by him, on consideration of $50. Elizabeth Cain signs with her mark, 2/5/1810 [?]. Witnesses: D. S. H. Miller and Joseph [?] Chifan [?] the latter of whom makes his mark.

13 [S. 5½ pp.:] Ysavel Kane to Zephaniah Kingsley for $120. Witnesses: Tomas de Aguilar, Juan de Entralgo and Bernardo Segui. Zubizarreta attests that copy agrees with original, 1/2/1809.

14 [E] Antonio Alvarez attests extract from descriptive list, No. 198, 300 acres to Zephaniah Kingsley. [Attached to 14 is copy of Marrot plat.]

15 [E] Unsigned plat conforming to Report No. 1, claim No. 55, 1825, confirmed to Zephaniah Kingsley, being in T. 4, R. 25 S&E, 286.60 acres. Nepomuceno Creek crosses through middle of plantation, running from William Pengree's claim on the west.

[Dossier has translations of all Spanish documents.]

Kingsley, Zephaniah        Con. K 19; DG IV 279

1 [E] claims, through George Gibbs, 150 acres on the west side of St. Johns River, opposite the mouth of Dunn's Creek, known as the Orange Grove in the Swamp; Governor Coppinger's grant, 12/13/1817, to William Hartley who sold to Zephaniah Kingsley, 8/30/1821.

2 [S] William Hartley petitions for 100 acres on Wilses/Will's Swamp, bordered on the west by lands of Roberto Cowin, and for 150 acres opposite Dunn's Creek, for 3 sons and 3 slaves, 12/13/1817, which Governor Coppinger grants.

3 [E] Picolata, 8/30/1821, William Hartley acknowledges receipt of $163 in various payments preceding this date in part payment of $300, for which he has sold and delivered to Zephaniah Kingsley his right and title to 150 acres which he warrants and defends. The balance is to be paid when titles are delivered. Witnesses: G. Guiber and John Ashton [illiterate.]

4 [S] Andreu Burgevin's certified plat of 150 acres. Indian Road leads northeast from the house on the southern corner opposite bend in river.

5 [E] Antonio Alvarez certified extract from descriptive list, No. 195. Attached is copy of 4.

[Dossier has translation of 3.]

Kingsley, Zephaniah          Con. K 20; DG IV 278

    1 [E] claims, through George Gibbs, 100 acres on the southern side of St. Johns River at a place called St. Johns Bluff, bounded on the east by lands formerly belonging to Francisco Estacholy, south by vacant lands, west by Ship Yard Creek; Governor Coppinger's grant of head rights to Manuel Romero, 3/17/1817, who sold to Zephaniah Kingsley, 3/27/1817.

    [Stitched together 2-11 in Spanish:]

2 - Title page: R. No. 6, Florida, March 17, 1817. Dona Ysabel Rodriquez, widow of Manuel Romero, asking title to 100 acres.

3 - Pierra certifies that Manuel Romero petitioned for permission to give up 50 acres conceded to him on two islets of the River St. John, because of the lack of fresh water for his negroes, and receive in exchange 100 acres near Port of San Vicente de Ferrer, which Governor White conceded.

4 - [On the back of 3 where the Pierra letter has inked through:] Don Manuel Cartilla [?], attorney of Ysabel Rodriquez, yields and renounces to Pedro Miranda her right in the above land in exchange for $200, 12/6/1816.

5 - Don Manuel Cartilla [?], Lieutenant colonel of the army, captain of scouts [Cazadores, Hunters] of the Cuban Line Infantry, attorney of Ysabel Rodriquez, widow of Manuel Romero, petitions to prove compliance with conditions, etc., 7/19/1817.

6 - Before Governor Coppinger appeared Bartolome de Castro y Ferrer, faithful interventor of the Royal Custom House of the town of Fernandina, married, native of Leon, more than 50, who swore it was

well known that Manuel Romero, with some negroes, cultivated the lands near San Vincent Ferrer until in 1812 came the insurrection in the Province.

7 - At once appeared Lorenzo Solano, married, native, farmer, 40, who swore it was well known that the late Manuel Romero cultivated with slaves the lands in San Vincent Ferrer till insurrection drove them out.

8 - Sebastian Ortega, native, rower in the . . . bar of this port, swore to the cultivation by slaves, animals raised, etc., but did not sign because he did not know how to write.

9 - Entralgo states conditions of grant.

10 - Governor Coppinger concedes; Entralgo attests.

11 - Governor Coppinger's royal title to Ysabel Rodriquez, 3/17/1817, of the 100 acres conceded to Manuel Romero on 3/29/1805.

12 [S] Don Manuel de Castilla, attorney of Ysabel Rodriquez, now absent in Havana, sells her 100 acres to Zephaniah Kingsley for $200.

[Stitched together 13-14 in Spanish:]

13 - Zephaniah Kingsley says that on 3/27 of last year he bought of Ysabel Rodriquez 100 acres of which he obtained absolute title from the government; and now it appears that 50 of these acres were granted to Antonio Suarez previously, who renounced them at the time he asked to be sent title of 500 acres granted him on Amelia Island. Zephaniah Kingsley petitions for a copy of this translation to protect himself against any sinister claim, 3/27/1818. Governor Coppinger grants, 4/1/1818.

14 - Antonio Suarez says that the governor granted him land in San Vicente Ferrer, of which only 50 acres remain his, and other land

on Punta Negra on Amelia Island, when he was in the King's service.
He now asks to abandon this first tract and have it all on Amelia
Island with the same date as the original concession. Governor
White and Licenciado Ortega agree. Juan de Pierra certifies that
land granted to Antonio Suarez at Punta Negra now consists of 500
acres and 50 acres in San Vicente Ferrer, which is what was granted on 5/5/1797 as head rights for him, his wife, 4 children and
3 slaves. Fernando de la Puente, administrator of His Majesty for
the Rivers San Juan and Santa Maria, certifies that the above is
according to government order to Captain John McQueen, juez
pedaneo of this district, 8/26/1803. Entralgo attests copy, 4/1/1818.

15 [E] Entralgo's translation of above to which is appended a
copy of a letter from Pedro Miranda in which he assures Zephaniah
Kingsley that he [Pedro Miranda] had asked Entralgo and has been
assured by him that Antonio Suarez had now no interest in the land
at San Vicente Ferrer.

16 [S] Clarke certifies plat of land at San Vicente Ferrer to
Manuel Romero, 3/29/1825. The River St. John is at the north, the
land of Francisco Estacholy on the east, the Creek of the Ship
Yard is shown on the southwest.

[Dossier has the usual Murphy translation of all Spanish documents.]

Kingsley, Zephaniah          Con. K 21; DG IV 279

1 [E] claims, through George Gibbs, 50 acres on St. Johns
Bluff on the southern side of said river, bounded on the north
by St. Johns River, and lands now or lately belonging to Manuel
Romero, west by lands now or lately belonging to Bartolome de

Castro, east by creek and marsh, according to Clarke's survey. Royal title to Francisco Estacholy; Governor Coppinger's grant of head rights of 3/15/1817; sold, 3/27/1817, to Zephaniah Kingsley.

2 [S] Francisco Estacholy, boss of the post office canoes of the rivers San Juan and Santa Maria, says that since 1795 when he took charge, he and his family have lived in San Vicente Ferrer where they found on the east a little house which he bought of Jose Boney and near it there is land which he and his children can cultivate, since in these days they are not occupied, and with which he can help to support his family. He petitions, 2/3/1804, for 50 acres in this place on the same terms as favors granted to other inhabitants. Domingo Estecholy signs for his father who cannot write. On margin Governor White grants and Pierra sends certificate.

3 [S] Clarke certifies plat of 4/15/1817.

4 [S] Governor Coppinger's royal title, 4/15/1817; Entralgo attests.

5 [S] Jose Ximenes, attorney of Francisco Estacholy, now absent in Fernandina, sells to Zephaniah Kingsley. Witnesses: Jose Bernardo Reyes, Jose Mariano Hernandez and Eusebio Maria Gomez.

6 - Title page: Florida, year 1817. Francisco Estacholy seeking title to 50 acres. [Marked in blue pencil:] "K No. 17, Conf."

7 - Pierra's certificate. At the bottom the owner, who signs with a cross, renounces to Pedro Miranda for $30.

8 - Jose Ximenes, attorney, asks title; Governor Coppinger grants, 3/15/1817.

[Dossier has translation of all Spanish documents and a duplicate of 3.]

Kingsley, Zephaniah                    Con. K 22; DG IV 286

1 [E] claims, through George Gibbs, 1 marsh lot of about 120 feet in Fernandina, extending north and south and about 93 feet east and west (47 vv. N-S by 34 vv. E-W), making about 190 square yards, bounded on the north by Egan's Creek, east by a vacant marsh, south by other lands belonging to Zephaniah Kingsley, west by a canal belonging to Hibberson & Yonge; Governor Coppinger's royal title, 7/8/1815.

2 [S] Zephaniah Kingsley states that in front of the lot that was conceded to him there is a little piece of marsh which separates it from Egan's Creek, in which marsh he has made a dike for the conservation of his boat and a causeway to give his lot communication with this creek. Wishing to increase his improvements and lacking the necessary superior authority, he herewith petitions for same, 6/22/1815. On the margin Governor Estrada orders the petition, 7/8/1815, to Pangua, military commandant of Amelia Island, and to the surveyor, Clarke. [Below on margin:] Pangua orders Clarke to report, 7/15/1815.

3 [S. On reverse:] Clarke reports that it will be no injury to the town to have this district improved; and no one else has claimed it.

4 [S] Pangua reports that this will not prejudice defense. Governor Estrada orders petition and certificate sent, 8/15/1815.

5 [S] Zephaniah Kingsley, as certificate enclosed proves, has made various improvements, including a warehouse of capacity between his lot and Egan's Creek, and petitions for title, 3/27/1817.

On margin Governor Coppinger consents.

6 [S. Enclosed in 5:] Clarke certifies again as to improvements of Zephaniah Kingsley, 2/25/1817. [This document is signed below by Francisco Morales.]

7 [S] Governor Coppinger's royal title [4 pp.] according to plan to Clarke for the city of Fernandina. Entralgo attests copy.

8 [S] copied in one document and same attested by Aguilar.

[Dossier has translation of 7.]

Jacket show 1,498 square yards in Fernandina and descriptive list, No. 568.

Kingsley, Zephaniah          Con. K 23; DG IV 286

1 [E] claims, through George Gibbs, 1 lot of land, 17 vv. front by 34 vv. deep, in Fernandina, bounded on the north by the marsh of Egan's Creek, east by lot of John McClure, south by the street.

2 [S] Zephaniah Kingsley, as shown by enclosed certificate of Clarke, owns a lot in Fernandina for which he petitions title, 7/6/1815.

3 [S. Enclosed in 2:] Clarke certifies that he surveyed for Zephaniah Kingsley lot No. 6 of square 18, bounded on the north by the marsh of Egan's Creek, east by the lot of Juan McClure, south by the street Pasco de las Damas [Palmas?], west by the lot of Felipe Yonge.

4 [S] Governor Juan Jose de Estrada, *ad interim*, grants royal title [3 pp.] to Zephaniah Kingsley. Juan Blas de Entralgo, secretary *pro tem*, attests copy.

[Dossier has translation of title.]

Kunen, Mary                    Con. K 24; DG IV 160

1 [S] claims 200 acres on either side of Smith Creek, bounded on one side by lands of Mrs. Ormond, on the other by lands of Isaac Wickes and Patrick Lynch; Governor Coppinger's grant of 11/11/1817, confirmed 6/10/1818, by virtue of a royal order of 3/29/1815, on account of services of her late husband, Bernard Wickes, held since his demise by Mary Kunen, 8/15/1823.

[Bound together 2-10 in Spanish:]

2 - Title page: R. No. 6, Florida, year 1818. Mariana Kunen seeking fate corresponding to her and her slaves in virtue of her defunct husband, Bernardo Wickes, who served in the Urban Militia, and was granted 200 acres of land in two places in Mosquitoes.

3 - Mary Kunen petitions the governor to command that the Adjutant Major who has charge of the Sergeant Major's office state whether it was not true that her deceased husband, Bernardo Wickes, served in the Urban Militia in 1812, 10/30/1817. On the margin Governor Coppinger grants the request.

4 - [On bottom:] Juan Percheman, ensign with grade of lieutenant in the body of Dragoons of America and Lieutenant in Commission to the Third Company of the Second Squadron of aforesaid corps, certifies that Bernardo Wickes entered the Urban Militia, 9/7/1812, and served till 5/31/1813. Dated 10/31/1817.

5 - Mary Kunen petitions for 200 acres for herself, 1 daughter, and 5 slaves over the age of 16; 100 acres on Smith Point next to land of her father-in-law and vacant on other winds, and the other 100 acres in a thick wood in the swamp in front of lands of the heirs of Santiago Ormond of Smith Creek, 11/13/1817. On bottom Governor

Coppinger grants.

6 - Mary Kunen petitions to have Roberto McHardy authorized to act in default of a regular surveyor, 11/25/1817. Governor Coppinger grants and Entralgo attests. On reverse side Robert McHardy accepts.

7 - Robert McHardy certifies plats of 4/20/1818.

8 - Antonio Alvarez attests copy of 7 on blue paper.

9 - Another attestation on brown paper.

10 - Governor Coppinger's royal title [3½ pp.] to Mary Kunen.

[Dossier has duplicate McHardy plat in water colors with translation of plat and title both of the latter of which are torn off along left hand edge.]*

---

* The following data appeared in the translator's notes at this point:
Contents of bundle [?]
1. List of land claims confirmed in Superior Court of East Florida, and not reversed by Supreme Court. 2 typed pp. single space to which is added 10 pp. manuscripts sealed and signed by George R. Fairbanks (Clk.), 11/8/1844.
2. Minutes of Board of Land Commissioners, numbered 9-13 (1824-25), mostly in handwriting of Fatio, some little in handwriting of Murphy.
3. Five (5) copies of testimony before Board of Land Commissioners of East Florida.

Lamb, Thomas                           Con. L 1; DG V 377, 381

1 [S. badly mutilated] points out that on Amelia Island are 200 acres, more or less, on the creek known by name of Two Brothers. The tract is between the lands of Samuel Harrison and Francisco Teran and will serve Thomas Lamb to maintain his family, 10/24/1798. On margin Governor White refers the petition to the Engineer Commandant, Berrio, who stipulates that no claim may be registered if petitioner is forced to withdraw before invasions. Governor White grants, Pierra sends certificate.

2 [S] Thomas Lamb has not enough land. He is crowded in between Samuel Harrison and Francisco Teran, but farther on near the beach there are 200 acres vacant in places known as the Lagoons of the Two Sisters, for which he petitions. Governor White refers to Berrio who favors the concession. Governor White grants, 5/16/1799, and Pierra sends certificate.

3 [E] Copy of 1 attested by William Reynolds.

4 [E] Charles W. Clarke deposes before Fatio, 10/30/1825, that Lamb lived at a place called Lamb's Old Field, and he had heard him say he got the land from the Spanish government many years ago.

5 [E. On bottom of 4:] John Uptegrove, also before Fatio, testifies that he was on Lamb's land in 1802 and that he had a large family, consisting of wife, 5 daughters, 2 sons and a negro wench with 2 or 3 children.

6 [E] Charles Broward deposes before Isaac Carter, J. P., at the instance of Seymore Picket, that Thomas Lamb lived on land on Amelia Island in 1800 and by its looks he had been living there

some years; he had 8 children and 3 grown negroes, but does not recall the number of negro children, 12/5/1825.

7 [E] Henry Washington's plat of 6/30/1831, with Robert Butler's counter-signature of January, 1834, of land confirmed to Thomas Lamb, being in sec. 23, R. 28, T. 2 N&E, 200 acres.

8 [E] Francisco Jose Fatio's abstract of petition and grant.

[Jacket refers to descriptive list, No. 579.]

Lane, William            Con. L 2; DG IV 281

1 [E] claims, through Bellamy, 200 acres on Trout Creek, head rights of 2/10/1793.

2 [S. Pocket worn and faded nearly into illegibility:] Marrot-Dupont's certified plat of 212 acres.

3 [E] Antonio Alvarez' certified abstract from descriptive list, No. 207, 210 acres to William Lane.

4 [E. Attached to 3:] Antonio Alvarez' certified translation of 2, 6 caballerias and 12 acres [212 acres] surveyed for William Lane at Lane, Trout Creek, River St. John, 2/10/1793. William Lane does not sign, not knowing how to write.

5 [E] Murphy translation of 2, with Fatio's counter-signature.

[Dossier contains slip showing Board confirms claim on Marrot's plat.

Lang, Isaac, Heirs of            Con. L 3; DG V 376, 380

1 [S] Marrot-Eastlake's certified plat of 6 caballerias, surveyed to Isaac Lang, who has a wife and 1 child, on Santa Maria La Chica, 3/4/1792.

2 [S] William Reynold's copy of 1, 9/14/1827.

3 [S] Antonio Alvarez certifies extract of descriptive list, No. 578.

4 [E, Pasted to 3] Antonio Alvarez' translation of 1, 2/14/1845.

5 [E] Joseph Hagens deposes before William H. Allen that he knows the tract where Isaac Lang, wife and children lived and seemed settled.

6 [E] Francisco Jose Fatio's abstract of 1, to which Allen has added that Isaac Lang lived there 4 or 5 years which was as long as could be expected.

7 [E] Abstract in Thomas Murphy's handwriting says claim of Isaac Lang at Lang on Little St. Marys was filed by Thomas Murphy for claimants, 2[or 9]/14/1827.

[Jacket says: "See Drummond, William, for a paper connected with case."]

Larcey, Joseph                                    Con. L 4; DG IV 287

1 [E] claims 300 acres in 3 tracts. One hundred and fifty acres are on Trout Creek between the lands of Joseph Fenwick and River St. John. This tract has not been surveyed. The other half, to be pointed out to the surveyor general, lies near Six Mile Creek of the River St. John and is in two surveys, one of 100 acres, the other of 50 acres, according to plats of George J. F. Clarke of 5/28/1815. The land is a service grant by Governor Estrada, 8/21/1815.

2 [S] Clarke's certified plat of 5/28/1821 shows 2 tracts of 100 acres and 50 acres separated by the 500 acres of Jose Albarez.

3 [S] Clarke's certified plat of 150 acres north of Water Pond Creek and east of lands of Joseph Fenwick.

4 [S] Joseph Larcey petitions for service grant, 8/15/1815, which Governor Estrada allows; Aguilar attests.

5 [E] Antonio Alvarez attests extract from descriptive list, No. 212, 300 acres to Joseph Larcey, 11/30/1845.

6 [E. attached to 5:] Translation of Joseph Larcey's petition and Clarke's plat 3.

7 [E. loose:] Translation of Clarke's plat 4.

8 [E] David A. Burr plat, unsigned and without agreement with Joseph Larcey's land in 3, being in T. 1, R. 27, S&E on Water Pond Creek.

[Plat shows claim of Edward Turner on the northwest. The land of William Drummond lies far to the east on St. Johns River.]

[Dossier has translation of concession and copy of Joseph Larcey's memorial to U. S. Commissioners.]

Lasseter, Reuben                                     Con. L 5: DG V 69

1 [E] Hinchey Hollomon, illiterate, Harmon Hollomon and Lewis Bailey depose before James Green, J.P. of Nassau Co., that they knew Reuben Lasseter who on 2/22/1817 did inhabit and cultivate a tract of land on St. Marys River just below the land of Ellis Stafford and above the land of Diller Broadaway on upper Dunn's Creek; he is of age and head of a family, 6/5/1827.

2 [E] Same three, same place, depose that Reuben Lasseter has cultivated his land 15 or 20 years.

3 [S&E] Surveyor's plat, begun by George J.F. Clarke in Spanish alleging "disposition of S.S. of 10/20/1817",* to which is pasted

---

* See p. lv

Thomas T. Woods' English plat on pink paper, 250 acres surveyed to Reuben Lasseter on the Bluff on St. Marys River. Both of the same date, 10/14/1818.

4 [E] R. B. Ker's certified plat of 300 acres confirmed to Reuben Lasseter being sec. 1, T. 4, R. 23 N&E, 1st quarter of 1831.

5 [E] Surveyed by W. H. Allen, 640 acres, a donation on the south side of St. Marys River, confirmed for 300 acres to Reuben Lasseter, 9/26/1827.

[Dossier has duplicate of 3.]

Leath, Hartwell          Con. L 6; DG IV 281, Rept. 1, No, 171

1 [E] claims, through George J.F. Clarke, 300 acres, 200 of which are on Big Creek, St. Marys River (north arm), and 100 acres on Sweet Spring Branch; St. Marys River; Governor Coppinger's grant for head rights.

2 [S] Clarke's certified plat of 11/11/1818 claiming superior order* given 10/20/1817, 200 acres surveyed to Hartwell Leath, a part of 300 acres belonging to him, on Big Creek, north branch.

3 [S] Clarke's certified plat, same date as above, 100 acres surveyed to Hartwell Leath on Santa Maria River. [Sweet Spring Branch cuts across south and north.]

4 [E & S]

5 [E & S] Same plats made by Thomas T. Woods, 11/11/1818. Chain bearers: Stephen Sparkman and Jehu [?] Mizels or Hartwell W. Leath. Both plats certified before in Spanish by Clarke.

6 [E] Ellis Stafford deposes that Hartwell Leath took possession of land on Big Creek in 1815 and cut cedar for a year or two off and on; and last spring and winter he had a man, Meazles, working there.

---

* See p. 1v.

7 [E] Antonio Alvarez' attested extract from descriptive list, No. 208, 2/25/1845.

8 [E. pasted to 7:] Copy of T. T. Woods' certified plat with Clarke's attest in English.

9 [E. pasted to 7:] Translation of Clarke's plat of survey on Big Creek.

[6 is marked on back, T. 2, sec. 38, R. 23, E.]

[7 is penciled on back:] "Two copies of this, one returned in a former survey by Williams."

[Dossier has translation of surveys, and extra memorial in foolscap.]

Lecount, John                    Con. L 7; DG IV 287, Rept. 9, No. 4.
    of Cuba

1 [E] claims, through Bernardo Segui, 300 acres on the east side of Dunn's Creek or George's Lake on River St. Johns. Governor Estrada's service grant, 8/11/1815.

2 [S] Juan LeCount petitions for grant for his services in the Revolution, 8/11/1815. Governor Estrada grants, Aguilar attests and asserts it is a true copy.

3 [S] Clarke's certified plat of 4/26/1821.

[Pasted together 4-7, all English:]

4 [E] Antonio Alvarez' attested extract from descriptive list, No. 217, 300 acres confirmed to John LeCount, 6/25/1845.

5 [E] Translation of memorial.

6 [E] Translation of Clarke's plat, 6/26/1845.

7 [E] Duplicate of 6, 12/18/1848.

Dossier has Fatio translation of 2 and of 3.

[Jacket is marked "Insuf. Evidence".]

Ledwith, Garrett                                    Con. L 8; DG V 376, 380

1 [E] claims through Bellamy, 100 acres on Pearson's* Island, Nassau River, Governor White's grant of head rights to Garrett Ledwith, 6/22/1803.

2 [S] Garrett Ledwith has found vacant about 100 acres on Pierson's Island, for which he petitions. Barcelo sees no inconvenience to defense and Governor White grants; Pierra sends certificate.

3 [E] Charles Brofard [Broward?] deposes, 9/23/1828, before John Boward [Broward?], J.P., that he knows Garrett Ledwith, who in about 1804 or 1805 claimed a tract of land on Pierson's Island; that about 1813 Garrett Ledwith moved to Fernandina, but occasionally came to the Island still considered his property. [On the back of this paper is labeled, "Testimony for Cyrus Briggs on Land".]

4 [E] John Broward deposes, 9/23/1828, before Charles Broward, J.P., that he knows Garrett Ledwith, who claimed Pearson's Island and established a residence there, but moved to Fernandina, he said, on account of the unprotected state of the country in 1813.

5 [E] Clarke's certified plat, 2/2/1816, of 200 acres on Pierson's Island, 100 acres conceded to Garrett Ledwith and another 100 acres exchanged for 4 slaves.

[The River bounds the northeast and the northwest sides; Tucker's Creek bounds the southwest side. The road to the mainland is shown running across the southern end.]

6 [E] Antonio Alvarez attests translation of memorial and decree.

[Pasted together 7-9 in English:]

---

\* Pelot's/Pilot's Island according to the <u>American State Papers</u>, <u>Public Lands</u>. - - DG V 376, 380.

7 - Antonio Alvarez' certified extract of descriptive list, No. 440, 100 acres to Cyrus Briggs, 2/17/1845.

8 - Antonio Alvarez' translation of memorial and grant to Garrett Ledwith.

9 - Antonio Alvarez' translation of Clarke plat.

[Decree slip does not mention Cyrus Briggs.]

Leonardi, Roque, Heirs of        Con. L 9; DG V 376, Rept. 1, No. 5

[Stitched together 1-12 in Spanish:]

1 - Title page: L. No. 7, Florida, year 1819. Don Jose Maria Ugarte and heirs of the defunct Roque Leonardi asking title of property of 2,000 acres of land they own on North River.

2 - [Not stitched in] Andres Burgevin, named by the government surveyor, on the 5th of the current month, certifies plat of 600 acres conveyed to Roque Leonardi and Dona Aqueda Coll between the road to San Vicente Ferrer and lands of Juan Andreu, bordered on the south by lands of the heirs of Thomas Travers and on the north by vacant land, 4/28/1819.

3 - The heirs of Roque Leonardi, former neighbors of this place, are now absent and in their name Jose Maria Ugarte, co-heir through his legitimate consort now present, Maria Leonardy, claims 2,000 acres in several sections granted to the defunct in December 1792, April 1793, and January 1799, in consecutive places from the creek called the King's Landing, or Wharf, on North River, beginning with the limits recently verified for the heirs of Francisco Arnau. Roque Leonardi's land was located on the map and measured by Captain Pedro Marrot, but he never gave Roque Leonardi any receipt or title which Jose Maria Ugarte now asks of the Secretary's office. Governor Coppinger orders

this to be done.

4 - Roque Leonardi points out that 15 miles from this city there is a piece of land which in past times belonged to the King but which no one now claims or cultivates. He asks for this tract and signs his name Rocco Leonardi, 11/9/1792. Governor Quesada directs that his quota be given him, 12/24/1792, until the time of the survey.

Roque Leonardi, farmer, needs more land for his increased family, and asks for 300 acres more in the place that is confined within the King's wood cutting, and still more 4 miles north at the plantation called El Arruz. [Arroz - The Rice Plantation.] Governor Quesada directs Marrot to make the survey, 4/11/1793, Roque Leonardi points out that when the land was surveyed, a corner on the south was left next to the land of Teresa Pall which has now grown into a very dense chaparral, which he now asks for himself. Governor White refers this request to Berrio, who reports favorably, and Governor White makes the grant, 1/3/1799. Aguilar attests all of the above as correct copy.

5 - The heirs of Roque Leonardi and Dona Aqueda Coll claim, through Jose Mario Ugarte and Dona Maria Leonardi, only heirs present, the lands credited by the enclosed [missing] documents, and through the extended possession and perpetual cultivation of more than 26 years the territory described as follows: Beginning with the line that ought to run East-West, from its neighbors on the south [the heirs of Francisco Arnau on the Creek called the King's Landing], a district 12 miles north of this place extending along the West [North?] River, until it terminates on the north with the land belonging to the now ancient plantation called Mester Men [trade, craft, or occupation, now obsolete], amounting to 300 acres granted in 1799. Also the

plantation called "El Arros", 16 miles away on the same North River, and only anciently measured by Marrot, except the Chaparral district, for which Ugarte asks survey by Burgevin. Governor Coppinger grants; Entralgo notifies Burgevin who signs.

6 - Burgevin certifies plat of 600 acres just outside on the west side of which runs the 20 mile road to San Vicente Ferrer or Bluff.

7 - Burgivin certifies plat of 1,400 acres* on the west side of North River, 12 miles away from this place, extending from land of heirs of Francisco Arnau on the south to the first Salt Creek [called on plat "first tide creek"] on the north, where a landing is marked. Marshes of North River are shown on the east, from which runs in, clear across and branching on the west side, Sweetwater Creek. This creek is crossed by the road to San Diego, running N-S.

8 - Power of attorney from Clorinda Leonardi, widow, of Havana, to Santos Rodriguez of St. Augustine to act for her. This document is on official paper, marked at top "Second seal Twelve Reales, years 1818 and 1819," followed by the official royal seal, "Spain and Indies, Havana, Fernando" [illegible here], which is followed by four printed cyphers. Her act is witnessed by Juan Puentes, Andres Alvarez, and Fermin Ysquierdo, all of whom know her. Before Phelipe Alvarez, who as attorney, by three men of the notarial college of Havana; Joseph Francisco Rodriguez, Manuel de la Torre. The printed seal of the notarial college is affixed below. Each signature is followed by an official cypher.

---

*The concession is given in American State Papers as 1,400 acres on Pablo Road, 15 miles from St. Augustine.--DG, V, 377.

9 - Santos Rodriquez, General Guard of Fortification and Provisions in this place [St. Augustine], attorney of Josefa Clorinda Leonardy, and Jose Mario Ugarte, 2nd officer ad interim of artillery, together with Maria Leonardy, the only heirs present of the defunct Don Roque Leonardy and Dona Agueda Coll, for herself and in the name of Juan Leonardy, who is absent in the country, and Bartolome and Dona Antonia, who are in the U.S.A., we present our power of attorney, and lend voice and song for the absent, and say that in three concessions, copies enclosed, one each in 1792, 1793 and 1799, the government conceded 2,000 acres of which we enclose surveys and ask if we have not complied with the conditions stipulated. The government can name farmers of that epoch, or we will nominate the captains of the Provincial Militia, Jorge Fleming, Juan Gianopoly, and Pablo Sabats, the ancient [Senior?], all of whom will testify.

First, let them say whether Roque Leonardy took possession at once and cultivated continuously.

Second, whether after Roque Leonardy's death his family and slaves were not scattered and ruined, as fragments of concrete and fruit trees testify, during the revolt of the Indians.

Third, whether the family which was scattered in 1800 during the revolt, did not return when peace was restored in 1802.

Signed: Santos Rodriquez and Jose Mario Ugarte.

On bottom Governor Coppinger orders, 7/19/1819, the formalities of law, as Entralgo attests and notifies Santos Rodriquez and Jose Mario Ugarte.

10 - Jose Mario Ugarte petitions to present witnesses, 4/12/1821, which Governor Coppinger grants, 4/14/1821.

11 - Francisco Marin, married, carpenter, 50, deposes that Roque Leonardy took possession at once, and after his death, his sons, Juan and Bartolome, carried on, were driven out and returned; were ordered to withdraw during revolution but were back in 1812.

12 - Antonio Huertas, widowed, Indian interpreter, 62, testified that Roque Leonardy took possession and that his fruit trees and grape vines were famous, as were his experiments with wines.

13 - Joaquin Sanchez, Ensign of Militia, married, native of Cartagena in the Levant, 25, testifies that Roque Leonardy continued to farm until he died, then his widow carried on. His sons were ordered out during the insurrection, but returned. Governor Coppinger grants and orders title of absolute property sent.

[All in a bundle, 37 pp. in Spanish.]

Leslie, Flora (free black)    Con. L 10; DG V 383, 387
[Jacket marked "Rejected"]

1 [E] claims, through G.J.F.Clarke, 500 acres on the east head of Springer's Branch, about 10 miles northwest of St. Augustine, a grant by Governor White, of 4/12/1810, based on head rights. Plat and certificate will be filed when required.

2 [E] Clarke depositions before Charles Downing, 8/29/1828, that threats of Indian troubles followed by general revolution and invasion under South American auspices prevented settling lands.

3 [E] Clarke receipt for copy of concession, etc., from the Superior Court, 5/19/1832.

4 [E] Fatio's summary of grant and order for certificate marked in Downing's hand: "Signed Thomas Aguilar and not in office." -

5 [S] Clarke's certified plat of 6/17/1817. No details.

[Here follow three protocols of Superior Court action.]

[Tied together with yellow ribbon and written on brown paper in English are 6-9:]

6 - Flora Leslie claims 500 acres, etc.

7 - Statement of this case:

    a. Petition for confirmation filed in this clerk's office, 5/21/1831.

    b. Documents and testimony which include a Memorial of concession to Flora Leslie, 4/12/1810, as certified by Aguilar, together with Clarke's certified plat and testimony.

    c. Answer of U.S. Attorney, filed 8/22/1831.

    d. Decree of confirmation of 5/26/1832, to-wit.

8 - Flora Leslie petitions for 500 acres for herself and 12 children, to raise cattle. Aguilar certified it was granted, 4/14/1810.

9 - Clarke's certified plat and petition both translated by Anthelm Gay. Kingsley B. Gibbs certified translation and court action and seals, 8/29/1839.

[Another protocol, on white paper, bound with narrow blue ribbon:] Same material, but with decree of court in greater detail. Anthelm Gay translates and Kingsley B. Gibbs, clerk, attests, 2/21/1834.

[A third protocol on soiled white paper tied with a narrow brown ribbon, marked at top in pencil:] "Surveyed by Norris in 1850, Bundle 12", and at bottom: "Superior Court, May 1832. Surveyed by R. W. Norris, 1850, T. 6, 7, R. 28 SE. Surveyed 500, Dec. 4147 [sic]".

[Fastened together, 10-12 in English:]

10 - Flora Leslie's petition and Aguilar's attestation of Governor's action.

11 - Clarke's survey. Anthelm Gay's translation of 10 and 11.

12 - Summary of case and court action. Attorney for U.S.A. moves for a continuance on account of letter to him from the Secretary of State, 5/28/1830, but he is over-ruled and no further move for rejection is possible.

George R. Fairbanks, clerk, attests the above action and is in turn attested by Judge Isaac H. Bronson, no date.

[Dossier has extra jacket marked, "Rejected by Receiver and Recorder".]

Levy, Moses E.                 Con. L 11

.1 [E] Jacket notes: 65,800 acres confirmed by Superior Court, of East Florida, 5/27/1832, and decree confirmed by Supreme Court of U.S.A., 3/15/1834. [Below on jacket:]

```
12,000 acres [west side Second Lake]  Yonge, Traverse
 8,000 acres [Big or Long Lake      ]
10,400 acres [on stream running     ]  Clt.
             [from the west into    ]
             [St.Johns 12 m. south  ]  Huertas,
             [Lake George           ]  Clt.

 4,000 acres [Big Spring, 25 miles  ]  Miranda, Entralgo,
 3,400 acres [south of Lake George  ]  Clt.

 4,000 acres [5 or 6 miles east of  ]  Arredondo,
             [Spring Garden         ]  Entralgo,
 4,000 acres [near Black Creek &    ]  claimant
             [Doctor's Lake         ]

20,000 acres [Cuscavilla and Chacha-]  Clarke,
             [       la Hammocks    ]  Entralgo
                                    ]  claimant.
```

Descriptive list, Nos. 719, 720, 721, 722, 723.*

---

*"Private Claims, Descriptive List," of which the editor has a photostat copy for reference, gives the following list, all in the name of Moses E. Levy:

[Stitched together with braided silk lacing, 1/8", now very rotten and broken, 36 pp. headed: "Superior Court E. Fla., land claim, 65,800 acres, Moses E. Levy vs. U.S.A." In English:]

2 - List of land claimed mostly according to #1:

  12,000 acres known under the application of Valdes
   8,000  "  claimed under grant to Philip R. Yonge
  10,400  "  claimed under a grant of 15,000 acres to Antonio Huertas.
   7,400  "  granted to Pedro Miranda et al.
   8,000  "  of the 10,000 acres granted to Fernando M. Arredondo, Jr., et al.
   5,000  "  claimed by the same parties, located west of St. Johns River, contiguous to Black Creek near Flemming's Island and a pond called Doctor's Lake.
  20,000  "  claimed under a grant to George J.F. Clarke, at Cuscawilla and Chachala, situated west of the place on River St. John where there was a store of Panton, Leslie & Co., and about 45 miles from it.

[Translation of documents filed in this case and relating to a claim of Philip R. Yonge for 25,000 acres:]

3 - Memorial of Philip R. Yonge, who as commandant of militia without pay, built and maintained a ship called "The Emperor" until it was wrecked in a hurricane at a loss of $20,000; who also supplied beef

| #719, | 20,000 acres, of which 12,000 are on Lake Second, alias Valdez and |
|---|---|
| | 8,000 on Long Lake, both on St. Johns River. |
| #720, | 10,400 acres, on stream from west flowing into St. Johns River 12 miles above Lake George. |
| #721, | 7,400 acres, at Big Spring, in two tracts of 4,000 and 3,400 acres. |
| #722, | 8,000 acres, of which 4,000 are at Spring Garden and 4,000 at Black Creek. |
| #723, | 20,000 acres, in Alachua, Chacalas Hammock. |

These claims appear singly in Con. 12, 13, 14.

to troops and lent money to the royal treasury, for which he petitions for a service grant. Governor Coppinger grants. Anthelm Gay certifies translation.

4 - Governor Coppinger's royal title to Philip R. Yonge. Translation attested by Anthelm Gay.

5 - Andrew Burgevin certifies plat of 12,000 acres, a part of 25,000 acres granted to Philip R. Yonge [A.Gay translation], 5/20/1820.

"Indian Road" traverses the north end to "Second Lake" and begins again on the further side.

6 - Another of Burgevin's certified plats, 8,000 acres of the 25,000 acres granted to Philip R. Yonge on Long Lake.

[Papers in the case of Antonio Huertas, given 10,400 acres:]

7 - Memorial of Antonio Huertas. In spite of his receiving 10,000 acres on 3/27/1813 for growing cattle, his job for many years past, that land is mostly pine land and little fitted for cultivation. The Governor knows of his services when he provided food for garrisons during the Rebellion. He petitions for 15,000 acres which he asks to be located about 12 miles south of Lake George, beginning about 4 or 5 miles west so that said stream will divide the land into two parts; he petitions for a survey by some intelligent person, Clarke being absent, 9/15/1817. Governor Coppinger grants. Anthelm Gey, translator.

8 - Burgevin certifies plat, by authority granted, 12/13/1820, of 10,400 acres divided by stream and surrounded by vacant lands.

[Gay's translation of documents filed in claim of Pedro Miranda for 10,000 acres:]

9 - Pedro Miranda, First Pilot of the Bar and Captain of the Port, for services as far back as 1794, petitions for 10,000 acres as a

service grant, on a stream running from the west and entering into St. Johns River at place called in English, Big Spring, the stream dividing the tract. He petitions also to re-locate 2,000 acres granted him already, 9/16/1817. Governor Coppinger grants on the same day and orders certification filed. Anthelm Gay attests translation.

10 - Burgevin's certified plat of 4/5/1821.

11 - Additional plat certified by Burgevin, of 3,400 acres, part of the above. [Gay's translation.]

[Documents filed in this case in the claim of F. M. Arredondo Jr., for 8,000 acres:]

12 - F. M. Arredondo, Jr., who as commandant of cavalry, kept in touch with and reconnoitered the enemy in 1812, and with his 80 slaves supplied beef and provisions to garrisons, petitions for a service grant of 10,000 acres, of which 5,000 are in a Hammock 5 or 6 miles east of Spring Garden, and 5,000 west of River St. Johns on Black Creek near Flemming's Island and a pond called Doctor's Lake, 3/18/1817. Governor Coppinger grants, 3/20/1817, and orders certification sent. Anthelm Gay attests translation, 8/4/1829.

13 - Burgevin's certified plat, 7/25/1820, of 3,000 acres of the 10,000 granted to F. M. Arredondo, Jr.

14 - Ditto, another of 4,000 acres out of 10,000. Anthelm Gay translates both.

[Documents filed in this case, 20,000 acres to George J.F. Clarke out of 26,000 acres:]

15 - Clarke, holder of ten government positions without pay, listed elsewhere, petitions for a service grant, which he receives from

Governor Coppinger, 12/17/1817.

16 - Burgevin certifies plat of 20,000 acres out of 26,000 acres. Payne's house is shown on the south edge on the Picolata road, which curves to the north about the center and is marked "mickasuky Road". [No other important details. No deed of sale anywhere.]

17 - Florida Superior Court, having U. S. Supreme Court decree that case is straight except for survey to Antonio Huertas, now finds that matter straight, and reports back. The Supreme Court finds for Moses E. Levy. Gibbs signs and seals.

[This case apparently went to the Supreme Court and was sent back to the Superior Court of East Florida about five times, as the U. S. Attorney kept hammering at it and forced reconsideration of various surveys.]

18 - Three leaves of brown paper written by Antonio Alvarez [who was ordered to Washington to testify], pinned by spreading tacks to the remainder, and bound with white tape. Signed by Fairbanks who is attested by Judge Bronson, 3/13/1845.

[No less than 3 - all tied with brown ribbon - are dated 3/12/1845 and one 3/14/1845. All with Fairbanks' and Bronson's attestations. Various pencil notes of surveys by Randolph or McKeys, with notation of location, giving Township, Range and Section.]

19 - C. C. Tracy's certified plat, surveyed by order of Superior Court of East Florida to Moses E. Levy, August 1835, 3,159.76 acres, being in sec. 37, T. 19, R. 29 and in sec. 38, T. 19, R. 30. Countersigned by Surveyor General Butler, but not in his writing, 11/13/1848. Chainmen: Alexander Solana and William Reyes. Plat shows the Weekiwa Creek on the west and the corner of St. Johns River on the northeast.

Levy, Moses E.　　　　　　　　　Con. L 12; DG III  647
    Resident of Micconope

1. [E] claims, through Isaac N. Cox, 14,500 acres on the west bank of St. Johns River at Hope Hill. The first line runs south 25° west to a stake on an old path of the Chocochate Indians; the second north 25° west to a stake on the path of the Okeleoska Indians. It is bounded on the north by the trail mentioned, east by the river; the other sides vacant. Governor Coppinger's service grant to F. M. Arredondo, Sr., who sold the whole to Moses E. Levy.

[Papers included.]

    1. Title to F. M. Arredondo, marked A.
    2. Plat of survey               "     B.
    4-6. Other papers               "     C,D,E,G.

2 [E] Moses E. Levy receipts for the above papers from Antonio Alvarez according to the general order of the Superior Court.

3 [E] F. M. Arredondo, Sr., for his services of 20 years without pay, in the Department of Commissary to Indians, thus keeping peace with them; and as comptroller *pro tem* of the royal military hospital of St. Augustine; after leaving which employment he was aide-de-camp to Governor Estrada, 1812-13, and later a member of the provincial junta where his duties kept him in Havana, petitions for a service grant as a first settler, of 30,000 acres of which 15,000 acres are on the southwest side of the lagoon known as Lake George, survey to be made so that Sweet Water Creek may occupy the center front; the remaining 15,000 acres to be on the west side of St. Johns River, measurement to commence from the Old Indian Chocichatty, opposite the site where Panton, Leslie Co., had their "Upper Store". Clarke cannot attend to the survey at this time. Governor Coppinger grants, 3/24/

1817, and Entralgo attests. Fatio attests correct translation.

4 [E] F. M. Arredondo, Sr., petitions for survey by Andrew Burgevin who is to mark off 500 acres from the second tract, leaving 14,500 acres. Governor Coppinger assents; Entralgo attests and notifies Burgevin who signs. Fatio attests correct translation.

5 [S. On paper 17" x 10", broken:] Governor Coppinger's royal title to F. M. Arredondo. Copy attested by William Reynolds.

6 [E] Andrew Burgevin attests survey [not found] and Fatio attests translation.

7 [E] Bill of Sale "in the ever faithful city of Havana," 8/3/1820, Fernando de la Maza Arredondo for himself and for Fernando, his son, sells two tracts of 14,500 acres and of 38,400 acres, his own and his son's respectively, to Hernandez & Chauviteau for $5,000 and $20,000 respectively. Witnesses: Rafael Carcia, Tomas Gomez, and Buenaventura Calvet. Cayetano Ponton, public notary, attests. Charles Viscoles, public translator, certifies true translation, 6/5/1822.

8 [E] Special Power of Attorney "In the ever loyal city of Havanna," 11/2/1820, Hernandeau & Chauviteau to Moses Elias Levy, giving power to sell 52,900 acres "at the highest price". Manuel de Ayala attests. Fatio certifies true translation.

9 [S] Hernandez & Chauviteau, Habana, 11/10/1820, disclaim ownership of above tracts, declaring Levy as full owner.

10 [E] Decree of Superior Court of the District of East Florida, 8/28/1837, confirming claim and rejecting exclusion of water and marshes from the survey.

11 [E] Mandate of Supreme Court of United States, January term,

1839, affirming "in all respects" the decree of the Superior Court.
Witness: Roger B. Taney, Chief Justice, William Thomas Carroll,
clerk, attests. George R. Fairbanks, certifies true copy, 4/1/1845.

12 [E] Plat of claim being sec. 37, T. 15, R. 27 and 28 south
and east and T. 16, R. 27 and 28 south and east; surveyed in 1849
by Alexander McKay, approved, 7/7/1849, by B. A. Putnam, Surveyor
General.

[Dossier contains a copy each of 3, 4, 6 and 10; two translations of 5 and one of 6; and the decree.]

Levy, Moses E.                      Con. L 13

1 [E] Juan B. Entralgo claims, through George Murray, 3,400 acres
at Big Spring, 25 miles south of Lake George; Governor Coppinger's
royal title, 9/16/1817, to Pedro Miranda who sold to Entralgo.

2 [E] Deed of Sale, 12/5/1821, Pedro Miranda to Juan B. Entralgo,
of 3,400 acres for $1,400. Witnesses: Francisco J. Fatio and
Ruperto Saavedra. Fatio certifies true translation.

3 [S] Andres Burgevin certifies, 4/5/1821, plat of 3,400 acres
for Pedro Miranda.

4 [E] C. C. Tracy certifies plat of 4,150.34 acres surveyed
2nd quarter, 1847, for Levy. Chainmen: Alexander Solana and William
Reyes. Approved, 11/13/1848, Robert Butler, Surveyor General.

[Dossier contains translation of 3 and decree.]

Levy, Moses E.                      Con. L 14; DG IV 159, 175

1 [E] claims 275 acres on San Diego Plains; Governor Coppinger's
service grant, 2/16/1816, to Antonio Mier, who sold to Levy. It is
bounded on the north by Lazaro Ortega, south by Nicholas Sanchez,
east by the sea, west by the main road.

[Bound together 2-4 in Spanish:]

2 - Mier petitions, 10/4/1815, for all the vacant lands found north of Sanchez and south of Ortega for his services in the 1812 rebellio he challenges the claim of Simeon Sanchez and Felipe Devees to all of the Plains and requests the naming of Mr. McHarthi to arbitrate if Sanchez were to oppose the grant. Governor Estrada asks, 11/4/1815, Juan de Arredondo y San Felices, Auditor of War, who approves, 12/7, 1815. Governor Estrada grants, 12/13/1815, requesting certified lis of Mier's family.

3 - Mier certifies, 12/22/1815, list of his family of 6 children, wife, 7 slaves, and a dependent widow.

4 - Mier petitions, 2/16/1816, for his quota of land based upon his family list already submitted. Governor Coppinger grants, 2/16/181 275 acres at the place mentioned by Mier in his petition of 11/14/1815.

5 [E] Royal title, 2/16/1816, Governor Coppinger to Mier for 27 acres. Juan de Entralgo certifies true copy. F. J. Fatio certifies true translation.

6 [E] District of East Florida, Superior Court: 10/29/1832, Thomas Douglas, attorney for Levy, requests "rule Nisi" to force Antonio Alvarez to produce the bill of sale of Mier to Levy for 275 acres, 10/30/1832. Alvarez turns the papers over to Levy, obeying court order. Robert Raymond Reid, Judge.

[Dossier contains decree]

Lewis, Frankee              Con. L 15; DG IV 284

1 [E] claims, through Solomon Snyder, 640 acres under the donation act, located in Monroe County at Lewis' Place, 26 miles north c

Cape Florida on the southern branch of New River. It was in possession of Surl, her husband, for 30 years.

2 [E] Captain William Johnson deposes, 5/5/1825, before John Whitehead, Judge of County Court, Monroe County, that Frankee Lewis had for four years prior to 2/22/1819, cultivated the land claimed.

3 [E] George Mackay certifies plat of 640 acres in sec. 11, T. 50, R. 42, south and east. Chainmen: John Burke and Thomas Mitchell. Approved, 5/18/1846, by Robert Butler.

[Dossier contains copy of 3.]

Lewis, Johnathan            Con. L 16; DG IV 284

1 [E] claims, 640 acres under the donation act, located 2 miles south of Miami River,* one-half mile south of T. Paint's. He has been in actual habitation and cultivation for 10 or 12 years.

2 [E] George Mackay certifies plat of 613 acres in sec. 40, T. 54, R. 41, bounded on the east by Biscayne Bay. Approved, 5/18/1846, by Robert Butler, surveyor general.

Lewis, Polly**            Con. L 17; DG IV 284

1 [E] claims, 11/6/1824, 640 acres under donation act, 1 mile south of River Miami, near Cape Florida, of which he [or she?] has been in actual possession for 9 years.

2 [E] Mary Lewis claims, 12/13/1824, through Waters Smith, 640 acres under the donation act, on the east side of Miami River, near

---

\* Near Cape Florida, according to the reference shown in American State Papers.
\*\* Shown in American State Papers as Tolly

Key Beskene [Biscayne] at Cape Florida, where she settled in 1808 and is now in actual possession.

3 [E] George Mackay certifies plat of 634.17 acres in sec. 39, T. 54, R. 41, south and east. Chainmen: John Burk and Thomas Mitchell. Approved, 5/18/1846, by Robert Butler.

Lofton, William and John     Con. L 18; DG IV 208

1 [E] claim, 9/16/1823, through John B. Strong, 350 acres between St. Marys River and Nassau River. Peter Marrot's survey of 2/1792 to John Lofton, the claimants' grandfather.

2 [S] Marrot certifies, 2/24/1792, concession to John Lofton of 350 acres, his family consisting of himself, wife, 2 sons, and 2 slaves. Samuel Eastlake, surveyor, countersigns.

3 [E] Antonio Alvarez certifies, 2/25/1845, extract from descriptive list, "No 214 - William & John Lofton - 350 a."

[Dossier contains two translations of 2 and the decree.]

Lofton, William and John     Con. L 19; DG IV 160, 208

1 [E] claim, through John B. Strong, 350 acres between St. Marys and Nassau Rivers;\* Peter Marrot's survey, 2/24/1792, to John Lofton, Senior, their father. Claimants are in actual possession.

2 [S] Marrot certifies, 2/?/1792, plat of 350 acres for Juan Lofton whose family consists of himself, his wife, 2 sons, and 2 slaves. Samuel Eastlake, surveyor, countersigns.

3 [E] Antonio Alvarez certifies, 2/25/1845, extract from descriptive list, No. 210 - "William and John Lofton, 350 a."

[Dossier contains two translations of 2 and decree.]

---

\* Given in <u>American State Papers</u> as 160 acres located at St. John the Baptist.-- DG IV 160.

Lofton, William and John					Con. L 20; DG IV 281

    1 [E] claim, through George J. F. Clarke, 300 acres north of Julington Creek, St. Johns River; Governor Coppinger's grant for head rights.

    2 [S] Clarke certifies, 7/6/1819, plat of 300 acres bounded on the southwest by lands of George Long, for Guillermo and Juan Lofton.

    3 [E] David Thomas certifies plat of 240.03 acres surveyed in June, 1833. Chainmen: R. H. Green and William O'Neill.

    [Dossier contains translation of 2 and decree.]

Lofton, William and John					Con. L 21; DG IV 159, 176

    1 [E] claim, through John B. Strong, 50 acres on Amelia Island at Cabbage Spot; Governor Morales' grant, 9/18/1800, to Juan Lofton, their father. Claimants are in actual possession.

    2 [S] John Lofton petitions, 9/16/1800, for 50 acres. Governor Morales, 9/17/1800, refers to Pedro Diaz Berrio, commandant of engineers, who reports favorably. Morales grants, 9/18/1800; Pierra certifies.

    3 [S] Juan de Pierra certifies above grant.

    4 [E] Antonio Alvarez certifies, 2/26/1845, extract from descriptive list "No 215 - William & John Lofton - 50 acres."

    [Dossier contains two translations of 3 and decree.]

Lofton, William and John, Heirs of			Con. L 22; DG IV 245, 248

    1 [E] claim, through John B. Strong, 200 acres on the north branch of Nassau River, a British grant, 1768, to Cornelius Rain, who conveyed it, 1769, to John Lofton, grandfather of claimants. Details of the transaction are unknown to the claimants due to early death of parents and grandfather.

    2 [E] Indenture, 1768; Cornelius Rain sells to John Lofton 200

acres for "thirty pounds sterling", which had been granted by Governor Grant.  Witnesses· Joseph Rain, illiterate, and William Thompson, illiterate.

3 [E] Pedro Marrot certifies, 4/20/1792, plat of 200 acres for Cornelio Rain.  Samuel Eastlake, surveyor, countersigns.

4 [S] Loftin petitions, 5/30/1801, for 200 acres for the raising of cattle.  Governor White refers, 6/16/1801, to Pedro Diaz Berrio who approves.  Governor White grants.

5 [S] Juan de Pierra certifies, 6/16/1801, the above grant.

6 [E] Joseph Summerall deposes, 12/23/1823, before John B. Strong, Judge of the County Court, St. Johns County, that Lofton has for 20 years cultivated the land claimed.

7 [E] William Hartley deposes that after the senior Lofton's death, his sons occupied the land for 9 or 10 years.

8 [E] Antonio Alvarez certifies, 2/25/1845, extract from descriptive list, "No. 211, William & John Lofton - 200 a."

[Dossier contains decree.]

Long, George, Heirs of                    Con. L 23; DG V 382

1 [E] claim, through George J. F. Clarke, 350 acres at the head of Matanza River, on the west side of Graham's Creek, which has been cultivated about 25 years, but never surveyed.

2 [E] George Long claims, through M. Drysdale, 300 acres at Graham's Creek; Governor White's grant, 7/28/1803, to his father, who died in 1803, willing the land to claimant and his mother, the widow, "in fee as tenants in common".  Upon his mother's death claimant became owner of all the land.

3 [E] Benjamin and J. B. Clements certify plat of 599.5 acres, for heirs of George Long.  Chainmen:  John M. McGough and Joel F.

Yowell. Approved, March 1835, Robert Butler.

    4 [E] Above plat revised. "Approved, 9/30/1850."

[Dossier contains copy of 4]

Long, Jesse                      Con. L 24; DG V 69

    1 [E] claims 640 acres on Miss Nealey's Creek at Little St. Marys River.

    2 [E] Thomas J. Prevatt deposes, 10/20/1827, before James Green, J.P., Nassau County, that Jesse Long did cultivate "betwixt one and three acres," fulfilling requirements of donation claim.

    3 [E] Joseph E. Prevatt deposes in same manner.

    4 [E] R. B. Kerr certifies plat of 300 acres surveyed in the 1st quarter of 1831. Chainmen: Daniel Wells, Jr., and John Handley. Approved 1/1834, Robert Butler.

Lopez, Bartolome             Con. L 25; DG V 414.

    1 [E] claims, through Antonio Alvarez, $58\frac{1}{2}$ English yards fronting on the road "leading from the land gate of this city [St. Augustine]", bounded on the north by lands of Miguel Villalonga, south by those of Pedro Fujada, east by said road, west by St. Sebastian River; head rights by Governor White on 5/26/1807[*] to claimant.

    2 [S] Juan de Fierra certifies, 6/11/1807, that upon petition of Lopez $58\frac{1}{2}$ English yards on the road were granted to him.

    3 [E] Alvarez certifies, 12/4/1834, extract from descriptive list, "No. 582 - Bartolome Lopez - $58\frac{1}{2}$ yards in front."

---

    * Date of concession is given in <u>American State Papers</u> as June 3, 1807.--DG V 414.

Lopez, Francisco					Con. L 26; DG IV 102

1 [E] James W. Exum certifies plat of 679.24 acres on the north margin of Grand Bayou, surveyed in 3rd quarter of 1827 for [by ?] Frederic Ming and Wesley Inglish. Approved: Robert Butler.

Lorenzo, Juan, Widow of				Con. L 27; DG V 414

1 [E] claims, through Will Reynolds, a lot of land on the road "leading from the City gate" north of St. Augustine, in the "1500 varas",* bounded on the south by Jose Baya, east by road, west by St. Sebastian River, measuring north and south 185 Spanish yards; Governor White's concession, 6/5/1807, to Juan Lorenzo, whose widow is in actual possession.

2 [S] Juan de Pierra certifies, 6/5/1807, that upon Lorenzo's petition Governor White granted, 6/5/1807, 452 1/6 English varas.

Note: On 7/17/1807 Lorenzo ceded 277 varas leaving him only 180 varas. St. Augustine, 7/18/1807, Pierra.

[Dossier contains decree.]

Love, Alexander					Con. L 28; DG V 427

1 [E] Benjamin and J.B. Clements and James W. Exum certify plat of 1799.89 acres at Peridida Bay, West Florida; surveyed in 4th quarter of 1831. Chainmen: Manuel Suwarres and Sebastian Suwarres. Approved, January 1834, Robert Butler.

[Dossier contains copy of 1.]

Love, Charles					Con. L 29; DG IV 281

1 [E] claims, through Abraham Bellamy, 300 acres on St. Marys River, George Clarke's survey of 12/10/1819. Claimant is in actual possession.

---

* The mil y quinientas, see p. xxx.

    2 [S] Jorge J. F. Clarke, certifies, 12/10/1817, grant and plat of tract, bounded on the south by land of Shadrich Standley.

    3 [E] Antonio Alvarez certifies, 2/29/1845, extract from descriptive list No. 216.

    [Dossier contains a copy and two translations of 2.]

Lowe, John                    Con. L 30; DG IV 279

    1 [E] claims, through George J. F. Clarke, 750 acres at Bell's Old Field, on Bell's River, bounded on the north by Bell's Creek, east by McGirth's Creek, south by vacant lands, west by William Carney; Governor Estrada's grant for head rights, 1/30/1812, to John Lowe, who is in actual possession.

    [Bound together 2-10, in Spanish:]

2 - Juan de Pierra certifies, 10/10/1803, that upon petition of Lowe for the lands forfeited by Jacobo McGirt same were granted by Governor White, date *ut supra.*

3 - Juan Purcell certifies, 5/20/1807, plat of above tract.

4 - Lowe petitions, 11/5/1811, for royal title being willing to give $100.00 to the Royal Treasury or to whatever cause the government may direct. Governor Estrada grants, 11/6/1811. Jose de Zubizarreta certifies the above, notifies Lowe and

5 - Lists, 11/7/1811, conditions that must be met for a royal title.

6 - Bartolome de Castro y Ferrer deposes, 1/14/1812, before Zubizarreta that he has known Lowe for many years as settler in the St. Marys district where he has built a model plantation.

7 - Guillermo Lawrence deposes same.

8 - Fernando de la Maza Arredondo deposes, 1/18/1812, that due to his having a store in Fernandina he has known Lowe, who for many years has cultivated the land claimed.

9 - Zubizarreta certifies, 1/20/1812, the receipt of $100.00 from Lowe as promised, the same being by him turned over to the governor.

10 - Governor Estrada grants, 1/25/1812, royal title; Zubizarreta attests.

11 [S] Royal title, 1/30/1812, Governor Estrada to John Lowe. Zubizarreta attests and certifies true copy.

12 [S] Manuel Lopez, "Ministro Official Real y Contador de las Reales Cajas", and Jose Antonio de Yguiniz, Treasurer *interim* of same, certify Zubizarreta's signature.

13 [E] Antonio Alvarez certifies, 2/24/1845, extract from descriptive list, No. 206.

[Dossier contains decree and translation of 3 and 11.]

Lowe, John                     Con. L 31; DG V 58, 64

1 [E] claims, through George J. F. Clarke, 250 acres on Bell's River; Governor Coppinger's royal title to William Carney, who sold to claimant who is in actual possession.

[Bound together 2-7 in Spanish:]

2 - Tomas de Aguilar certifies, 11/9/1811, that upon petition, 7/12/1800, of Carney for 250 acres on St. Marys River, bounded south by Daniel McGirt, northwest by Doctor's Creek [Lake ?] and 250 acres at the northern extreme of O'Neil Swamp, Governor White granted same, 7/14/1800.

3 - Jorge J. F. Clarke certifies plat of tract, bounded on the northwest by Eleiaza Waterman, southeast by Juan Low, northeast by Bell River, southwest by vacant land.

4 - Carney petitions at Fernandina, 2/12/1816, the commandant of Fernandina, for a permit to prove cultivation and the right to receive the

original papers of the concession, which request Benito de Pangua grants. Bernardo Segui attests.

5 - Domingo Fernandez deposes, 2/20/1816, before Pangua that for 10 years Carney has cultivated his land, building thereon a model plantation.

6 - Luis Mattair deposes same. Segui attests the above.

7 - Carney petitions, 4/3/1816, through Eusebio Maria Cromer, for royal title, having by witnesses proved his worth, and Governor Coppinger grants, 4/4/1816. Juan de Entralgo attests, and notifies Carney.

    8 [S] Royal title, 4/4/1816, Governor Coppinger to Carney. Entralgo attests and certifies true copy.

    9 [E] Antonio Alvarez certifies, 2/13/1845, extract from descriptive list, No. 575.

    [Dossier contains a copy and translation of 3, and translation of 8.]

Lowe, John W.                      Con. L 32

    1 [E] claims, through George J. F. Clarke, 16,000 acres of which 6,000 acres are at Doctor's Branch on Bell's River, 10,000 acres northwest of Indian River's head, west of North Creek savannahs; Governor Coppinger's grant of a mill site, 4/6/1816, to claimant who is in actual possession.

    2 [S] Lowe petitions, 3/20/1816, for mill site as above. Governor Coppinger grants, 4/6/1816, title to be conditional upon the construction of the mill. Tomas de Aguilar certifies true copy.

    3 [S] At Santa Maria, 12/23/1819, Jorge J. F. Clarke certifies plat of survey by Thomas T. Woods on 12/18/1819 of Lowe tract of 7,080 acres from which must be deducted previous grants of 950 acres

and 130 acres to Daniel Vaughan and William Christopher, respectively, leaving 6,000 acres as the part of the mill grant to Lowe.

4 [S] Clarke certifies, 2/7/1820, plat of 10,000 acre tract, bounded on the north by Carlos Sibbald, south by Juan McIntosh, east by North Creek savannahs.

[Bound together 5-7 in English:]

5 - Decree of Superior Court, District of East Florida, 7/6/1840, confirming claim.

6 - Mandate of the Supreme Court of the United States affirming decree of superior court and ordering further proceedings. Witness: Honorable Roger B. Taney, Chief Justice of Supreme Court, 2nd Monday in January, 1842. William Thomas Carroll, Clerk.

7 - Opinion of Supreme Court, January term, 1842, in case of U. S. vs. John W. Low et al., heirs of John Low, deceased. Justice Catron delivered the same, affirming claim as surveyed by Clarke.

8 [E] Charles C. Tracy certifies plat of 10,000 acres surveyed in January and February, 1847. Chainmen: William Reyes, Alexander Salina and Domingo Pacetty. Approved, 4/16/1847, Robert Butler.

9 [E] David H. Burr certifies plat of 10,016 acres for John Low and others. Approved, 11/26/1850, B. A. Putnam.

10 [E] Brief [27 pp.] on appeal to Secretary of the Interior from decision of the Commissioner of the General Land Office: Drummond and Bradford "of counsel for Administrators of heirs of John T. Lowe, deceased," S and F Sts., NW, Washington City, Wednesday, 7/4/1883, to Commissioner of the General Land Office, Division D, Interior Department. It claims error in decision delivering patent [to heirs of John T. Lowe] to Charles R. King of Lake City, Fla., as attorney for part of the Lowe heirs. It reviews the case, asks that the commissioner's

decision be reversed, and insists that the surveyor general be ordered to recover the patent and deliver it to the administrator.

Robert H. Bradford of Drummond & Bradford deposes, 7/5/1883, before Emma M. Gillett, N.P., Washington City, that a certified copy of above brief was sent by registered mail to King. M. Martin, surveyor general, certifies, Tallahassee, 7/25/1883, that the above "is a true and correct copy."

[Dossier contains 2 translations each of 2 and 3, and 3 translations of 3, and a copy each of 2, 5, 6 and 7.]

Maestre, Louis                Con. M 1; DG IV 102

   1 [E] Benjamin Clements and James E. Exum certify, first quarter of 1809, plat of 646.78 acres on the east side of the Bay of St. Mary de Galves and being in Sec. 19, T. 1, R. 27, and Sec. 14, T. 1, R. 28, S&W, to Louis Maestre. Chainmen: J. B. Clements, S. L. Ming, James Ming and Wesley Inglish, approved by Butler.

Malagosa, Juan                Con. M 2; DG IV 103

   1 [E] James R. Donelson certifies plat of 644.29 acres at Turvin's, or Red Shoes Bluff, on the west margin of Scambia River, being in Secs. 14, 15, 22, and 23, T. 4, R. 31, for Andrew Mitchell. Chainmen: Robert Mosely and William Washington; approved by Butler, 1/?/1834.

   [Dossier contains duplicate of 1.]

Malloy, Daniel                Com. M 3; DG IV 157

   1 [E] Benjamin and J. B. Clements and James W. Exum certified, 4th quarter of 1831, plat of 638.96 acres, being in Sec. 42, T. 5, R. 29 N&W, for Daniel Malloy. Chainmen: James M. Sawyers and Andrew A. Crawford. Butler approves, 1/?/1834, a donation grant.

   [Dossier contains duplicate of 1.]

Manning, Drury                Con. M 4; DG IV 117

   1 [E] Benjamin and J. B. Clements and James W. Exum certified, 4th quarter of 1831, 639.40 acres at Turvin's Bluff on Scambia River, northeast of land of Henry O'Neal, being in Sec. 42, T. 4, R. 31 N&W. Chainmen: Thomas McClelland, Jesse Evans, Albert Sebastian, Charles Sims, J. M. Sawyers and A. A. Crawford. Butler approves, 1/?/1834.

Marin, Francis           Con. M 5; DG V 57

1 [E] claims 2,000 acres at Cabbage Hammock on the west side of St. Johns River. Governor Estrada's grant, 11/15/1815.

2 [E] Marin petitions, 11/15/1815, for 2,000 acres on the west side of St. Johns River at the head of a creek that flows into said river about 4 or 5 miles from the place where Panton & Leslie had their store. He had rendered numerous services to the provinces and actually is a sergeant of the urban militia. Governor Estrata grants.

3 [S] George J. F. Clarke certifies, 4/24/1821, plat of 200 acres, above, for Marin.

4 [E] Bernardo Segui deposes, 9/27/1824, that he has seen the original and believes the signature on the copy to be that of Thomas Aguilar, that he wrote the original memorial himself and that the signature attached to the original concession is that of Governor Estrada. George J. F. Clarke deposes that the plat was made by one of his deputy surveyors, either Andres Burgevin or William Garvin. Horatio G. Dexter deposes that Marin claims and has claimed the above tract of land. Before the board in session, 9/27/1824.

5 [E] Letter, 1/10/1831, Marin to Robert Butler, Tallahassee, submitting certificate of grant and copy of survey of tract claimed by him, "in obedience to your advertisements in the Florida Herald."

6 [E] Randolph and Putnam certify, 11/16/1850, plat of 1,721.94 acres, being T. 16, R. 28 S&E, for Marin.

[Dossier contains 1 copy and 2 translations of 2 and 3.]

Marshall, Theresa, Heirs of      Con. M 6; DG IV 278

1 [E] Eliza Burnell for herself and the heirs of Theresa Marshall, claims, through Drysdale, 533 1/3 acres at Santa Teresa on

the west side of North River, about 9 miles from St. Augustine, granted to Theresa Marshall, then T. Hill, [Gill?], 10/10/17 [?].

[Bound together 2-4 in Spanish:]

2 - Theresa Gill, widow of Teofilo Gill, through Joseph Sanchez, petitions, 8/4/1791, for permit to make a temporary ranch about 9 miles from the place where she now stays, which is low land very unhealthy to her children and hard to be cultivated. Governor Quesada requests, 8/13/1791, information from the ministers of the royal domain.

3 - Gonzalo Zamorano and Bartolome Benitez y Calvez, ministers of the royal domain, report favorably.

4 - Governor Quesada grants, 10/10/1791, permit to establish herself for the present at the place which she solicits until the next survey when she would be allotted her quota. William Reynolds certifies true copy, 9/20/1823.

5 [S] Theresa Marshall petitions, 5/6/1819, for Clarke's certificate of the plat of 6 caballerias and 17 acres made by Pedro Marrot.

6 [S] Marrot certifies, 5/18/1793, plat, above, to T. Marshall as curator of her children, Juan, Juana, Maria, Ysabela and Ana Hill. Clarke certifies true copy, 5/6/1819. Antonio Alvarez' extract, 5/26/1845, from descriptive list, No. 240, Theresa Marshall, 533 1/3 acres.

[Dossier contains translation of 2, 3, 4, 5 and 6.]

Martin, George W.                    Con. M 7; DG IV 159, 169

1 [E] claims, through George J. F. Clarke, 300 acres on the west side of St. Johns River, at Big Swamp in front of Dutch Island, Governor Coppinger's grant, 11/29/1790, to Charles W. Clarke who sold to Martin.

[Bound together 2-3 in Spanish:]

2 - At Fernandina, 3/15/1817, Carlos Clarke petitions for 300 acres, the quota that corresponds to himself and 10 slaves. He also petitions for another tract in place of his pay for services rendered as Lieutenant of the provincial militia for 18 months during the insurrection. These lands he wished to be measured in two different places, one at Big Swamp west of St. Johns River near Turkey Buzzard, the other at Big Hammock above Dutch Island.

3 - Governor Coppinger grants, 4/10/1817, 300 acres, instructing that claimant's second petition be presented separately.

4 [S] Royal title, 4/10/1817, to 300 acres at Big Swamp west of St. Johns River to Carlos Clarke. Entralgo attests. Fatio certifies true copy.

5 [S] Clarke certifies, 5/30/1820, plat of 300 acres above.

6 [E] Deed: Camden County, Georgia, 4/23/1822, Charles W. Clarke sells the 300 acres described above to George W. Martin of St. Marys, Camden County, Georgia, for $180 cash.

7 [E] Benjamin and J. B. Clements certify plat of 304.87 acres, being in Sec. 40, T. 10, R. 27 S&E, for George W. Martin. Chainmen: Joel F. Owel [Yowell ?] and John M. McYowell.

[Dossier contains one copy of 5 and one translation each of 5 and 6.]

Martin, Henry B., Heirs of     Con. M 8; DG IV 161, 213
Charleston, N. C.

1 [E] claim, 8/17/1823, through John B. Strong, 400 acres at Mosquitos, granted, 9/3/1803 to Martin, who immediately took possession of it until 1808, when he had to abandon it for a time as his home was burned and all the plantation improvements destroyed by the

Indians. Later he had his father-in-law to again take possession of the land until 1812 when on account of the commotion and famine he had to abandon it. He has had a tenant there.

2 [S] Henry B. Martin, new resident, petitions 9/3/1803, for 400 acres in Mosquitos, bounded on the south by lands of Ambrosio Hull. Governor White grants until Martin's quota be surveyed to him. Juan de Pierra and William Reynolds certified true copy, 8/15/1823.

Martinely, Geronima                    Con. M 9; DG V 58

1 [E] claims 366 2/3 acres at Guana Creek on San Genaro's place, Governor White's grant to Jose Peso de Burgo of whom claimant is heir.

2 [S] Jose Peso de Burgo petitions, 11/19/1792, to have survey of his quota of land in the place called del Gobernador Grant which was granted to him, 7/15/1786. He has now 2 slaves. Governor Quesada grants, 11/19/1792, and William Reynolds certifies true copy, 8/16/1827.

3 [S] Pedro Marrot and Josiah Dupont certify, 6/3/1793, plat of 11 caballerias for Jose Peso de Burgo with a family of wife, 1 child and 18 slaves.

4 [S] Juan de Pierra certifies, 9/11/1798, that upon petition of Jose Peso de Burgo and Francisco and Juan Triay for a permit to exchange lands granted to them, the former's being 9 miles north of this town and known as Gobernador Grant, and the latter's west to the San Sebastian River, which land had belonged to Juan Forbes during the British possession, Governor Quesada grants.

5 [S] Jose Peso de Burgo petitions, 2/14/1818, for permit to present proof of continuous cultivation of his 366 2/3 acres at Guana Creek and 1,000 acres on San Sebastian River. Governor Coppinger

grants, 2/14/1818.

6 [S] Entralgo lists, 2/16/1818, conditions necessary to the title.

7 [S] Fernando de la Maza Arredondo, married, 30, deposes, 2/16/1818, before Entralgo that Burgos has cultivated for 10 years his San Genaro plantation at Guana Creek where he has built houses and made other improvements necessary to the title to the land. Burgos had to flee from this plantation in 1812 during the revolution when all his houses were destroyed. As for his other plantation on San Sebastian River, Burgos has been cultivating it for more than 10 years with his slaves, and comes to town every day to bring eggs and vegetables for sale. He has built houses and made all improvements necessary to obtain title to the land.

8 [S] Pedro Miranda, Habana, married, 45, deposes before Entralgo confirming above.

9 [S] Governor Coppinger grants, 2/26/1818. Entralgo attests and notifies Burgos.

10 [S] Royal title, 2/28/1818. Governor Coppinger grants to Burgos 11 caballerias, or 366 2/3 acres, at Guana Creek.

11 [S] Upon Burgos' petition, 11/19/1792, for the quota for his family and 12 slaves, Governor Quesada grants until his quota is surveyed according to his number. On 2/28/1818, Governor Coppinger issues him a royal title to 11 caballerias, or 366 2/3 acres. [Fatio's abstract is attached to the decree of the Board.]

12 [S] Alvarez' extract, 5/25/1845, from descriptive list, No. 595, Geronima Martinely, 366 2/3 acres.

[Dossier contains 1 translation of 3.]

Mason, Littleberry            Con. M 10; DG IV 103

    1 [E] James R. Donalson certifies plat of 620.47 acres for Littleberry Mason, being in Secs. 35 and 36, T. 6, R. 30 N&W, situated near the "Conicut" River and touching the Alabama line. Chainmen: Robert Mosely and William Washington.

Mattain, Lewis            Con. M 11; DG IV 173

    1 [E] claims 300 acres at Box's on the south side of St. Johns River, Governor Estrada's service grant of 10/4/1815.

    2 [S] L. Mattain petitions, 9/12/1815, for 300 acres on Amalia Island between the lands of Domingo Fernandez and Santiago Cashen. He was forced in 1812 and later again in 1813, because of revolution, to abandon the plantation that was granted to him on the main land of the frontier which he believes is too insecure to go back. Governor Estrada asks the commandant for information; Pangua reports favorably, 10/21/1815. Governor Estrada grants, 10/24/1815. Aguilar certifies true copy.

    3 [S] Clarke certifies, 8/3/1817, plat of 300 acres, above, for L. Mattain.

    4 [E] Antonio Alvarez' extract of 12/23/1844 of proceedings of the Board, 9/18/1823, showing that Lewis Mattain presented a claim for 300 acres, and on 4/30/1824, the claims of:

           Frederick M. Munon for . . . 450 acres
           Abraham Bellamy for . . . . 350 acres
           Moses E. Levy for . . . . . 275 acres
           L. Mattain for . . . . . . . 150 acres

being called were submitted and confirmed.

    5 [E] Antonio Alvarez' extract of 12/23/1844 from descriptive list, No. 233, L. Mattain for 300 acres.

[Dossier contains 1 translation of 2 and 1 copy and 1 translation of 3.]

Mattain, Lewis          Con. M 12; DG IV 159, 174

1 [E] claims 150 acres at San Ramon at the head of Pablo Creek, Governor White's grant, 12/5/1811, to the heirs of Josefa Espinosa who sold, 1/18/1819.

[Bound together 2-11 in Spanish:]

2 - Jose Sanchez, heir and executive of Josefa Espinosa, for himself and his brothers petitions for permit to present proof of the continuous cultivation for 10 years of the 12 caballerias and 43 acres granted, 5/13,14/1793, to his aunt, Josefa Espinosa. Zubizarreta attests and notifies Jose Sanchez.

3 - White requests, 3/4/1809, them to prove that they are the heirs of J. Espinosa. Zubizarreta attests and notifies Jose Sanchez.

4 - Pedro Marrot and Josias Dupont certify, 5/3/1793, plat of 3 caballerias and 20 acres, a part of the quota due to her, on the plantation, Fuerte de San Diego, for Josefa Espinosa, who has a brother, 2 nephews, and 7 slaves.

5 - Marrot and Dupont certify, 5/14/1793, plat of 4 caballerias and 17 acres, as part of the quota due to her, at the San Ramon plantation.

6 - Jose Sanchez petitions to have the secretary of the government certify his appointment as administrator by his aunt in her will. Governor White grants, 4/8/1809; Zubizarreta attests and notifies J. Sanchez.

7 - The will, 10/6/1797, of Josefa de la Encarnacion Espinosa, legitimate daughter of Diego Espinosa and Josefa Torres, names her nephew, Jose Sanchez, and Francisco Zavier Miranda as administra-

tors of her estate and bequeaths half of it to her brother, Sabastian Espinosa; the other half to be divided in three parts, two of which she leaves to her nephews, Nicolas, Barnardino, Jose and Ramon Sanchez and her nieces, Maria de la O Sanchez and Andres Sanches, the last two to share one fifth of two-thirds; the other third she leaves to Diego Juan Jose, Antonio Abad and Fania Espinosa, nephews also, and to Dolores Gavilan, as legitimate daughter of Andres Espinosa, "my dead niece". Witnesses: Bernardo Segui, Francisco Rovira and Juan Entralgo. Zubizarreta certifies true copy, 4/11/1809. Governor White grants, 4/5/1809, permit for presentation of witnesses to prove the cultivation of the land for 10 years and other conditions to obtain title. Zubizarretta attests and notifies J. Sanchez.

8 - Zubizarreta lists conditions required for title.

9 - Bartolome Castro y Ferrer, married, 51, deposes, 1/16/1811, before Jose Gregorio Quintana that on passing through the place of J. Espinosa at San Diego he has seen it cultivated both while she was alive and after her death when her place has been inhabited by the heirs. The place has been built and all other improvements made necessary for the title.

10 - Fernando de la Maza Arredondo, married, 45, deposes, 1/18/1811, before Quintana confirming above as all conditions having been fulfilled by Josefa Espinosa and her heirs. Governor White grants, 1/19/1811, and Quintana countersigns. Zubizarreta attests and notifies Jose Sanchez. Zubizarreta lists, 1/19/1811, dues as follows:

```
        To Governor White for 5 signatures . . . .   10
        "  Quintana  . . . . . . . . . . . . . . .   74
        "  Zubizarreta . . . . . . . . . . . . . .   71
                                                    155 or -
```

19 pesos and 3 reales.

11 - Royal title, 1/25/1811, to 4 caballerias and 17 acres on San Ramon Plantation granted by Governor White to the heirs of Josefa Espinosa.

12 [S] Deed, 1/18/1819: Cristina Hill, Maria Hill, Magdalena Joaneda, widow of Jose, Bernardino Sanchez, Nicolas Sanchez, Bernardo Segui, executor of Ramon Sanchez; Fernando de la Maza Arredondo, representing the heirs of Maria de la O Sanchez, and Pedro Miranda, representing heirs of Maria Andre Sanchez, all heirs of the late Josefa Espinosa and Sebastian, her brother, sell to Luis Mattain 4 caballerias and 7 acres, 150 acres, at San Ramon for 150 pesos cash. Witness: Francisco Medicis, Santos Rodrigues, Jose Mariano Hernandez. Juan de Entralgo certifies true copy.

13 [S] Burgevin certifies, 11/4/1819, plat of 150 acres at the head of Pablo Creek for Luis Mattain who bought it from the heirs of Sebastian Espinosa.

14 [E] Washington certifies plat of 190.91 acres at San Ramon in Sec. 39, T. 3, R. 29 S&E, for Luis Mattain. Chainmen: John W. Townsend and Isaac Varnes. Robert Butler approves, 6/20/1836.

[Dossier contains 1 translation each of 11, 12 and 13.]

Maxey, Robert C., Heirs of     Con. M 13; DG V 376

1 [S] Jose Dil [Dell ?] new settler, petitions, 12/30/1802, for 500 acres on St. Johns River at Milergue place, about 40 miles from St. Augustine, bounded on the north by the plantation of Capin Dil. White asks, 12/30/1802, information from the commandant, Barcelo, who reports favorably, 1/3/1803. Governor White grants, 1/3/1803.

[Bound together 3-10 in Spanish:]

3 - Pierra certifies, 1/3/1803, that upon petition of Jose Dell for

500 acres north of St. Johns River at Mill Crike [Creek], 40 miles from St. Augustine, bound on the north by lands of Captain Dell. Governor White made the grant.

4 - Peter Maxey petitions, 4/12/1821, for himself and other heirs of Roberto Clarke for permit to have the Small Hope place, 500 acres which R. C. Maxey bought from Jose Dell, surveyed by Lynch. Governor Coppinger grants. Entralgo attests and notifies Maxey. He also notifies Lynch who countersigns.

5 - Lynch certifies, 5/2/1821, plat of 500 acres, more or less, at Small Hope west of Miller [Mill] Creek, about 2 miles from St. Johns River, for Pedro Maxey.

6 - Maxey, for himself and other heirs, petitions Roberto Clarke, 5/8/1821, for title and to present testimonial of their fulfillment of the conditions necessary to title. Entralgo attests and notifies P. Maxey.

7 - Jan Eduardo Fate, of London, married, school teacher, deposes, 5/17/1821, before Governor Coppinger that R. C. Maxey died at Small Hope plantation at the place at which his son, Peter Maxey, has lived and has cultivated and improved for more than 10 years with no interruptions.

8 - Felipe Dewes [Dewees ?], married, 36, deposes before Entralgo confirming above No. 7.

9 - Fernando de la Maza Arredondo, Jr., married, 33, also deposes confirming above.

10 - Governor Coppinger grants, 5/18/1821. Entralgo attests and notifies P. Maxey.

Mazells, John                 Con. M 14; DG IV 281

1 [E] claims, through Clarke, 800 acres, 400 of them in Long's

Hammac on the south side of Mozell's Lake, 200 on "Hiccory" Bluff, St. Marys River, and 200 on Brandy Branch, St. Marys River, Governor Coppinger's grant as head rights.

2 [S] Clarke certifies, 5/6/1818, plat of 400 acres, above, for John Mozells.

3 [S] Clarke certifies, 10/11/1818, plat of 200 acres on Hickory Bluff, St. Marys River, for John Mozells. Thomas T. Woods also certifies plat in English.

4 [S] Clarke certifies, 11/10/1818, plat of 200 acres on Brandy Branch, St. Marys River, for John Mozells. Thomas T. Woods certifies same plat in English.

5 [E] Alvarez' extract, 2/26/1845, from descriptive list, No. 224, John Mozells, 200 acres at Brandy Branch.

[Dossier contains 1 copy of 1, 1 copy and 1 translation of 2 and 3, and 1 copy and 2 translations of 4.]

McCully, William            Con. M 15; DG IV 281

1 [E] claims, through Clarke, 300 acres on St. Marys River, Governor Coppinger's grant as head rights.

2 [S] Clarke certifies, 9/8/1818, plat of 300 acres on the bank of St. Marys River, above the lands of Carlos Hovey, for William McCully.

[Dossier contains 1 copy and translation of 2.]

McDavid, Joel A.            Con. M 16; DG IV 117

1 [E] Benjamin and J. B. Clements and James W. Exum certify, 4th quarter of 1831, plat of 639.52 acres in Sec. 39, T. 4, R. 32 N&W, for Joel A. McDavid. Chainmen: James M. Sawyers and Andrew A. Crawford. Butler approves, January 1834.

McDonell, Ferdinand D.				Con. M 17; DG IV 301

1 [E] claims, through Farquhar Bethune, 800 acres at John Stout's, at Matanzas Bar, Governor Quesada's concession, 10/8/1790, to William McHenry, whose granddaughter married F. D. McDonell.

2 [S] Tomas Aguilar certifies, 12/19/1817, that on page 23, Sec. 2 of the Register, William McHenry, carpenter and dealer in spirits and beer, "native of Ireland, married, Roman Catholic, as such attached to the Minorcans, swore allegience and fidelity 8/12/1790, and was placed upon the list by the parish priest, Pedro Campos."

3 [S] F. D. McDonell and his wife, Marria Monrro, legitimate heiress of her late grandfather, W. McHenry, petition, 12/9/1817, for certified copy of the concession of 800 acres, above, and they would like to know the number of slaves McHenry had at the time. Governor Coppinger grants the request for certified copy of concession to McHenry and the concession by Aguilar follows.

4 [E] Arthur M. Randolph certifies plat of 783.58 acres, being in Ts. 9 and 10, R. 30 south, for F. D. McDonald [McDonell]. Putnam approves, 11/16/1850.

[Dossier contains 1 translation each of 2 and 3.]

McDowell and Black				Con. M 18; DG V 62

1 [E] claims, through Drysdale, 900 acres on Graham's Swamp, between Matanzas and Halifax Rivers, bounded on the south by lands of Francisco Pillion, granted, 5/20/1805, to Joseph M. Arredondo, Governor Estrada's royal title, 6/30/1815.

[Bound together 2-9 in Spanish:]

2 - Pierra certifies, 9/15/1803, that upon petition of Santiago Toole for 3,000 acres on Pantano [Swamp] de Graham, Governor White granted

900 acres, the quota corresponding to petitions for land for his wife and 14 negroes.

3 - Aguilar certifies, 5/20/1805, that upon petition of Jose de la Maza Arredondo for the 900 acres granted to Toole, who had relinquished them on leaving with his family for the U. S. A., Governor Kindelan grants.

4 - J. M. Arredondo petitions, 5/26/1816, for permit to present the testimonials proving that he has fulfilled all conditions required to title.

5 - Entralgo lists, 5/27/1815, conditions necessary to the title.

6 - Juan Gaiger, North American, married, 34, tanner, deposes, 5/27/1815, before Juan de la Maza Arredondo y Sanfelices that J. M. Arredondo has cleared, cultivated and made other improvements, and has lived on the land for 10 years, which is a dairy farm. Entralgo attests.

7 - Felipe Solano, married, 32, farmer, deposes confirming above. Entralgo attests.

8 - Juan Huerta, 26, married, farmer, also deposes confirming above.

9 - Governor Estrada grants, 5/27/1815. Arredondo countersigns. Entralgo attests and notifies J. M. Arredondo. Fees 24 *reales*.

10 [E] Royal title, 6/20/1815, to 900 acres granted by Governor Estrada to Jose de la Maza Arredondo. Entralgo attests and certifies true copy.

11 [E] Robert McHardy, upon petition of J. M. Arredondo, 6/20/1815, certifies, 3/12/1818, plat of 900 acres.

12 [E] Deed, 6/12/1820: Fernando de la Maza Arredondo, Jr., attorney in fact for his brother Jose, absent in Habana, Cuba, sells

to Francisco Pasqual Sanchez 900 acres for $2,137.40 cash. Witnesses: Jose Mariano Hernandez, Gabriell Perpall, Andres Burgevin. Entralgo countersigns and certifies, 6/14/1820, true copy.

13 [E] Deed, 6/10/1823: Francisco P. Sanchez sells 900 acres, above, for the sum of 1 dollar cash to Andrew McDowell and Alexander Black.

14 [E] Antonio Alvarez' extract, 7/12/1845, from descriptive list, No. 589.

[Dossier contains 1 copy and 1 translation of 11.]

McDowell and Black    Con. M 19

1 [E] claims, through Drysdale, 500 acres east of St. Johns River, about half a legua northeast of Little Orange Grove. Governor Coppinger's grant, 12/4/1818, to Andres Burgevin, who sold to Francisco P. Sanchez, who in turn sold, 1/10/1833.

2 [S] Burgevin of North Carolina petitions, 1/13/1818, for the quota corresponding to himself and his slaves, of which he inserts a list. Governor Coppinger grants, 1/24/1818, 500 acres. William Reynolds certifies true copy.

3 [S] Burgevin petitions, 1/26/1818, to have a survey made by McHardy, which Governor Coppinger grants. Entralgo attests and notifies Burgevin. He also notifies McHardy who countersigns. William Reynolds certifies true copy, 9/19/1823.

4 [S] McHardy certifies, 3/27/1818, plat of 500 acres on Spring Garden Creek near the lands Burgevin possesses on the St. Johns River.

5 [S] Royal title, 4/24/1819, to 500 acres east of the St. Johns River to Burgevin. Entralgo attests and certifies true copy.

6 [S] Deed, 6/12/1820: Andres Burgevin sells 500 acres on St. Johns River, about one league from Little Orange Grove, to Francisco Pascual Sanchez for $1,075.00 cash.

7 [E] Deed, 6/10/1823: F. P. Sanchez sells to Andrew McDowall and Alexander Black of Charleston, S. C., the 500 acres mentioned above, for the sum of 1 dollar. Witness: G. W. Perpall and C. Zully. Tingle certifies true copy.

8 [E] Antonio Alvarez' extract, 6/20/1845, from descriptive list, No. 539, McDowall and Black, 500 acres.

[Dossier contains 1 translation of 3 and 4.]

McDowell and Black          Con. M 20; DG IV 196

1 [E] claim, through Drysdale, 490 acres east of St. Johns River at Little Orange Grove, south of the old Indian or Chocochate Road, on the eastern bank of St. Johns River and Little Lake, about 8 or 10 miles from Lake George. Governor Coppinger's grant, 12/11/1814 [?], to Burgevin who sold, 6/12/1820, to Francisco P. Sanchez who sold, 1/10/1823, to McDowell and Black.

2 [S] Burgevin petitions, 12/9/1817, for the quota of land corresponding to himself, his family and slaves, lists of whom he includes, on Little Orange Grove. Governor Coppinger grants, 12/11/1817, 490 acres.

3 [S] List of Burgevin's family and slaves, 12/9/1817, includes Burgevin, his wife, Julia Guillet, daughter, Carolina, nephew, Constantino Burgevin, and 14 slaves from 45 to 17 years.

4 [S] Burgevin petitions, 1/2/1818, to have the land surveyed by McHardy. Governor Coppinger grants, 1/5/1818. Entralgo attests,

notifies Burgevin and McHardy, the latter of whom countersigns.

    5 [S] McHardy certifies, 3/27/1818, plat of 490 acres above.

    6 [S] Royal title, 4/24/1819, to the 490 acres, granted to Burgevin by Governor Coppinger.

    [Bound together 7-21 in Spanish:]

7 - Aguilar's certified copy of 2 above.

8 - Burgevin petitions, 1/13/1818, for the rest of his quota of land in Little Orange Grove, and Governor Coppinger grants, 1/24/1818, 500 acres. Aguilar certifies true copy.

9 - Burgevin petitions, 7/17/1818, for permit to present proof of the fulfillment of conditions required for the title, which request Governor Coppinger grants. Entralgo attests and notifies Burgevin.

10 - Santiago Pellicer, 7/20/1818, single, 24, deposes, 7/20/1818, before Governor Coppinger, that Burgevin has taken possession of the land, that he has cleared some of it, built shacks for the slaves and is ready to start cultivation.

11 - Patricio Lynch, Irish, single, 32, deposes confirming No. 10 above.

12 - Pablo Dupon of Borguet, Santo Domingo Island, 38, single, also deposes confirming above No. 10.

13 - Duplicate of 4 above.

14 - McHardy certifies, 3/27/1818, plat of 490 acres on Spring Lake Garden.

15 - Burgevin petitions, 4/21/1819, for permission to present proof of his cultivation of the land and the further building of houses, which request Governor Coppinger grants, 4/22/1819.

16 - Entralgo attests and notifies Burgevin.

17 - Patricio Lynch deposes, 4/23/1819, before Governor Coppinger, that it is true Burgevin built houses, fences and other improvements, fulfilling the conditions necessary to the title. Entralgo attests.

18 - Paul Dupon also deposes before Governor Coppinger, confirming above, No. 17. Entralgo attests.

19 - Governor Coppinger grants, 4/24/1819; Entralgo attests and notifies Burgevin.

20 - Deed: Andres Burgevin sells, 6/24/1820, 490 acres on the east side of St. Johns River to Francisco Pascual Sanchez for $1,040.00 cash. Witnesses: Pedro Miranda, Antonio Alvarez and Julian Avice. Entralgo attests and certifies true copy.

21 - Fernando de la Maza Arredondo, Jr., Mayor, and Jose Mariano Hernandez, rexidor [regidor], vouch for Entralgo's signature.

22 [E] Deed: F. P. Sanchez sells, 6/10/1823, to Andrew McDowall and Alexander Black, 490 acres for $1.00 cash. Witnesses: W. Perpall and C. Zully.

23 [E] Alvarez' extract, 6/26/1845, from descriptive list, No. 234, McDowall and Black, 490 acres.

[Dossier contains 1 copy of 2 and 1 translation each of 2, 14 and 20.]

McDowall and Black          Con. M 21; DG V 416

1 [E] claim, through Drysdale, 450 acres, being part of the 1,300 acres granted, 2/23/1792, to Honoria Blake [Black ?] by the Spanish government in exchange for lands owned by her under a British grant, at Graham Swamp between the heads of the Halifax and the

Matanzas Rivers. Margarita Black who was bequeathed this 450 acres upon the death of her mother, Honoria Black, in 1809, sold it, through J. M. Ugarte, to Fernando de la Maza Arredondo, Jr., on 8/23/1820, who sold, 8/25/1820, to Francisco P. Sanchez, who sold, 5/31/1823, to McDowell and Black.

2 [S] Clarke certifies, 3/12/1818, plat of 450 acres for F. M. Arredondo, which he bought from Margarita Black.

3 [S] Deed: Jose M. Urgate, with power of attorney from Margarita Black, sells to F. M. Arredondo, Jr., 450 acres for 12 pesos 4 reales cash, 8/23/1820. Witnesses: Francisco P. Sanchez, Antonio Alvarez and Pedro Miranda. Entralgo attests; Reynolds certifies true copy, 9/7/1823.

4 [S] Deed: F. M. Arredondo sells, 8/25/1820, to Francisco P. Sanchez 450 acres for 1,068 pesos 6 reales. Witnesses: Bernardo Segui, Pedro Miranda and Jose Bernardo Reyes. Entralgo attests and certifies true copy.

5 [E] Alvarez' extract, 6/20/1845, from descriptive list, No. 606, McDowell and Black, 450 acres.

[Dossier contains translation of 2.]

McFee, Constance, Heirs of       Con. M 22; DG IV 256

1 [E] claim, 12/1/1823, through G. W. Perpall, 446 acres on St. Johns River, on Julington and Cunningham Creeks, Governor Quesada's grant of December 1791, to Angus Clark, their ancestor.

2 [S] Pedro Marrot certifies, 11/17/1791, plat of 13 caballerias and 17 acres at Liberty Hall for Angus Clark who has 7 slaves.

[Bound together from 3-10 in Spanish:]

3 - Gabriel Guillermo Perpall, attorney-in-fact for Constancia McFee, petitions for a certified copy of the concession of the above land, granted 12/1/1791, to Constance McFee's father by Governor Quesada. Governor Coppinger grants, 7/9/1818. Entralgo attests and notifies Gabriell Perpall.

4 - Entralgo certifies, 7/11/1818, copy of the concession of 13 <u>caballerias</u> and 17 acres at Liberty Hall, granted, 12/10/1791, by Governor Quesada to Angus Clark. Witnesses: Miguel Rengil and Francisco Rovira.

5 - Gabriell G. Perpall petitions for certified copy of the will of Angus Clark and of the decree of execution.

6 - Will of Angus Clark, dated 11/7/1794, in which he nominates Francisco Felipe Facio, Sr., and Leslie Escoderos administrators and curators of his only heir, his daughter, Constancia McFee, to whom he leaves the place, tools, 6 negroes [Dublin, Jack, Cyrus, Albion, Pagui and Rosa] and everything else left of his after giving: to Alejandro McDowell all his clothing and his riding horse, to Randolph McDonald his small rifle and to Sara Crosby, widow of Tomas Crosby, all the house furniture and the fowls. In case of anyone's being dissatisfied and commencing any law suit or causing any difficulty to the administrators and curators, his legacy shall pass to Constancia McFee. Witnesses: Francisco Felipe Facio, Jr., Alejandro Creighton, Jorge Fleming, Felipe Fatio, Juan Creighton, Jose McCullock and Miguel de Ginaudy.

7 - Governor White decrees, 12/12/1804, the will valid and that C. McFee shall enter in possession. The delivery of the property should be made by John Forrester, the actual holder, "immediately upon the

request of this decree or of an authenticated copy." Fees 80 reales.

.8 - G. Perpall petitions for certified copy of the general power of attorney given before Zubizarreta. Governor Coppinger grants, 7/9/1818. Entralgo attests and notifies Perpall.

9 - General power of attorney given by Constance McFee to G. G. Perpall. Entralgo certifies, 7/11/1818, true copy.

10 - Perpall petitions, 8/6/1818, to present the information of his having fulfilled all conditions necessary to title. Governor Coppinger grants permission. Entralgo attests and notifies Perpall.

11 [E] Washington certifies plat of 444.04 acres at Liberty Hall on the St. Johns River, being Sec. 37, T. 5, R. 27 S&E; Sec. 43, T. 4, R. 27 S&E, and Sec. 39, T. 4, R. 26 S&E, for C. McFee. Chainmen: John W. Townsend and Isaac Varnes. Robert Butler approved, 6/20/1836.

[Dossier contains a translation each of 4 and 7.]

McGirt, James                    Con. M 23; DG V 393

1 [E] The heirs of J. M. Girt [McGirt] claim, through E. R. Gibson, 300 acres on St. Marys River, bounded by James Wheeler's plantation; granted to J. M. Girt in January, 1793.

2 [S] J. M. Girtt petitions, 1/7/1793, for 300 acres on Cano de Bell on the Santa Maria River, as a part of the quota corresponding to himself and his large family. He petitions also for the land to be surveyed.

3 [S] Governor Quesada, 1/19/1793, requests from Marrot information as to whether J. M. Girtt has any lands surveyed to him, and if so in what place they are located, and at what distance from those he now solicits.

4 [S] Marrot replies, 1/20/1793, that J. M. Girt has been granted, 2/24/1792, 300 acres at Governor Grant, 9 miles from St. Augustine; 200 acres on the Guano; and 300 acres between Nassau and St. Marys Rivers, but none of this land has been surveyed; on 3/8/1792, he was permitted to exchange the 300 acres at Governor Grant for 300 acres at Black Creek on St. Johns River, 35 miles from St. Vincent Ferrer. As to the lands J. M. Girt now solicits, they are vacant and are 35 miles from St. Vincent Ferrer. Governor Quesada grants, 1/24/1845.

5 [E] Antonio Alvarez' extract, 2/14/1845, from descriptive list, No. 598, J. M. Girt's heirs, 300 acres.

[Dossier contains 1 copy and 2 translations of 2, 3 and 4.]

McGirt, James, Heirs of          Con. M 24; DG V 377

1 [E] claim through E. R. Gibson, 300 acres of the plantation formerly belonging to James Grant, the British Governor, 9 miles from St. Augustine; 200 acres at Guano Creek bounded on the north by Juan Capo and south by Pedro Mestre; and 300 acres for the raising of cattle on the Nassau River, formerly inhabited by M. Bell, Governor Quesada grants and orders Marrot to survey the land.

2 [S] James McGirt petitions, 2/24/1792, for 300 acres on the plantation formerly belonging to James Grant, the British Governor, 9 miles from St. Augustine; also 200 acres at Guano Creek, bounded on the north by Juan Capo and south by Pedro Mestre; and for the raising of cattle, 300 acres on the Nassau River, formerly inhabited by M. Bell. Quesada grants and orders Marrot to survey the land.

3 [E] Antonio Alvarez' extract, 3/6/1845, from descriptive list, No. 599, J. M. Girt's heirs, 300 acres.

[Dossier contains 1 translation of 2.]

McGirt, James, Heirs of        Con. M 25; DG V 377

1 [E] claim, through Edward R. Gibson, Martin's Island of 80 acres on St. Marys River, opposite the place formerly occupied by J.M. Girt, which was a grant by Governor White, 4/26/1798, to J. M. Girt.

[Bound together 2-4 in Spanish:]

2 - J. M. Girt petitions, 4/25/1798, for the Martin Island [above], formerly granted to Tomey Grair who abandoned the land to move to Georgia; he also desires a piece of land on the lower part of Rose's Bluff next to Bell's Old Plantation in order that he may cut timber for building houses and fences. He has already been granted a place on St. Marys River, opposite Martin Island, but there is not enough land there for his quota. Governor White requests information from the Commandant of Engineers who reports favorably concerning the petition for Martin's Island, but opposed the second petition stating that Girt should be only allowed to cut the timber he needs.

3 - Tomas de Aguilar certifies, 2/3/1796, that upon Jaime McGirt's petition for the vacant lands on St. Johns River, formerly belonging to the Widow Ashley, Governor Quesada granted until his quota could be measured to them.

4 - Manuel Rengil certifies, 8/26/1794, that upon Jayme McGirt's petition, 8/12/1794, for 200 acres on St. Johns River, between the plantations of Angus Clark and Magarita Jones, Governor Quesada granted the tract, 8/18/1794.

5 [E] Antonio Alvarez' extract, 2/14/1845, from descriptive list, No. 600, J. McGirt's heirs, 30 acres.

[Dossier contains 1 copy and 2 translations of 2.]

McHardy, Caroline E., Heirs of    Con. M 26; DG V 61

1 [E] The infant children of Caroline E. McHardy, deceased, through their guardians, John Rodman and James W. Sibley, claim 1,100 acres, 500 of which are in McDougal's Swamp in the Mosquitos district, bounded on the south by Bisett's lands and east by the Manglar Islands. The other 600 on Bissit's Swamp is bounded on the south by lands of Antonio Giralde, north by McDougal's lands and east by Manglar Islands, Governor Estrada's grant, 8/26/1815, to Caroline E. McHardy, then named Caroline Isabel Williams. The following documents are presented:

  1. Grant by Governor Estrada
  2. Petition and order for survey.
  3. Certificate of survey and plat of 500 acres.
  4.      "         "      "     "     "   " 600  "
  5. Petition for absolute title and order to examine witnesses.
  6. Certificate of improvements made on land.

2 [S] Roberto McHardy, for his wife, Carolina Isabel Williams, petitions, 7/1/1815, for 1,100 acres, 500 of them on McDugal's Plantation and the other 600 on Bisset's place. Both places are vacant since the evacuation of the English subjects. Caroline I. Williams has inherited 20 slaves, all of whom are field workers, so she needs this land.

3 [S] Governor Estrada grants, 8/20/1815, the 1,100 acres. Aguilar attests and certifies true copy.

4 [S] Roberto McHardy petitions, 8/2/1818, to have the land surveyed by Andres Burgevin, to which Governor Coppinger assents. Entralgo attests and notifies McHardy and Burgevin, the latter of whom countersigns.

5 [S] Burgevin certifies, 8/8/1818, plat of 600 acres at Bisset's, bounded on the south by Antonio Giraldo, north by McDougal, and east by the Manglar Islands, for Caroline Ysabel Williams.

6 [S] Burgevin certifies, 8/8/1818, plat of 500 acres at McDougal's place, bounded on the south by Bisset's and east by Manglar Islands, for C. Ysabel Williams.

7 [S] McHardy petitions, 3/20/1819, for royal title and order to examine witnesses, which Governor Coppinger grants. Entralgo attests and notifies R. McHardy.

8 [S] Andres Burgevin and Esteban Arnau certify that coming from the Ys River where they had gone to measure some lands, they stopped at a place on Hillsborough River belonging to C. Y. Williams and her husband, R. McHardy, in order to see the house McHardy had recently built, but they only saw the ruins of it as the Indians had burned it. Francisco Guez and John Geiger vouched for Burgevin's and Arnau's signatures.

9 [E] Stephen Arnau deposes, 8/21/1825, before D. Floyd that "about the latter end of 1818 or the beginning of 1819" he passed by McHardy's place and saw some negroes at work improving the place; that about 6 months afterwards again passing by he was requested by McHardy to call and see the improvements, which he did. He found the house lately burned down. Cross examined, he said that the land had the appearance of having been cultivated or prepared for cultivation many years ago.

[Dossier contains 1 translation each of 2, 4, 5, 6, 7 and 8.]

McHardy, Robert                    Con. M 27; DG IV 287

1 [E] John Rodman, as assignee of all the estate, both real

and personal, of R. McHardy, claims, 10/23/1823, 1,600 acres on the west side of St. Johns River, at Old Stores, a district where there is a spring and a stream of fresh water. McHardy was prevented by the Seminole Indians from erecting the saw mill he mentions in his petition accompanying the grant made previous to the cession of Florida to the U. S. A.

[Bound together 2-8 in English:]

2 - McHardy petitions, 11/8/1814, for a "square of 5 miles" at the place called Aprecale Spring opposite the Old Store of the House of Panton & Leslie. He wishes to erect a water saw mill for commercial purposes in order that he may make up the many losses he experienced through his loyalty to the province during the rebellion of the year of 1812. Governor Kindelan grants the "square of 5 miles" as a service grant. Aguilar attests, 11/9/1814, and certifies true copy. Antelm Gay certifies true translation, 5/21/1830.

3 - McHardy petitions, 2/7/1815, for permit to have the land surveyed by John Addison. Governor Kindelan grants and orders that bordering neighbors be notified. Fatio certified true translation. Gay also vouches for the translation, 5/21/1830.

4 - Burgevin certifies, 10/5/1819, plat of 16,000 acres for McHardy, on the west side of St. Johns River at a place where there is a spring and a creek of fresh water, next to the Old Store. Gay certifies true translation, 5/21/1830.

5 - The superior court of the District of East Florida finds this claim valid and confirms it to Malvina, Rickey and Carolina Ann, and Mary Eliza McHardy, heirs of R. McHardy.

6 - The Supreme Court of U. S. A. on a mandate [2nd Monday of January

of 1841] orders further proceedings by the judge of the superior court of the District of East Florida and a new survey of the land to be made by the surveyor of public lands. Roger B. Taney, Chief Justice.

7 - The opinion of the Supreme Court of U. S. A. [January term 1841] is that the decree of the superior court should be reversed upon 3 grounds:

1. The evidence is insufficient to prove the grant was ever made.

2. Even if it is proved that the grant was made, it is void because it is not in conformity to the Royal Order of the 29th of October, 1790, under which "grants can only be made to foreigners and that the number of acres granted must be in proportion to workers."

3. The grant was made upon condition that the grantee should build a water saw mill, a condition that was never performed.

The court affirms the decree of the superior court of East Florida, but directs a new survey to be made. W. T. Carroll, clerk.

8 - George R. Fairbanks certified, 3/1/1845, true copy of supplementary order of the superior court of East Florida, November 1844, for a new survey to be made with a map or plat showing the township, range and sections on which the lands are situated, in case they are within surveyed government lands. Signature. Bronson vouches for Fairbanks.

[Dossier contains 1 copy of 2, 4, and 5, and a jacket and clip as follows: McHardy, Robert, assignee of 16,000 acres. Insufficient evidence. American State Papers, Vol. 4, p. 287. Report 9, No. 1 - 1825 - Claimant - Old Store on the west side of St. Johns River.]

McHardy, Robert            Con. M 28a; DG IV 278

1 [E] John Rodman, assignee of R. McHardy, claims, 10/23/1825,

1,000 acres in Tomoka, bounded on the north by lands of the heirs of James Ormond, east by Tomoka River, south by John Bunch and west by the public road. Governor Estrada's grant, 7/3/1815, to R. McHardy, founded on a previous grant made to him, 9/5/1808.

2 [S] Royal title to the 1,000 acres above granted, 7/3/1815, in exchange for those that had been granted to him in the Mosquitos territory on 8/5/1808. Entralgo attests and certifies true copy.

3 [E] A. M. Randolph certifies plat of 745.42 acres, in Sec. 38, T. 13, R. 31 and Sec. 38, T. 13, R. 32 S&E, for R. McHardy. Chainmen: Paul Sabote and John Reyes.

[Dossier contains 2 translations of 2.]

McIntosh, John H.            Con. M 28b; DG III 643-44

1 [E] Juan de Pierra certifies, 5/18/1803, that J. H. McIntosh petitioned for the necessary land for his family of 250 slaves and 5 white men, 2 of whom have their families, at the following places: on Stony Point, or Mants, Island and in the Riverde [Indian River section]. McIntosh petitions for these lands and for the following:

- 300 acres - containing about 150 acres of hammock, at Stuart's Swamp, northeast of the north part of Stony Point Island, between the lake of Indian River near said island and Mosquitos Lake, and a break of said river running through the swamps on the east side of the above island;

- 1,000 acres - containing Cabbage Swamp on the east side of Indian River, opposite the narrows of the river about 20 miles distant from its head;

- 6,000 acres - west of Indian River, commencing 1 mile below its head, running from thence 2 miles in a westerly direction to a certain point, from thence in a northerly direction 3 miles to another point, from thence in a direct line south 3 miles until it stops opposite and 1 mile distant from the first point, containing about 6 miles square.

Governor White granted, 5/18/1803, without injury to a third person, until his quota should be surveyed to him and on condition that he should take possession within 12 months.

NOTE: McIntosh states that the 6,000 acres are on the west side of Indian River about 1 mile from its head although the boundaries described in the memorial are not very clear to him because of his not having seen said lands and having petitioned for them through information given him by others. F. J. Fatio certifies true translation.

2 [S] Clarke certifies, 12/2/1817, plat on Mantas Island in Indian River to J. H. McIntosh as part of the lands granted him 5/18/1803.

3 [S] Carlos Clark's letter, 8/2/1815, not addressed, notifies of the dispatch of the Lieutenant of the Provincial Militia, "for his good services", with congratulations, adding that although the name of Juan is mentioned in the dispatch by mistake, it is meant for him [supposedly McIntosh], and that the mistake will be mentioned to the Captain General so it can be amended.

4 [S] Clark's certified plat, 12/2/1817, of 1,000 acres at Cabbage Swamp west of Indian River for McIntosh.

5 [S] Clark's certified plat, 12/2/1817, of 6,000 acres at the head of Indian River for McIntosh.

6 [S] Clark's certified plat, 12/2/1817, of 300 acres at Stuart's Swamp for McIntosh.

Decree is confirmed.

[Dossier contains 3 translations of 2, and 1 copy of 4, 5 and 6.]

McIntosh, John H.            Con. M 28c; DG III 758

    1 [E] claims 9,600 acres at Mantas Island, a part of a concession granted to him as head rights by the Spanish government.

    2 [S] [See No. 1 of Con. M 28½.]

    [Dossier contains 1 copy and 1 translation of 2.]

McIntosh, John H.            Con. M 29; DG V 419

    1 [E] claims, 8/5/1823, 6,000 acres at the head of Indian River; another tract of land of an indefinite number of acres at Stony Point or Mantas Island on Indian River; 300 acres between north and east on the north side of Mantas Island; 1,000 acres at Cabbage Swamp on the east side of Indian River.

    He would have been granted a royal title for this land but he took an important part in the insurrection of 1812 and had to leave to save his life. Later, before the cession of the province, he came to St. Augustine and inquiring of the Governor whether he would be responsible for the safety of his person, the Governor replied that he would be responsible only while your memoralist was in his sight.

    He also claims 96 caballerias and 8 acres at St. Juan Nepomuceno on St. Johns River which McIntosh bought from Juan McQueen; 800 acres at Mulberry Grove which he bought from Timothy Hollingsworth; and 2,000 acres at Miame River, bought from McQueen.

    [Bound together 2-9 in Spanish:]

2 - Juan McQueen, captain grenadier of the militia, petitions for a royal title to 273 caballerias and 20 acres on both banks of St. Johns River, surveyed to him in 1792 and 1793 by Marrot. McQueen had cultivated and improved all this land except Monte Hermoso next to the Sa

Pablo place, and that called San Juan Nepómuceno, which he had to abandon during the invasion of the province when all the houses and everything there was destroyed.

3 - Licenciado Ortega informs the Governor, 2/17/1804, of the regulation by which it is legal to grant McIntosh title to the land. Governor White grants, 2/18/1804.

4 - Marrot and Eastlake certify, 1/14/1792, plat of 98 caballerias and 8 acres on San Juan Nepomuceno plantation for Mc-Quin [sic].

5 - Marrot and Eastlake certify, 2/3/1792, plat of 78 caballerias, as part of McQuin's quota on San Pablo plantation.

6 - Marrot and Eastlake certify, 2/5/1792, plat of 3 caballerias and 4 acres on the Monte Hermoso plantation for Mc-Quin.

7 - Marrot and Eastlake certify, 4/27/1792, plat of 21 caballerias and 20 acres, as part of McQuin's quota.

8 - Marrot and Eastlake certify, 5/10/1793, plat of 75 caballerias and 30 acres as part of McQuin's quota on the plantation called Sierra del Agua.

9 [S] Marrot and Deupont [Dupont?] certify, 4/18/1793, plat of 3 caballerias and 26 acres, as part of McQuin's quota on the Favorito plantation.

10 [S] Royal title, 2/27/1804, to 98 caballerias and 8 acres, on San Juan Nepomuceno to McQueen.

11 [S] Deed: Juan McQueen sells, 3/13/1804, to Juan Houston McIntosh the 2 places called San Juan Nepomuceno and Isla de San Jorge for 25,000 pesos cash, 10,000 for the former and 15,000 for the latter. Witnesses: Guillermo Lawrence, Fernando de la Maza Arredondo,

Bartolome de Castro y Ferrer. Zubizarreta attests and certifies, 3/20/1804, true copy. William Reynolds certifies true copy 4/2/1824.

12 [S] Andres Burgevin, at St. Johns, Duval County, certifies 5/5/1830, plat formerly thought to contain 98 caballerias and 8 acres [3,274 2/3 acres] but actually containing 5,500 acres [including 1,500 acres of water between the different parts of which it is composed], situated on the west side of St. Johns River, on Migert [McGirt] and Cedar Creeks, about 5 miles above Jacksonville, for McIntosh.

13 [S] Andres Burgevin, Duval County, certified, 6/4/1830, Marrot-Eastlake plat above, No. 4.

14 [E] Burgevin certifies, 6/14/1830, the plat of Migert showing the difference between his first and second plats made for McIntosh depicting by red dotted lines the two old lines recently traced.

15 [S] Burgevin certifies, 6/16/1830, plat of 4,500 acres on the west side of St. Johns River, on Migert and Cedar Creeks, 5 miles above Jacksonville, for McIntosh.

16 [E] Tracy certifies, 1st quarter of 1848, plat of 7,034.10 acres on McGirt's Creek and St. Johns River, in Sec. 53, T. 2, R. 26 S&E, and Sec. 38, T. 3, R. 26 S&E. Chainmen: John Manucy and Alexander Solana. Butler approves, 11/13/1848.

17 [E] Antonio Alvarez' extract, 12/7/1844, from descriptive list, No. 607, J. H. McIntosh, 3,274 acres.

[Dossier contains 1 copy and 3 translations of 4; and 1 translation of 10 and 11.]

McIntosh, John H.        Con. M 30; DG V 381.-

1 [S] Timothy Hollingsworth petitions, 9/13/1790, for 800

or 900 acres next to La Arbolada de los Morales, where he has lived for 6 years. He has a family of 8, 9 negroes, 8 heads of cattle, 6 horses, 3 donkeys and about 30 or 40 pigs. Governor Quesada requests, 10/4/1790, documents showing how many acres he already has, and what his rights are to the land.

[Bound together 2-7 in Spanish:]

2 - T. Hollingsworth petitions for title and to present proof of his having inhabited and improved his plantation, Moral Grueso [Mulberry Grove], from 1787 when it was granted to him, until 1794, when by governmental order he had to leave it, losing almost everything he had, all his houses being burned. Later, after the insurrection had been quelled, he started over again and now actually he has all the improvements required to the title. Governor White grants, 2/23/1805. Zubizarreta attests and notifies Hollingsworth.

3 - Marrot and Eastlake certify, 12/11/1731[?], plat of 27 *caballerias* on the Moral Grueso plantation for T. Hollingsworth whose family of 16 consists of husband, wife, 4 children and 11 negroes.

4 - Zubizarreta lists conditions necessary for the title, 3/4/1805.

5 - Francisco Zavier Sanchez, married, 68, deposes, 3/5/1805, before Zubizarreta that Hollingsworth had inhabited and improved Moral Grueso as he had testified, having left the place only by order of the government during the 1794 insurrection and coming back to it as soon as it was quieted down. He also said that Hollingsworth had made all the required improvements. He stated that Hollingsworth served as captain of militia during the revolt.

6 - Fernando de la Maza Arredondo deposes confirming the above.

7 - Jose Fleming, Captain of militia, deposes that Hollingsworth had inhabited and cultivated the land for 16 years leaving it only because of the revolt when he, as all others, had to leave the St. Johns banks by government orders; he also confirms Hollingsworth's having fulfilled all conditions required to title. Governor White grants, 3/7/1805, and Ortega countersigns. Zubizarreta attests and notifies Hollingsworth. Zubizarreta's note: Title was granted on 3/5/1805.

Fees:

```
To the Governor for 4 signatures . . . . .  4 reales
 "    "   Auditor of War  . . . . . . . . . 68    "
 "    '   Zubizarreta . . . . . . . . . . . 92    "
```

8 [E] Royal title, 3/9/1805, to 27 caballerias at Mulberry Grove to T. Hollingsworth. Zubizarreta attests. Fatio certifies translation.

9 [S] Sale: T. Hollingsworth sells, 5/2/1805, to Juan Houston McIntosh 27 caballerias at Moral Grueso for 3,000 pesos cash. Witnesses: Fernando de la Maza Arredondo, Bernardino Sanchez and Bernardo Jose Segui.

10 [E] David Thomas certifies, 4/?/1833, plat of 1,157.99 acres on the west side of St. Johns River at Mulberry Grove in Secs. 27, 28, 33, and 34, T. 3, R. 26 S&E, for J. H. McIntosh. Chainmen: William O'Neill and Augustus Tibbit.

[Dossier contains 1 translation of 3 and 8.]

McMurren, Frederic          Con. M 31; DG IV 171

1 [E] claims, through Bellamy, 450 acres on St. Marys River at Wilder's Plantation, Governor Estrada's grant, 12/?/1815.

2 [S] Frederico McMarrin [McMurren] petitions, 12/11/1815, for

title to ~~the~~ 450 acres located about 8 miles from Trader's Hill, granted to him in 1801 or 1802, which he has cultivated since. Governor Estrada refers request, 12/12/1805, to Benito de Pangua, military commandant of Amelia Island, who reports favorably on 1/8/1816; Governor Coppinger grants, 1/30/1816.

3 [S] Clarke certifies, 2/10/1816, plat of 450 acres at Wilder's plantation on St. Marys River, for F. McMarrin.

4 [E] R. B. Ker certifies, first quarter, 1831, plat of 451.70 acres, being in Sec. 18, T. 3, R. 23 N&E, for F. McMarren. Chainmen: Daniel Wells and John Handley. Robert Butler approves, 1/?/1834.

[Dossier contains 1 copy and translation of 2 and 3.]

McQueen, John, Heirs of        Con. M 32; DG V 57, 61

[Bound together 1-7 in Spanish:]

1 - Roberto Clark Maxey petitions, 5/25/1804, for permit to present information of his having fulfilled conditions for a royal title to the land at Punta del Caño de San Pablo, which was granted to him 10 years since. Governor White grants. Ortega countersigns.

2 - Marrot and Eastlake certify, 1/29/1793, plat of 30 <u>caballerias</u> at Punta del Cano de San Pablo for R. C. Maxey, whose family consists of 19, of whom 5 are white and 14 are negroes.

3 - Zubizarreta lists conditions to the acquirement of title.

4 - Jean Eduardo Fate, of London, bachelor, 28, deposes, 5/26/1804, before Ortega that Maxey with his family and negroes had lived on and improved the Punta de San Pablo Creek plantation since the year 1791, and had fulfilled all the conditions. Zubizarreta attests.

5 - Juan Holzendorff of South Carolina, married, 52, deposes through Bernardino Sanchez, public interpreter, confirming above.

6 - Dr. Tom Travers, physician in charge of the hospital, also deposes confirming No. 4.

7 - Governor White grants title. Ortega countersigns. Zubizarreta attests and notifies Maxey. Fee: 10 reales.

8 [S] Royal title, 6/6/1804, to 30 caballerias on Punta de Pablo Creek granted by Governor White to Maxey. Zubizarreta attests. [All of the following are bound together:]

9 [E] Andrew Atkinson relinquishes, 3/24/1806, in favor of Juan McQueen, all his rights to a tract of land called Ship Yards, on St. Johns River, near Vincente, which was granted to him years ago, but which he relinquished afterward and sometime later it was granted to said McQueen. Witness: Daniel Delany.

10 [S] Guillermo Lawrence petitions, 7/15/1813, to have the above document translated into the Spanish language and archived. Governor Kindelan grants, 7/20/1813, and orders translation to be made by Gabriel Guillermo Perpall. Arredondo countersigns. Entralgo attests and notifies Lawrence and Perpall, the latter of whom countersigns.

11 [S] Perpall's translation of 9 above, 7/28/1813. Governor Kindelan orders the document to be archived, 7/29/1813; fee: 12 reales. Entralgo attests and notifies Lawrence; fee: 4 reales to the Governor, 39 to the Auditor of War and 22 to Entralgo.

12 [S] Deed, 10/18/1811: Bernardo Segui sells to Juan Travers for 5,000 pesos cash 30 caballerias on the Punta del Cano plantation, which he bought from the heirs of Juan McQueen through Bartolome Castro y Ferrer. Witnesses: Juan de Entralgo, Bernardino Sanchez

and Jose Lorente. William Reynolds certifies translation.

13 [S] Reynolds certifies, 6/28/1825, that Robert Clarke Maxey sold, 11/23/1804, 1,000 acres at Point on San Pablo Creek to John McQueen who sold, 1/22/1805, to George Taylor, who sold, 12/19/1808, through Fernando de la Maza Arredondo to Bartolome de Castro y Ferrer, acting as attorney for the heirs of John McQueen. The heirs of McQueen, through B. Castro y Ferrer sold, 9/13/1811, to Bernardo Segui.

14 [E] Henry Washington certifies plat of 1,000 acres at the Point of St. Pablo Creek being Sec. 37, T. 2, R. 28 S&E. Chainmen: John W. Townsend and Isaac Varnes. Butler approves, 6/20/1836.

McQueen, John, Heirs of        Con. M 33; DG V 58, 66

1 [E] claim, through Joseph S. Sanchez, 400 acres on Amelia Island, bounded on the north and west by St. Marys River and south by Hagen's Creek, Governor White's grant, 11/24/1798, to John McQueen; surveyed by John Purcell on 11/24/1809.

2 [S] Juan McQueen petitions, 11/22/1798, for 400 acres on Amelia Island north of Hagen's Creek for the purpose of raising cotton. Governor White requests information from Berrio, commandant of engineers who reports favorably, 11/23/1798. Governor White grants, 11/23/1798.

3 [S] Juan de Pierra certifies, 11/24/1798, that upon McQueen's petition for the 400 acres mentioned above, Governor White made the grant. William Reynolds certified true copy.

4 [S] Purcell's certified plat, 11/24/1809, of 400 acres on Amalia Island, bounded on the north and west by Santa Maria River and south by Hagen's Creek, for John McQueen.

5 [E] Henry Washington's certified plat of 400 acres, being Sec. 10, T. 3, R. 28 N&E, for the heirs of John McQueen. Robert Butler approves, January 1824.

[Dossier contains translations of 2 and 4.]

Medicis, Francis      Con. M 34; DG V 377

1 [E] Francis de Medicis and the heirs of Juan Solon claim 400 acres on a small island on the west side of North River about 9 miles from St. Augustine, bounded on the north by lands of Mialls, south by Henderson, east by North River; Governor White's grant, 9/27/1798. The land was sold by the heirs of Juan Solon to Lewis Ricardo who sold, 5/18/1822, to Miguel Solon, one of the heirs of Juan Solon, who executed a quit-claim, dated 3/23/1820, to Francis Medicis.

2 [S] Juan de Pierra certifies, 9/27/1798, that upon Juan Solon's petition for title to 400 acres at Grotto, 2 miles north of Casacola, of which he is in possession, in which Solon stated that he had misplaced the title which had been granted in response to his memorial of 8/12/1792, another was issued to him by the secretary's office in virtue of which he was to continue in possession on the same conditions as formerly.

3 [S] Miguel Solon, 3/23/1820, relinquishes all his rights to a piece of land bequeathed to him by his father, Juan Solon, in favor of Lewis Ricardo to whom he has sold it. Before Juan Entralgo. Witnesses: Francisco Sanchez, Guillermo Burch and Juan Cavedo.

4 [E] Deed: Lewis Ricardo sells, 5/18/1822, for $60.00 cash, 100 acres of land in St. Johns County, East Florida, on the west side

of North River, about 9 miles from St. Augustine. Witnesses: John A. Cavedo and Thomas H. Penn. [On the back: J. Tingle certifies that this deed, with notarial certificate, was given to him by the grantee to record.]

    5 [E] Antonio Alvarez' extract, 5/27/1845, from descriptive list, No. 601, Francisco Medicis, 400 acres.

    [Dossier contains 2 translations of 2 and 1 of 3.]

Meers, Samuel, Heirs of          Con. M 35; DG IV 278

    1 [E] Susana Cashen, on behalf of the orphan children of Samuel Meers, claims 200 acres on Tyger Island; Governor Estrada's grant to Samuel Meers, with royal title dated 10/17/1811.

    2 [S] Samuel Meers, of Georgia, new resident, petitions, 3/16/1799, for 200 acres on the Isla del Tigre on the north side of Santa Marias Port. Governor White requests information from Berrio, commandant of engineers, who reports favorably but states that buildings should be of light construction as they may have to be demolished in case of the necessity to defend the province. Governor White makes the grant on that condition. Pierra certifies true copy.

    [Bound together 3-8 in Spanish:]

3 - Pierra certifies, 3/16/1799, that upon Samuel Meers' petition for 200 acres, Governor White made the grant.

4 - Margarita Meers, widow of Samuel Meers, petitions, 8/26/1811, for title to the 200 acres granted to her husband, also for a permit to present witnesses to prove that all conditions necessary to the title had been fulfilled. Governor Estrada grants, 9/5/1811, Zubizarreta attests and notifies Margarita Meers.

5 - Zubizarreta lists conditions necessary to title.

6 - Fernando de la Maza Arredondo, married, 45, deposes, 10/12/1811, before Zubizarreta that he has visited Tiger's Island both during Samuel Meers' life and after his death, noticing always that Meers had all the land suitable for cultivation planted, and that he had, besides the dwelling house, others for the crops, animals and tools, having fulfilled all conditions to title.

7 - Bartolome Castro y Ferrer, married, 52, deposes confirming above.

8 - Governor Estrada grants, 10/17/1811, and orders title to be extended to Margarita Meers.

9 [E] Royal title to 200 acres on Tyger's Island to Margarita Meers and her children, granted 10/17/1811, by Governor Estrada.

10 [E] Antonio Alvarez' extract, 2/18/1845, from descriptive list, No. 66, Juan Cashen for the heirs of Samuel Meers, 200 acres.

11 [E] Memorandum of papers delivered by order of the court.

[Dossier contains 1 copy of 9.]

Mestre, Pedro                    Con. M 36; DG IV 284

1 [E] Antonio Alvarez' certificate from descriptive list, No. 226, Peter Mestre, 640 acres, from the Journal of the Board of Commissioners, 10/31/1825, "received claim of Peter Mestre under the donation act", and from the Journal, 12/2/1825, "confirmed the claim of Mestre".

2 [E] Henry Washington certifies plat of 640 acres lying north of the head of North River, being in Sec. 54, T. 4, R. 29 S&E, for P. Mestre as donation. Chainmen; John W. Townsend and Isaac Varnes. Robert Butler approved, 6/20/1836.

Mestre, Bartolome                Con. M 37; DG V 65

1 [E] claims 600 acres at Holmes' Old Plantation, or "Savanico",

on the west side of Matanzas River, bounded on the north by Holmes Creek, east by Matanzas River; Governor Quesada's concession to Antonio Mestre and Joseph Yus [Hughes ?] on 8/8/1794.

2 [S] Bartolome Mestre petitions, 1/8/1820, for certificates of memorial and of decree granted and the documents concerning deed of sale, 8/2/1794, of 600 acres at "Savanica" [sic], on Matanzas River, from Jose Huges [Hughes/Yus] to his father. Governor Coppinger grants.

3 [S] Jose Yus [Hughes ?] and Antonio Mestre make joint petitions, 8/7/1794, for permit to the latter to take possession of the "Savanica" plantation on the west side of Matanzas River, which the former has possessed and cultivated for many years. Now he is old but Mestre is young and has slaves to cultivate the land. Governor Quesada grants until the general survey is finished when Mestre is to be alloted his quota.

4 [S] Clarke certifies, 1/12/1820, plat of 600 acres at Holmes Old Plantation on the west side of Matanzas River, for Bartolome Mestre, ceded by his father and Jose Huges [Hughes/Yus].

5 [E] Benjamin and J. B. Clements certify plat of 597.30 acres at Holmes Old Field, being in Sec. 39, T. 9, R. 30 S&E, for Bartolome Mestre. Chainmen: Joel F. Yumell [Yowell ?] and John McGough.

Mestre, Bartolome                    Con. M 38; DG IV 285

1 [E] claims for himself and his mother, Mariana Mestre, through John B. Strong, 300 acres on Thompson's Branch opposite Little Bar on the Matanzas River; Governor White's grant, 1/28/1790, to Bartolome Mestre not specifying the number of acres, but according to the number of his family which consisted of himself, his wife, and children.

B. Maestre has abandoned his family which Mariana Maestre is supporting.

2 [S] B. Mestre, through Jose de Zavalia, petitions, 6/21/1796, for the quota of land for himself and his family at Thompson's Branch on Matanzas River opposite the Little Bar. Governor White requests, 6/23/1796, information from Berrio, commandant of engineers, who reports favorably, provided the land Mestre petitions for is on the mainland and not on the Penon or Barreton where Dupont was given permission to settle but where instead he raised stones from the walls of the bar in order to sell them to the people in the city thus ruining the port. Governor White grants; Abreu attests. Rengil certifies true copy; Tingle certifies true copy.

3 [E] Francisco Pellicer, Jr., deposes, 4/26/1825, before W. H. Allen that about 20 years ago Mestre settled on 250 or 300 acres of the above mentioned land, granted him by the Spanish government; and that Mestre made improvements for sometime, although he later abandoned his wife, Mariana, and his children and moved to Darien where he has since lived with a colored woman by whom he has children. Mariana had herself reared her children.

4 [E] Benjamin and B. J. Clements certify plat of 301.78 acres on the west side of Matanzas River for Bartolome Mestre. Chainmen: Joel Yumell and John McGough.

[Dossier contains 1 translation of 2.]

Mestre, John                Con. M 39; DG V 377

1 [S] Juan Mestre, admiral of the King's gunboat, petitions, 11/18/1816, for 100 acres on the opposite side of St. Nicolas Battery and by the plantation of Daniel Slogans. Governor Coppinger

grants, 12/3/1816. Tomas de Aguilar's note: There were granted to Mestre 50 acres on the southern point of San Juan Bar about half a mile from Quesada's Battery.

2 [S] Juan Mestre, captain of the gunboat called "Immutable", petitions, 6/2/1818, for a small island of 50 acres more or less about half a mile from the place where stood the Quesada Battery, the tract to be a part of the 100 acres granted him on 12/3/1816 opposite San Nicolas Port where he could find only 50 acres vacant. Governor Coppinger grants.

[Bound together 3-6 in Spanish:]
3 - Clarke certifies, 2/21/1817, plat of 50 acres on the west side of St. Johns River at Cowford, or Feria del Camino Real, as part of 100 acres granted, 12/13/1816, to Juan Mastre [sic].
4 - Juan Mestre petitions, 4/2/1821, for permit to present testimonial of his having cultivated and improved the land granted on 12/3/1816, at Cowford until July 1817, when during the occupation of Amalia Island by the rebels he was forced to leave it. Governor Coppinger grants.
5 - Juan Jose Robles, 25, deposes, 4/21/1821, before Juan Blas de Entralgo, that he knows Mestre to have cultivated and improved his land until 1817 when he had to leave his house, crops and furniture in the hurry of withdrawal.
6 - Blas Crespo, lieutenant of the infantry of Cuba, deposes confirming above. Governor Coppinger grants, 4/3/1824, and orders a royal title extended to Mestre. Entralgo attests and notifies Mestre.

[Dossier contains copies of 1 and 2.]

Middleton, John                    Con. M 40; DG IV 279

    1 [E] claims, through Farquhar Bethune, 200 acres at Cedar Branch on the west side of St. Johns River; Governor Coppinger's grant, 3/29/1817, to William Garvin. This grant was made at Langley Bryan, but the land there having been previously claimed, the Governor had Cedar Branch surveyed by Clarke.

[Bound together 2-5 in Spanish:]

2 - William Garvin petitions, 9/4/1816, for 200 acres on the west side of St. Johns River. He has a family of himself, wife and 5 slaves. Governor Coppinger requests information from the military and political commandant as to the number and ages of the slaves belonging to Garvin.

3 - Francisco Morales informs the Governor, 10/10/1816, that the number of slaves is exact, and their ages are, as shown in an accompanying list, from 22 to 50 years, there being 2 males, Jack and Ben, and 3 females, Zabel, Hannah and Cumba.

4 - Francisco Ribera certifies, 12/2/1815, that William Garvin had served very loyally in the defense of the territory since the beginning of August 1813 until the present time; moreover, that he was one of the first to volunteer for service.

5 - William Garvin, 10/7/1816, wishes to make clear that the place he desires on the west side of St. Johns River is Langly Bryan's old plantation which he had forgotten to mention in his former petition. Governor Coppinger grants him the 200 acres, 3/29/1817. Entralgo attests and notifies William Garvin.

    6 [S] Royal title to 200 acres on the west side of St. Johns River to William Garvin granted by Governor Coppinger, 3/29/1817.

Entralgo attests and certifies true copy.

7 [S] Clarke certifies, 4/6/1817, plat of 200 acres at Cedar Branch west of St. Johns River for Guillermo Garvin, in exchange for the same number of acres which were granted to him at Langly Brian's old plantation but which had been claimed by someone else.

8 [E] Deed: William Garvin sells, 12/3/1831, to John Middleton 200 acres at Cedar Branch, west side of St. Johns River, for $200.00 cash. Witnesses: Charles Sibbald and Francisco Dorr.

9 [E] Farquhar Bethune, judge, of St. Johns County, certifies that William Garvin personally appeared before him and acknowledged the above document to be his "act" according to the "true intent and meaning thereof".

10 [E] Antonio Alvarez' extract, 11/28/1844, from descriptive list, No. 223, J. Middleton, 200 acres.

[Dossier contains translations of 6 and 7.]

Middleton, John                    Con. M 41; DG IV 286

1 [E] claims, through Farquhar Bethune, two half-lots in Fernandina, No. 3 and No. 4, in Sq. 14, granted by Governor Kindelan, 5/21/1814, to Anna Wiggens who sold them to Henry Yonge, who sold, 8/25/1819, to Middleton; also lot No. 6, in Sq. 14, granted, 3/4/1814, by Governor Kindelan to Guillermo Bauson, who sold to Middleton.

2 [S] Guillermo Bauson, who lives with his mother, petitions, 12/15/1813, for a lot on which to build a house as he is planning to marry and establish himself in business. Governor Kindelan requests information from the district captain and the surveyor general. Felipe Roberto Yonge certifies that it is true that Middleton lives with his mother and little brother, whom he supports, being very

dependable, 2/15/1814. Clarke reports, 2/15/1814, that lot No. 6 in Sq. 14 is vacant. Governor Kindelan grants, 3/4/1814. Yonge and Clark certify at Fernandina, 3/16/1814, that the lot was given in possession to Bouysson [Bauson].

3 [S] Ana Wiggins, through Jose de Zavalia, petitions for a lot to establish herself in the town, 12/15/1813. Governor Kindelan requests information from the captain and surveyor general. Yonge and Clarke report favorably, 5/9/1814. The 2 half-lots, No. 3 and No. 4, on Sq. 14, are vacant. Governor Kindelan grants, 5/21/1814. Yonge and Clarke certify that in Fernandina, 6/8/1814, Ana Wiggins took possession.

4 [E] Deed: Henry A. Yonge of Fernandina, Amalia Island, sells to John Middleton lot No. 6, and two half-lots, No. 3 and No. 4, on Sq. 14, for $100.00 cash. Witness: J. Brown.

5 [E] F. Bethune deposes, 12/26/1825, before Davis Floyd that Middleton had fenced and erected dwellings and other houses and had been in possession of the lots since 1819. The original grantee had been in possession since 1814.

[Dossier contains 1 translation each of 2 and 3.]

Middleton, John  Con. M 42; DG IV 286

1 [E] claims, through Farquhar Bethune, in Fernandina, lot No. 8, Sq. 21, bounded on the north by lot of Samuel Harrison, east by Benjamin Ayres, south by Damas Street and west by New Street. The lot was granted originally to Benjamin Ayres, who sold it to W. P. Yonge, who sold to Middleton.

2 [S] Benjamin Ayres petitions for a lot for the purpose of building a home, 9/21/1811.

3 [S] Clarke certifies, 6/26/1817, plat of half-lot No. 8, Sq. 31, containing 17 varas in front and depth for Benjamin Aires.

4 [E] Deed: W. P. Yonge, Fernandina, sells, 7/10/1818, to Middleton, the above mentioned lot for $60.00 cash. Yonge appears personally before J. Bankhead and acknowledges his signature and seal.

[Dossier contains translation of 3.]

Middleton, John and John Sibley      Con. M 43; DG 286

1. [E] claim, through Farquhar Bethune, in Fernandina, lot No. 6 on the first square containing 16 varas in front and 34 in depth, bounded on the north by Jane Sibbald's lot, east by William Hall's, south by Constitution Square, and west by Joseph Arredondo. It was Governor Kindelan's grant of 3/30/1814 to James Cashen who sold it to Middleton and Sibley, 11/20/1817.

2 [S] Royal title to the above mentioned lot, granted, 3/30/1814, by Governor Kindelan to James Cashen. Entralgo attests and certifies true copy.

3 [E] Deed, dated 11/20/1817: James Cashen and his wife, Susanna, sell to John Middleton and John Sibley a lot of land, with the shop and dwelling house and all the appurtenances, in Fernandina, for $800.00. Witness: J. Brown.

[Dossier contains 1 translation of 2.]

Miles, Francis [Guardian of]      Con. M 44: DG IV 279

1 [E] claims, through J. M. Hanson, his guardian, 300 acres at the Feria on St. Johns River; Governor White's grant, 2/4/1811, to the heirs of Francisco Zavier Sanchez of whom F. Miles is one.

2 [S] Royal title to 9 caballerias at the Feria plantation on St. Johns River, to the heirs of Francisco X. Sanchez.

3 [E] Unfinished plat of 320 acres being in T. 3, R. 27, S&E, claimed by J. M. Hanson.

4 [E] Antonio Alvarez' extract, 12/14/1844, J. M. Hanson, guardian to Francis Miles, 300 acres.

[Dossier contains 1 translation of 2.]

Miles, Francis [Guardian of]    Con. M 45; DG IV 279

[Bound together 1 to 6:]

1 [E] John M. Hanson, guardian of Francis Miles, an infant, claims 200 acres on North River, bounded on the north by land of Manuel Marshal, and southeast by land of John Salom; a British grant to Barbara Hainsman later confirmed by the Spanish Government.

2 [S] Royal title to 200 acres 9 miles northwest of St. Augustine on North or Yolemato Creek granted to Anthony Heintsman, 10/11/1770, by Governor James Grant; signed by David Yeats, Deputy C.C., Governor in Council. [On back:] Recorded, 10/24/1770, in Book A, p. 203 in Register's Office.

3 [E] C. M. de Brahm certifies, 9/2/1769, a plat of 200 acres, 9 miles from St. Augustine on "a creek of the North or Yolemato River

4 [E] Governor Tonyn and David Yeats certify, 10/24/1776, the will of A. Heintsman in favor of his wife, Barbary Heintsman.

5 [S] Barbara Heintsman petitions, 9/21/1797, for the title granted to her husband by the British government to be translated into Spanish and permission to sell her land as she is in need and could sell the land to Francisco X. Sanchez for 200 pesos. The petition is granted.

6 [S] Translation into Spanish of the royal title, will, and plat.

7 [S] Marrot and Dupont certify, 6/2/1793, a plat of 6 _caballerias_ for Barbara Straburg and "Hansman" whose family consists of herself and one daughter.

8 [S] Deed: Barbara Hainsman sells, 9/11/1797, to Francisco X. Sanchez 200 acres at Marota Naranjo, or Sabana de los Alemanes, for 200 _pesos_. Zubizarreta attests. Witnesses: Thomas Aguilar, Juan Entralgo and Lorenzo Capo. T. H. Penn certifies true copy.

9 [E] Henry Washington certifies plat of 211.20 acres on North River and Sec. 44, T. 6, R. 29 S&E, for Francis Miles. Chainmen: John W. Townsend and Isaac Varnes. Robert Butler approves, 6/20/1836.

[Dossier contains translation of 2 and 8.]

Miller, Robert                    Con. M 46; DG IV 301

1 [E] claims 200 acres in Duval County at Martin's Island on St. Marys River, bounded on the northeast by Tyger Island, east by a small creek which divides both islands, north by a marsh that runs into St. Marys River, southwest by Lowes Creek which separates it from the body of Duval County. It was a donation grant.

2 [S] The U. S. Land Commission of East Florida authorizes James T. O'Neal, Justice of the Peace, to examine the witness produced by the claimant. Fatio attests, 5/13/1824, and certifies true copy. J. T. O'Neill [_sic_] countersigns, 6/24/1824.

3 [E] The U. S. Land Commission of East Florida authorizes William Gibson and Samuel Clarke, Justices of the Inferior Court of Camden County, Georgia, to examine the witness produced by the claim-

ant. Fatio attests, 5/12/1824.

4 [E] John Boog, answering to the interrogatory, deposes before William Gibson and Samuel Clarke concerning the claim of Robert Miller and Margaret, his wife [formerly James Baird's wife], Robert Delany and his wife, Maria, and her sister Ann Baird [daughters of James Baird], for 625 acres, declares that:

He knows the parties who are connected as mentioned above; he also knew James Baird from 1805 until his death in 1815, and knew that he had 25 slaves in East Florida, though he does not know their ages. John Boog states further that the family was established on Martin's Island from about 1814 until 1822. In 1823 they planted on Cumberland Island, and this year they are at Martin's Island and the mainland. The province of East Florida was in a very restless condition from 1812 until the transfer to the United States.

5 [E] Interrogatories made to John Boog of Camden County, Georgia, by William [sic] O'Neil and Samuel Clark:

1. As to his acquaintance with Robert Miller and Margaret, his wife, formerly the wife of James Baird; Robert Delany and his wife, Maria, and Ann Baird, daughters of said James Baird, claimants to 625 acres between the rivers Is and Jupiter.

    Were the claimants connected to James Baird as mentioned in 4?

2. Whether he knows James Baird, how long, and about what time did he die? Also, how many slaves did he possess in East Florida around 1812-15, and their ages?

3. About what time of the year in 1815 did James Baird die? How did the claimants establish themselves in Martin's Island from 1815 to 1822?

4. What was the situation in East Florida in regard to the security of property from 1812 to the time of the transfer to the United States?

5. ~~Do~~ all the parties above mentioned live in Camden County, Georgia?

6 [S] Interrogatories concerning the same matter made to John Lord and James Armstrong of Duval County, by J. O'Neal.

7 [S] J. Armstrong answers, 6/23/1824, the above questions saying that he knows the parties and that they are connected with each other and also with James Baird of Camden County, Georgia. He has known James Baird since 1809 and until his death 1815, and knew him to possess 22 slaves on Martin's Island; also that his representatives have continued to establish and plant the land and have also purchased slaves within the time mentioned in the interrogatory. Armstrong adds that the security of property was very limited because the province was in a state of revolution; also that James Baird had applied for a piece of land at St. Marys River, but as it was previously claimed he applied for another piece elsewhere.

8 [S] John T. Lowe deposes, 6/24/1824, before O'Neill answering the above questions. He confirms No. 7 and says that the claimant has two plantations adjoining his own, which have been under the management of James Armstrong since 1815.

9 [E] James Armstrong of Duval County, 40, deposes, 11/19/1824, that he knows Robert Miller well, as he has been in his employ since 1805 as overseer of Miller's plantation of which plantation Miller has been in actual and peaceable possession and has cultivated the whole part of it during said time.

10 [E] John T. Lowe deposes, 11/19/1824, that since 1815 he has known Robert Miller, who had cultivated and peaceably possessed these 200 acres at Martin's Island, Duval County.

11 [E] Alvarez' extract, 2/16/1845, from descriptive list, No. 603, Robert Miller, 200 acres.

[Dossier contains 1 copy each of 1 and 7.]

Mills, Maria            Con. M 47; DG V 58, 65

1 [E] Maria Mills, widow of William Mills, claims, through Farquhar Bethune, for herself and her children, 150 acres contiguous to Johnson's Creek, south of Matanzas; Governor White's grant, 11/15/1798, to William Mills who possessed, cultivated and improved the land until his death in 1818, but neglected to take out a title. After his death Governor Coppinger granted her the title, 7/9/1819. She is and was at the time of the cession in actual possession of the land.

2 [S] Guillermo Mills petitions, 11/13/1798, for 190 acres on Johnson's Creek for the purpose of raising cattle, of which he already has 90 head. Governor White requests information from the commandant of engineers, and on 11/14/1798, Berrio reports favorably. Governor White grants to Mills the quota that corresponds with himself and his workers, 11/15/1798. Pierra certifies true copy.

[Bound together 3-11 in Spanish:]

3 - Pierra certifies that upon Mill's memorial for 150 acres, Governor White granted same.

4 - Juan Pucell certifies, 7/20/1804, plat of 150 acres on Matanzas about half mile west of Graham Creek for Guillermo Mills.

5 - Santiago Gonzalez, attorney-in-fact for Maria McIntosh, widow of Guillermo Mills, petitions, 12/17/1818, for a certified copy of the memorial of her husband's petition for 150 acres on Matanzas about

8 miles south of Barra Chica and the decree granting them. Governor Coppinger grants, 12/17/1818.

6 - Copy of the memorial and grant.

7 - Santiago Gonzalez petitions, 6/25/1819, for permit to present testimonials that Guillermo Mills had fulfilled all conditions necessary to the title. Governor Coppinger grants. Entralgo attests and notifies Santiago Gonzalez.

8 - Francisco Pellicer deposes before Entralgo that he knew Jose Mins, who worked for 7 years on Mills' plantation taking care of the cattle of which there were about 150 to 200 head. He said also that Mills planted maize, pumpkins and other things, and undertook to operate a water saw mill.

9 - Gabriel Guillermo Perpall, 50, deposes that since 1803, when he came to this province, Guillermo Mills was already in possession of the land which he improved and used to raise cattle until 1812 when there was a revolution. His father-in-law, Jorge Long, helped with the Mills' cattle after Jose Mins left.

10 - Governor Coppinger grants title to Maria McIntosh, 7/8/1819. Entralgo attests and informs Santiago Gonzalez, her attorney.

11 - Clarke certifies, 5/12/1819, plat of 150 acres on Johnston Creek, west of Matanzas River, for Guillermo Mills.

12 [S] Royal title to 150 acres above as shown, granted, 7/9/1817, by Governor Coppinger to Maria McYntosh.

13 [E] Benjamin and J. B. Clements certify plat of 151.60 acres west of Matanzas River on Johnston Creek being in Sec. 41, T. 10, R. 30 S&E, for Maria Mills. Chainmen: John Hagens and Jesse P. Warrs. Robert Butler approves, 3/?/1835.

14 [E] Benjamin A. Putnam certifies, 11/16/1850, plat of 144.40 acres, being in T. 10, R. 30 S&E, for Maria Mills.

[Dossier contains 1 copy of 2 and 2 copies of 11.]

Mills, Maria             Con. M 48; DG V 72

1 [E] claims, through Farquhar Bethune, in behalf of herself and her children, 2 half-lots in Fernandina, Nos. 1 and 2 of the 5th Square, bounded on the east by Amelia Street, south by Joseph Bergallo's lot, west by Joseph Fenwick's lot and north by St. Fernando Street. It was a grant of Governor Kindelan, 3/2/1814, to Samuel Betts who sold to William Mills, her husband.

2 [S] Royal title to the half-lot No. 1 of the 5th Square having 17 varas in front and depth, and being bounded on the north by San Fernando Street, east by Amelia Street, west by Jose Fenwick and south by a lot belonging to himself; Governor Kindelan's grant, 3/2/1814, to Samuel Betts. Entralgo attests and certifies true copy.

3 [S] Royal title to half-lot No. 2, of the 5th Square having 17 varas in front and depth, and being bounded on the north by the lot of Samuel Betts, east by Amelia Street, south by Jose Bergallo and west by Jose Fenwick; granted by Governor Kindelan to Benjamin Armstrong. Entralgo attests and certifies true copy.

4 [E] Farquhar Bethune deposes, 11/26/1825, before David Floyd that he knew Samuel Betts, who had possession of the 2 half-lots and built on or fenced them and sold in 1814 to William Mills, who improved by fencing and building thereon a black-smith shop, where he carried on his trade until his death. There was no deed of conveyance as the transfer was made by delivery of title and premises.

[Dossier contains 1 translation each of 2 and 3.]

Mill, Maria                               Con. M 49; DG V 413

    1 [E] claims, through Farquhar Bethune, for herself and her children, lot No. 12 of the 17th Square in Fernandina, containing 17 varas in front and 34 varas in depth, bounded on the east by the lot of Thomas Turdas, south by Mathew Gonzalez and west by Charles Sibbald; Governor Coppinger's grant, 12/19/1818, to her and her children.

    2 [S] Clark certifies, 6/10/1816, plat of the above mentioned lot for Guillermo Mills.

    3 [S] Santiago Gonzalez, attorney-in-fact for Maria McYntosh, widow of Guillermo Mills, petitions, 12/19/1818, for a royal title to the lot. Governor Coppinger grants.

    4 [S] Royal title to the lot granted, 12/19/1818, by Governor Coppinger to Maria McYntosh, widow of Guillermo Mills. Entralgo attests and certifies true copy.

    5 [E] Farquhar Bethune deposes, 9/26/1828, before W. H. Allen that the claimant's husband improved the property and built a house on the above mentioned lot for his black-smith shop some years before his death in 1817.

    6 [E] Fatio's abstract of the claim.

Minchin, Christopher                      Con. M 50; DG IV 287

    1 [E] claims, through Clarke, 400 acres in Durbin's Swamp to the east of Twenty Mile House and southwest of Big Bend, Governor Coppinger's grant of 10/11/1817.

    2 [S] Christopher Minchin, Santa Maria District, petitions, 11/2/1817, for 400 acres at Twelve Mile Swamp or elsewhere. He has served in the defense of the government during the years 1812 and

1813 and in the invasion of the present year. Governor Coppinger grants, 11/10/1817. Aguilar attests and certifies true copy.

3 [S] Clarke certifies, 7/11/1819, plat of 400 acres for Christopher Minchin.

4 [E] Unfinished plat of 400 acres being in Sec. 48, T. 4, R. 28 S&E, for Christopher Minchin.

5 [E] Alvarez' extract, 5/16/1845, from descriptive list, No. 238, Christopher Minchin, 400 acres.

[Dossier contains a copy of 1, 2 translations of 2 and a translation of 3.]

Miralla, Jose Antonio          Con. M 51; DG IV 106

1 [E] James W. Exum certifies, 3rd Quarter 1827, plat of 661.52 acres on the west margin of Pensacola Bay and east of Bayou Taxar, being in Sec. 18, T. 1, and Sec. 2, T. 2 S&W, for Jose Antonio Marialla Chainmen: Frederick Ming and Wesley Inglish. Robert Butler approves.

Miranda, Pedro          Con. M 52; DG IV 159, 176

1 [E] claims, through Waters Smith, 2,000 acres at Bernard, west of St. Johns River, bounded on the west by Spring Garden Plantation and on the north by lands of Zephaniah Kingsley, Governor Coppinger's grant of 3/29/1815 and royal title of 12/12/1817.

2 [S] Pedro Miranda petitions, 7/1/1817, for the above mentioned 2,000 acres. He served in defense of the territory during 1812. Governor Coppinger grants.

3 [S] Royal title to 2,000 acres granted on 12/12/1817, by Governor Coppinger to Pedro Miranda. Entralgo attests, William Reynolds certifies true copy, 7/21/1823.

4 [E] C. C. Tracy certifies, 2nd Quarter 1847, plat of 815.39

acres on Wekima in Sec. 39, T. 19, R. 29 S&E for Pedro Miranda. Chainmen: Alex Solana and William Reyes. Robert Butler approves, 11/13/1848.

5 [E] Alvarez' extract, 6/26/1800, from descriptive list No. 230, Pedro Miranda, 2,000 acres.

[Dossier contains 2 translations of 3.]

Miranda, Peter            Con. M 53; DG III 643, 644

1 [E] claims, through Waters Smith, 1,000 acres in St. Johns County, East Florida, at Blide's Oil Field, bounded on the north by Cabbage Swamp, south by lands of John Andreu and east by North River, Governor Estrada's grant, 1/2/1816, to Joseph J. Sanchez who sold on 3/15/1823.

2 [S] Jose Simon Sanchez petitions, 1/2/1816, for the above mentioned 1,000 acres. He has served in the militia at any time the government has needed him; he also was on the boats fitted in Fernandina to pursue the rebels at Rose's Bluff. Governor Estrada grants. William Reynolds certifies, 8/6/1823.

3 [E] Deed: Jose S. Sanchez sells 1,000 acres to Peter Miranda for $15,000.00, before J. S. Tingle.

4 [E] Henry Washington certifies plat of 1,000.26 acres, being Sec. 55, T. 4, R. 29 S&E, for Peter Miranda. Chainmen: J. W. Townsend and Isaac Varnes. Robert Butler approves, 6/20/1836.

[Dossier contains decree and 1 translation of 2.]

Miranda, Pedro            Con. M 54; DG V 376

1 [S] Clarke certifies, 3/18/1818, plat of 790 acres for Pedro Miranda, situated west of Matanzas River and about 10 miles south of

St. Augustine, between the lands of Fernando de la Maza Arredondo and Jaime Falaney. This land was granted to Miranda in absolute property on 7/6/1816.

Miranda, Pedro           Con. M 55; DG V 58

1 [S] Clark certifies, 12/20/1816, plat of 100 acres at the head of Santa Maria la Chica Creek near Mount Ford for Pedro Miranda, which was granted to him on 11/28/1816.

2 [E] Antonio Alvarez' extract of 2/14/1845, from descriptive list, No. 592, Pedro Miranda, 100 acres.

[Dossier contains 1 translation of 1.]

Mitchel, Robert          Con. M 56; DG V 413

1 [E] claims, through Robert Mitchel, 13 acres fenced and 13 acres of marsh, called Mitchel's Grove, within the city limits of St. Augustin, originally granted to Don Bosquet who sold to Paul Dupont, who sold to Octavius Mitchel, who sold, 2/25/1822, to Robert Mitchel.

2 [E] Plat of Mitchel's Grove certified by P. Mitchel, 11/14/1823.

3 [E] Alvarez' extract, 12/24/1834, from descriptive list, No. 605, Robert Mitchel, 13/10 acres.

Molina, Antonio          Con. M 57; DG IV 103

1 [E] James W. Exum certifies, 4th Quarter 1824, plat of 1,590 acres on the west margin of the Bay of St. Marys de Galves, being in Sec. 14, T. 1, R. 28 S&W, for Antonio Molina. Chainmen: Enos Evan and John Byrd. Robert Butler approves.

2 [E] Register's certificate No. 63, dated 9/20/1831, G. W.

Ward to Antonio Molina for 1,590 acres on the Bay of St. Maria de Galves, being Sec. 14, T. 1, R. 28 S&E.

[Dossier contains 1 copy of 1.]

Mollere, Maria D.                    Con. M 58; DG IV 103

1 [E] Benjamin and Jesse B. Clements and James W. Exum certify plat of 514.46 acres, being in Sec. 40, T. 1, R. 31 S&W, for Maria D. Mollere. Chainmen: Manuel Sumaras and Sebastian Sumaras. Robert Butler countersigns, June 1834.

[Dossier contains 1 copy of 1.]

Montero, Antonio, Heirs of       Con. M 59; DG IV 161, 210

1 [E] claim, through John B. Strong, 25 acres on the road to Capuaca and adjoining the lands of John Gianopoly. Governor White's grant to Antonio Montes, 1/23/1808.

2 [S] Antonio Montero petitions, 1/22/1808, for 25 acres of scrub oak land at Macaris, outside of the fifteen hundred yards* and bounded on the north by the creek that divides the land from Moses [Mosse ?] west by the road to Capuaca and south by lands of Juan Gianopolis. Governor White grants, 1/23/1808; Pierra certifies true copy.

[Bound together 3-8 in Spanish:]

3 - Pierra certifies, 6/1/1807, that upon petition of J. Gianopoly for 10 acres adjoining the former Votrero de los Dragones, in exchange for 600 acres granted, 7/21/1801, in Mosquitos territory; Governor White made the grant.

4 - Pierra certifies, 1/23/1808, that upon petition of Antonio Montero

---

* Outside the Mil y quinientas, see p. xxx

for 25 acres at Macaris, 2 above, Governor White made the grant.

5 - Juan Purcell certifies, 6/27/1809, plat of 35 acres bounded on the west by the Mosse's Road, and south by the lands of Bernardino Sanchez.

6 - Juan Gianopoly, through Jorge Gianopole, his son, petitions, 5/4/1821, for permit to present testimonials of his having inhabited and improved for 13 years the 35 acres as it is required in order that he may obtain the royal title to the 35 acres granted to him and to Antonio Montero. Governor Coppinger grants, 5/5/1821. Entralgo attests and notifies petitioner.

7 - Esteban Arnau, 26, deposes, 5/10/1821, before Entralgo that he knows Juan Gianopoly to have lived on, cultivated and improved the land and raised cattle on it for more than 10 years.

8 - Lorenzo Capella, 63, deposes confirming 7 above. Governor Coppinger grants, 5/11/1824. Entralgo attests and notifies Juan Gianopoly.

9 [E] G. Darling certifies, 10/3/1823.

Napier, Thomas  
   of Charleston, S. C.          Con. N 1; DG V 415, 416

1 [E] claims, through Thomas F. Cornell, 1,000 acres on the west side of Hillsborough River, at Mosquito South Lagoon, bounded on the north by land of William Hale, south by Robert McHardy, being part of 4,000 acres of a Spanish grant of 5/3/1816 to George J. F. Clarke, who sold in 1823 to the memorialist.

2 [E] Andres Burgevin certifies, 5/8/1819, plat of 1,000 acres at McDougal's Old Plantation in Turnbull's Swamp for George J. F. Clarke. Charles S. Tucker, Register, Charleston District, certifies, 6/21/1823, recording in Book N. No. 9, p. 1. Clarke certifies translation, 5/12/1823. Antonio Alvarez certifies true copy, 12/29/1846.

3 [E] Deed, 1823: Clarke sells to Napier for $1,500.00 the following tracts of land:

    1,000 acres, a part of Governor Coppinger's grant of 5/3/1816, as shown above;

    1,000 acres, a part of a 2,000-acre grant made by Governor Coppinger on 11/26/1817 to William Garvin who sold, 1/8/1821, to Clarke in Camden County, Georgia;

    100 acres, a moity of the 2,000-acre tract granted by Governor Coppinger on 6/12/1816 to Charles Clarke who sold, 12/29/1820, to George J. F. Clarke in Camden County, Georgia.

Witnesses: James Hibben, Jr., and Charles M. Furman. James S. Tingle certifies, 7/17/1823, recording in Deed Book B, p. 29, St. Johns County. Charles S. Tucker certifies, 6/21/1823, recording in Charleston, as shown in No. 2 above.

4 [E] Clarke certifies, 11/1/1817, plat of 2,000 acres at Chachala, west of Payne's Savannah in Alachua, for Charles Clarke.

5 [E] Clarke certifies, 12/16/1817, plat of 2,000 acres at Flounder Creek and Youngblood's Hammac for Garvin. Clarke certifies, 3/11/1822, 4 and 5 as true translations. Tucker certifies recording as shown above.

6 [E] Testimony taken by the Board of Commissioners, 7/11, & 12/1825, in the claim of Napier for 3,000 acres in three tracts of 1,000 each. G. W. Perpall declared the signature of Governor Coppinger on the grants was genuine and testified that governors often wrote their own decrees. Antonio Alvarez declared the signatures genuine, and stated that before the exchange of flags it was rumored that the archives were to be moved to Havana.

[Dossier contains copy of 2.]

Napier, Thomas                  Con. N 2; DC V 415, 416
of Charleston, S. C.

1 [E] claims, through Thomas F. Cornell, 1,000 acres, a part of a Spanish grant, 6/10/1816, of 4,000 acres to Charles W. Clarke, at Chacala, west of Payne's Savannah in Alachua, which was conveyed by deed, 12/29/1820, by Charles Clarke to George J. F. Clarke, who in 1823 sold it to the claimant.

2 [S] Carlos W. Clarke petitions, 6/9/1816, for 4,000 acres at Chacala for his services to the "fatherland" under commissions of Governors Quesada, White and Kindelan, without reward. Governor Coppinger grants, 6/10/1816.

3 [E] Deed, 12/29/1820: C. W. Clarke sells to George J. F. Clarke, Spanish vice-consul in the Town of St. Marys, for $500.00, a tract of 20,000 acres, west of Payne's Savannah. Witnesses: William

Garvin and Belton A. Coppinger, N. F., Camden County, Georgia. James S. Tingle, clerk of St. Johns County Circuit Court, certifies, 6/11/1823, recording in Book B at page 52.

4 [E] Antonio Alvarez certifies, 7/5/1845, extract from descriptive list, No. 611.

5 [E] George J. F. Clarke certifies, 11/1/1817, plat of his 2,000 acres showing it as cut into two tracts of 1,000 acres each, one sold to Napier and the other to Duncan L. Clinch. Alvarez certifies, 7/5/1845, true copy.

[Dossier contains translation of 2.]

Napier, Thomas       Con. N 3; DG V 415, 416

1 [E] claims, through Thomas F. Cornell, 1,000 acres, being half of a 2,000-acre Spanish grant of 11/26/1817 to William Garvin at Flounders Creek, west of River Ys, which was conveyed by deed of 1/8/1821 to George J. F. Clarke, who sold in 1823 to the claimant.

[Jacket refers to claim Con. N 1 for other papers connected with this claim.]

Napier, Thomas       Con. N 4; DG IV 279

1 [E] claims, through Richard B. Herman, 800 acres 3 miles west of New Smyrna; a Spanish grant to Juan de Entralgo, who sold to Isaac Wickes, who sold to the claimant.

2 [S] Entralgo petitions, 5/20/1817, for title to:

  2,000 acres west of St. Johns River, south of the mouth of Cedar Swamp Creek;

  1,000 acres 30 miles west of Buena Vista;

  800 acres 3 miles west of New Smyrna;

for services rendered. Governor Coppinger grants, 5/20/1817. William Reynolds certifies true copy, 10/28/1823.

3 [S] Royal title, 11/15/1817, Governor Coppinger to Entralgo for 800 acres. Tomas de Aguilar, by Antonio Alvarez, attests.

4 [S] George J. F. Clarke certifies, 2/20/1818, plat of 800 acres. William Reynolds certifies, 10/8/1823, true copy.

5 [S] Entralgo petitions, 2/26/1818, for filing of survey above, which Governor Coppinger grants. William Reynolds certifies, 10/8/1823.

6 [S] Deed, 8/20/1818: Juan de Entralgo to Isaac Wickes, 800 acres for $1,500.00. Witnesses: Jorge Fleming, Guillermo Travers and Bartolome de Castro y Ferrer. William Reynolds certifies true copy, 10/27/1823.

7 [E] Deed: Charleston, 4/22/1820, Wickes to Napier, 800 acres for "good and valuable considerations". Witnesses: P. Lynch and Thomas Murphy.

8 [E] Frederick L. Ming certifies plat of 788.8 acres. Chainmen: Thomas C. Ellis and James Story. Approved, 5/20/1836, by Robert Butler.

9 [E] Antonio Alvarez certifies, 1/24/1835, extract from descriptive list, No. 245.

[Dossier contains translations of 3, 4, 5 and 6, a copy of 4, and decree.]

Nelson, Joseph                  Con. N 5; DG IV 117

1 [E] Benjamin and J. B. Clements and James W. Exum certify plat of 638.12 acres, a donation claim of Joseph Nelson "confirmed by an act of congress passed the 22nd day of April, 1826." Chainmen: Thomas McCleland, Albert Sebastian, James M. Sawyers and Andrew Crawford. Approved January 1834, by Robert Butler, surveyor general.

[Dossier contains a duplicate of above.]

Nelson, WilliamCon. N 6; DG IV 281

1 [E] claims, through George J. F. Clarke, 350 acres on St. Marys River, near Mill's Ferry, bounded by lands of Richard Lang and Jesse Youngblood, and 100 acres between St. Marys and Nassau Rivers. The grants were made by Governor Coppinger as head rights to claimant who is in actual possession.

2 [S] Clarke certifies, 10/8/1818, permit to Nelson to occupy 250 acres, a part of those granted him.

3 [E] Antonio Alvarez certifies, 3/3/1845, extract from descriptive list, No. 244, William Nelson, 350 acres.

4 [E] Ellis Stafford deposes that Nelson settled about 10 years ago on St. Marys River. [Not dated.]

[Dossier contains 2 translations of 2 and a copy of 1.]

Nobles, HannahCon. N 7; DG IV 279

1 [E] claims, through George Gibbs, 280 acres more or less on St. Johns River, bounded on two sides by lands of Isaac Bowden; Governor Kindelan's royal title of 4/24/1815, to Susana Cowan and confirmed to Robert Cowan, who willed same to claimant who is in actual possession.

2 [S] Susana Cowin petitions, through Juan de Entralgo, for a certified copy of the plat of the tract, "Beaclure" [Beauclere?], which she bought of the heirs of Isaac Bordin, Jr., that she may settle several boundary disputes which she has with her neighbors. Governor White grants, 8/4/1805.

[Bound together 3-10 in Spanish:]

3 - R. Cowin petitions, 5/18/1804, for royal title to lands he was

granted and has cultivated for 10 years. Governor White grants Licenciado Ortega countersigns. Assessment: 12 <u>reales</u>.

4 - Pedro Marrot certifies, 12/12/1791, plat of <u>cuatro caballerias y diez y siete acres</u>\* for R. Cowin and wife, at Punta Negro. Samuel Eastlake, surveyor, countersigns.

5 - Jose de Zubizarreta lists, 5/19/1804, requisites for royal title.

6 - Isaac Wickes deposes, 5/19/1804, before Ortega and by Bernardino Sanchez, interpreter, that R. Cowin did cultivate and improve his lands; that in the invasion of 1795 R. Cowin and his family left his land, coming to the east side of the river, but soon after the return of quiet Cowin again cultivated his tract.

7 - Daniel McGirtt deposes same.

8 - George Cook, native, deposes same, saying that R. Cowin returned to his land after the rebellion, rebuilt his burned houses, and is there now cultivating the land.

9 - Governor White grants, 5/24/1804. Ortega countersigns. Assessment: 16 <u>reales</u>.

10 - Zubizarreta attests all the above documents and lists costs, 5/24/1804:

```
        To Governor for 2 signatures . . . . 4 reales
        To Auditor of War . . . . . . . . . 50    "
        To Notary . . . . . . . . . . . . . 48    "
             Total  . . . . . . . . . . .  102    " or 12 pesos, 6 rr.
```

[Bound together 11-18 in Spanish:]

---

\* 4 <u>caballerias</u> and 17 acres.

11 - Marrot certifies, 12/21/1791, plat of <u>seis caballerias y ocho acres</u>* at Punta de Beauclere for Isaac Bowden, Jr., his wife and four sons. Eastlake countersigns.

12 - Juan de Pierra certifies, 6/18/1801, that upon petition of Maria Bowdin, widow of Isaac, for permit to transfer her Beauclere land to Robert Cowin, Governor White granted; Ortega countersigned.

13 - R. Cowin petitions, 11/28/1814, for royal title to Beauclere. Governor Kindelan refers the petition to Juan de Arredondo, who approves, and the petition is granted.

14 - Entralgo attests the above, and lists requisites to royal title. Date <u>ut supra</u>.

15 - Santiago Hall, "Hampshire state", deposes, 11/28/1814, before Juan de Arredondo that he knows that for more than 10 years R. Cowin has cultivated the Beauclere land, building a complete plantation.

16 - Juan Bautista Collins, free mulatto, deposes same.

17 - Juan Gonzalez Montesdeoca deposes same.

18 - Governor Kindelan grants, 4/24/1815; Arredondo countersigns. Assessment: 24 <u>reeles</u>. Entralgo attests.

19 [S] Royal title, 4/24/1815, Governor Kindelan to Robert Cowin for Beauclere. Entralgo certifies true copy.

[Dossier contains translations of 2, 4, 11 and 19; also decree.]

Nobles, Hannah                      Con. N 8; DC IV 280

1 [F] claims, through George Gibbs, 100 acres on Will's Swamp, south of St. Johns River; Governor Coppinger's royal title of

---

\* 6 <u>caballerias</u> and 8 acres.

3/26/1819, to claimant who is in actual possession.

[Bound together 2-8 in Spanish:]

2 - Nobles petitions, 4/23/1816, through Juan Bautista Collins, for 100 acres at the Major Bridge of the St. Nicholas Road. Governor Coppinger grants. Tomas de Aguilar certifies true copy.

3 - Jorge J. F. Clarke certifies, 5/13/1817, plat of 100 acres for Ana [Hannah?] Nobles.

4 - Hannah Nobles petitions, 3/22/1819, through Robert Cowin, for royal title, asking permit to prove her claim. Governor Coppinger grants.

5 - Horatio S. Dexter, native of United States, deposes, 3/22/1819, before Juan de Entralgo that Hannah Nobles has continuously cultivated her land with the protection of Robert Cowin.

6 - Daniel Sweney, illiterate, deposes the same.

7 - Enrique Sweney, illiterate, deposes the same.

8 - Governor Coppinger grants, 3/24/1819, royal title. Entralgo attests.

9 [S] Royal title, 3/26/1819, to 100 acres at Will's Swamp, Governor Coppinger to Hannah Nobles.

10 [E] Unfinished plat of Nobles' 100 acres, being in T. 3, R. 27 S&E.

11 [E] Antonio Alvarez certifies, 12/24/1844, extract from descriptive list, No. 242.

[Dossier contains two copies of 2, two translations and a copy of 3 and decree.]

Noda, Joseph                                 Con. N 9; DG V 414

1 [E] claims a lot extending north and south 85 varas between

North River and the road leading north out of St. Augustine, bounded on the south by I. R. Hanham; Governor White's concession of 2/9/1808 to claimant.

2 [S] Juan de Pierra certifies, 2/9/1808, Governor White's grant to Josede Noda of 85 varas, a lot in the mil y quinientas.[*]

3 [E] Antonio Alvarez certifies, 12/24/1834, extract from descriptive list, No. 609.

Noda, Joseph                           Con. N 10; DG V 414

1 [S] Jose de Noda petitions, 2/9/1808, for 85 varas of land laid out by the commandant of engineers for Nicolas Perez. Governor White grants; Pierra certifies.

2 [S] Jose Garcia, free black, through Juan A. de Aguilar, certifies, 12/4/1824, a sale by himself of a lot outside the city gates, to Jose de Noda for six pesos. James S. Tingle, clerk, St. Johns County Court, records, 3/31/1824, in Book D, p. 70.

3 [E] Antonio Alvarez, keeper of the public archives, certifies, 12/24/1834, extract from descriptive list, No. 608, Joseph Noda, 84 2/3 acres in front [4 acres.--DG V 414.]

Noriega, Joseph                        Con. N 11; DG IV 102

1. [E] Benjamin Clements and James W. Exum, certify plat of 1,526.63 acres on an island in the Escambia River at the head of Escambia Bay, surveyed in 4th Quarter of 1828, for Joseph Noriega. Chainmen and markers: Jesse B. Clements, C. J. Drake, John Gaylor, Frederick L. Ming, James Ming and Wesley Inglish. Note: The above survey is marked "Subsequent survey."

---

[*] Supra, p. xxx.

[Dossier contains 2 copies of 1.]

Noriega, Joseph                    Con. N 12; DG IV 106

1 [E] James W. Exum certifies plat of 689.3 acres on the west margin of Escambia or Pensacola Bay, surveyed in the 3rd quarter of 1827 for Joseph Noriega. Chainmen: Frederic Ming and Wesley Inglish. Approved by Robert Butler.

Noriega, Joseph                    Con. N 13; DG IV 106

1 [E] James W. Exum certifies plat of 656.84 acres on the west margin of Escambia Bay, surveyed 3rd quarter of 1827 for Noreaga. Chainmen: Frederic Ming and Wesley Inglish. Approved by Robert Butler.

Noriega, Joseph                    Con. N 14; DG IV 102

1 [E] James W. Exum certifies plat of 353.65 acres on Escambia Bay, surveyed in the 3rd quarter of 1827 for Joseph Noriega. Chainmen: Frederic Ming and Wesley Inglish. Approved by Robert Butler.

2 [E] Register's certificate No. 59: To Joseph Noriega from Pedro Jack for 353.65 acres on the Bay of Escambia. By G. W. Ward, register.

3 [E] Letter written from Tallahassee, 2/27/1832, by J. G. Searcy for the surveyor general to Benjamin Clements and J. W. Exum, asking if the stream that makes of Noriega's claim an island is navigable.

4 [E] Letter written from Tallahassee, 2/28/1832, by Exum and Clements to Colonel Robert Butler, replying that the stream has "sufficient depth of water for any craft that can enter" Escambia River.

5 [E] Letter written from Tallahassee, 4/18/1832, by Surveyor General Butler to the Honorable Elijah Hayward, Commissioner of the

General Land Office, Washington, reviewing Noriega's claim. He showed that Colonel Joseph M. White was not entitled to the land below the channel and stated that Colonel White had admitted the fact and withdrawn his claim upon being shown the original plat.

    6 [E] Unfinished plat of Noriega Island [see Con. N 11 above].

[Dossier contains copy of 1.]

Noriega, Joseph                    Con. N 15;   DG IV 102

    . 1 [E] James W. Exum certifies plat of 263.4 acres on the west margin of Escambia Bay, surveyed in the 3rd quarter of 1827 for Joseph Noriega. Chainmen: Frederic Ming and Wesley Inglish. Approved by Robert Butler.

Oliver, John                           Con. O 1; DG IV 284

1 [E] claims, through S. Streeter, 640 acres, a donation on the east side of Dunn's Lake, about a mile from River St. Johns. Claimant was in actual possession from 1818-1822 but not since, though his improvements remain.

2 [E] Horatio S. [?] Dexter swears before the U. S. Commissioners that John Oliver occupied and got his buildings up before the exchange of flags, then was ill 12 months; but he had 8 or 9 negroes on his plantation and planted 25 acres of corn, rice, some sugar cane, etc., 8/31/1825.

3 [E] Antonio Alvarez certifies translation of 1.

4 [E] certified extract from descriptive list, No. 246, 6/28/1845.

Oliveros, Raphael                      Con. O 2; DG V 69

1 [E] claims 640 acres, a donation [under act passed 5/6/1824]* about 2 miles north of Doctor's Lake, adjoining Cypress Swamp.

2 [E] Manuel Crispo swears before the U. S. Commissioners that Raphael Oliveros was established on his land before 1815, built houses and cultivated; he has a wife and 5 children. On the bottom Andres Papy swears the same. Before W. H. Allen, 10/12/1827.

3 [E] Antonio Alvarez certifies extract from descriptive list, No. 613, 12/19/1844.

4 [E] Antonio Alvarez certifies that Raphael Oliveros' claim was

---

* Supra, p. xlvi

confirmed, 5/27/1833. [On the back is a note in ink: "Came to hand while in range 25, surveying, there being no evidence". Below in pencil: "Claim surveyed by D. H. Barr". Also on back in ink is a note: "This came to hand in July 1833, while surveying, but there being no specific calls [?] therein, I had intended locating the donation on sec. 12 [?] in T. 4, R. 25 S&E. and, on examination at office of surveyor general I find a claim of Raphael Oliveros identifying the same as being surveyed, etc., - Paul M. Caniche/Corniche/Camiche."]

Pasted to 4 is Alvarez' copy of a certified plat by J. A. Coffee, located about 2 miles north of Doctor's Lake on the head branch of McGirt's Creek. The Trail runs across the west end. Chainmen: John M. Bowden and Elijah Petty.

5 [E] Original Coffee survey.

[Jacket refers to descriptive list, No. 613.]

O'Neal, Henry     Con. O 3; DG IV 117

1 [E] A Clement-Exum certified plat in conformity with Report 10 of the West Florida Commissioners and the Act of Congress of 4/25/1826, 640 acres as a donation grant to Henry O'Neal, being in T. 4, R. 31 N&W, on the west side of Escambia River. The first line begins at southeast corner of Turner Stark's survey and runs south to Juan Mallagossa's line, thence west along Celestino Gonzalez' line. Robert Butler countersigns. Chainmen: James M. Sawyers and Andrew A. Crawford. Surveyed in 4th quarter of 1831. John Rues [Rua ?] dotted off in the southeast corner. [Discolored and broken out where paper has been wet.]

[Dossier has duplicate without Butler's signature, and a Murphy slip attesting, 8/23/1825.]

O'Neal, Margaret, Heirs of    Con. O 4; DG V 379
from Georgia

1 [E] Heirs of Margaret O'Neal claim, through Lancaster, two tracts of land surveyed for Pedro Marrot by Samuel Eastlake, one of 9 caballerias and 7 acres, 4/16/1792, on Langford's Creek, and one for 7 caballerias on the same creek, dated 4/17/1792. The lands are being cultivated.

2 [S] Ebero O'Neilly petitions, 7/8/1800, for copies of surveys of his lands made by Marrot. On the margin Governor White and Ortega grant. The plats follow below and on next four pages. Zubizarreta attests copies. [Document much worn and broken].

[Stitched together 3-9 in Spanish:]

3 - Marrott-Eastlake's certified plats.

4 - Asa O'Neilly in the name of his other brothers, heirs of the defunct Margarita O'Neilly, who was granted 16 caballerias and 17 acres at the plantation called Nueva Esperanza, which was cultivated ten years, a house built, etc., petitions for title. Governor White and Ortega will grant when documents are filed, witnesses heard and fees paid. Zubizarreta attests actions, 3/11/1807.

5 - Zubizarreta states conditions of grant.

6 - Asa O'Neilly presented Juan Paredes of St. Augustine, captain of the schooner, married, Minorcan, 57, who since the province returned to the Spanish 22 years ago, had been on Margarita O'Neilly's plantation various times and can testify.

7 - Asa Pons, Minorcan, married, farmer, 52, swears same. Ortega and Zubizarreta sign for him.

8 - Manuel de la Puente, distinguished soldier of the Third Batallion

of Cuba, single, 30, accompanied his father, Fernando de la Fuente, captain of the same batallion, when by order of the government he visited all the old plantations and among them one where there were three brothers, a sister, and their mother, a widow, Margarita O'Neilly, who had a well provided plantation. Governor White and Ortega approve and grant title.

9 - Fees:

    To the Governor for 2 signatures . . . 4 reales
    To the Assessor General . . . . . . . 60 "
    To the Notary . . . . . . . . . . . . 124 "
                188 " or -
          23 pesos 4 "

10 [S] Title [5 pp. badly faded]. Zubizarreta's attested copy.

11 [E] Alvarez attests extract from descriptive list, No. 615, 243 acres on Lanceford Creek on St. Marys River, at a place called O'Neill's, 2/14/1845.

12 [E] Pasted to 11 is a copy of survey.

13 [E] Patio summary: That Marrot surveyed 2 tracts of land side by side, one of 9 caballerias and 10 acres, or 307 acres, on Lanceford Creek at a place called New Hope; the other tract containing 7 caballerias and 10 acres, or 243 acres, at the same place, and that Governor White issued a title to Margarita O'Neilly for the last tract which is marked "confirmed". Jacket note: "See No. 5".

O'Neal, Margaret, Heirs of    Con. O 5; DG IV 278

1 [E] Thomas Andrew, through Farquhar Bethune, claims title, as guardian of the heirs of Margaret O'Neal, defunct, to 307 acres on Langford Creek, Amelia Island, granted by Governor White to Margaret O'Neal, 3/12/1807. The heirs are now in actual possession.

2 [S] Asa O'Neilly, for himself and other heirs of the late Margaret O'Neal to whom the government conceded 300 acres contiguous to her plantation on Lanford Creek, petitions for survey by Juan Purcell who is now surveying on Amelia Island, 3/14/1801. Governor White grants request.

3 [S] Governor White's royal title for head rights to Margaret O'Neal. Zubizarreta attests.

4 [E] Alvarez attests extract from descriptive list, No. 250, 2/20/1845.

5 [E. Pasted to 4:] Alvarez' certified copy of Marrot's certified plat, same date.

[Dossier has Murphy translation of 3, decree slip of confirmation and top of jacket of descriptive list.]

O'Neal, Margaret, Heirs of                Con. O 6; DG IV 278

1 [E] Thomas Andrew, through his attorney, Farquhar Bethune, claims, as guardian of the children of Margaret O'Neal, 300 acres on Langford Creek, bounded on the south by land of William Carny; Governor White's grant of head rights, approved, 6/15/1810. The heirs are in legal possession.

2 [S] Margaret O'Neal finds that the land she has on Langsford's* Creek is not sufficient for her family and slaves and petitions for 300 acres more next to the rest, 4/24/1799. Governor White refers to Pedro Diaz Berrio, the engineer in command, who sees no inconvenience

---

* The name appears also as Landsford, Lanford, Langford and Lanceford; in Con. O 7 it appears as Sanford. The Creek is in Nassau County and empties into St. Marys River.

Governor White grants, Pierra sent certificate.

3 [S] Governor White's title [5 pp.] to Margaret O'Neal, 6/15/1810. Zubizarreta attests copy.

4 [E] Antonio Alvarez certifies extract from descriptive list, No. 249, 3/6/1845.

5 [E. Pasted to 4:] Alvarez attests translation of title.

6 [E] Another Alvarez translation of title to which is pasted a slip saying: "This is the same as claim described under No. 64".

[Dossier has Murphy translation of title, and decree slip, confirmed.]

O'Neal, William, Heirs of          Con. O 7

1 [E] Charles Seton, administrator of the estate of William O'Neal, late of Nassau County, claims through John Rodman on behalf of the heirs of William O'Neal, 300 acres on the point formed by St. Marys River and Sanford [Lansford] Creek, bounded on the north by the plantation of Margaret O'Neal, east by marsh of St. Marys River, west by the creek, south by William Carney; Governor White's grant to Margaret O'Neal on whose death the tract fell to William O'Neal, 9/29/1825.

2 [S. Inked through and badly blurred:] Governor White's title to Margaret O'Neal, widow, of 300 acres surveyed by Juan Purcell, 6/15/1810. Attested by Jose de Zubizarreta and by William Reynolds.

[Dossier has Fatio's summary and jacket of descriptive list, No. 614, marked "confirmed".]

Ordozgoity, Vincent          Con. O 8; DG IV 103

1 [E] James W. Exum certifies plat with Butler's signature, of

109.54 acres confirmed to Vincent Ordozgoity's heirs by the commissioners of West Florida and Congress, being sec. 30, T. 2, R. 30 S&W. Chainmen: Ming and Inglish. [Document is water-stained and broken.]

2 [E] Certificate No. 50 from G. Ward, Tallahassee register's office, that the plat and certificate of survey to him of Vincent Ordozgoity from Juan Cortez has been deposited in his office and a patent will be issued to heirs of Vincente Ordozgoity.

[Dossier contains duplicates, unbroken.]

Ormond, James and Emanuel        Con. O 9; DG III 643 rejected
                                                              IV 218 confirmed

1 [E] claim, through Murray, 2,000 acres at a place called Damietta on Halifax River, bounded on the south by lands of McHardy, east by vacant land, north by land of Robert Bennett, west by public road, Governor Coppinger's royal title as head rights; in actual possession.

[Stitched together 2-8 in Spanish:]

2 - Title page:             Florida
                            Year 1816
              Dona Russell Ormond, widow of Santiago Ormond, seeking title of 2,000 acres on Halifax River, known by name of Damietta.

3 - Pierre certifies that Santiago Ormond abandoned, 3/8/1803, 2,000 acres in Mosquitoes, which had been conceded to him, and petitioned for an equal amount at the head of Halifax River ceded before by the British government to Mr. Moncrief, bounded on the south by lands of Mr. McLean, east by a pine forest, north by vacant lands, on consideration that he shall not lose by the exchange, and that Governor White granted, 5/16/1807.

4 - McHardy certifies plat [in Sepia] according to Governor Coppinger's order of 2/10/1816 of 2,000 acres surveyed for Santiago Ormond in Mosquitoes, bordered on the south by lands of McHardy, east by vacant lands, north by Roberto Bennet, west by public road. Surveyed, 2/19/1816. Plat shows a creek on the west, Smith Creek on northeast, cleared land [200 acres more or less] and buildings on south end.

5 - Isaac Wickes, agent of Dona Russell Ormond, widow of Don Santiago Ormond, having fulfilled 10 years' compliance with terms of grant, petitions for title. Governor Coppinger, 4/6/1816, demands proof.

6 - F. M. Arredondo, Jr., married, neighbor, 28, testifies to 10 years cultivation of Santiago Ormond and his widow.

7 - Jose Mariano Hernandez, married, native, 28, testifies that the plantation is one of the best known and has a large number of slaves.

8 - Governor Coppinger deems the plantation worth a title and Entralgo so notifies Isaac Wickes.

9 [S] Governor Coppinger's title, 4/19/1816, as copied by the undersigned notary pro tem. [Entralgo.]

10 [E] Testimony of J. H. Lawrence: He knew the mother well and resided at their house many times. [Unsigned.]

11 [E] Isaac Wickes swears that about 1814 he had charge of their estate for several years and knew the family and the improvements they made. Before Alexander Hamilton, January 12, 1824.

12 [E] Alvarez certifies translation of McHardy plat.

13 [E] Slip in writing of Charles Downing: "Interfered with by British grants, not reported in American State Papers, Duff Green edition, Vol. III, p. 643, 1st Report, 1824."

[Dossier has jacket of descriptive list, No. 248, translation of title with Fatio's attest, the original of Isaac Wickes' petition for survey with Fatio's attest of translation. The translation of the McHardy plat and survey are not countersigned.

14 [E] A. M. Randolph certifies plat, pursuant to order of surveyor general of Florida and in conformity with Report 1, claim 122, confirmed by Congress 3/22/1826, of 2,195.87 acres in sec. [blank] T. 21, R. 31, sec. 37, T. 13, R. 31, and sec. 37, T. 13, R. 32 S&E; State highway is called King's Road.

Ortega, Ann                      Con. O 10; DG V 399
    St. Augustine

1 [E] claims 100 acres 12 miles south of Lake George, a service grant to Antonio Hertas, who sold to Andrew Burgevin, 7/14/1821, who sold to Ann Ortega, 5/29/1822, who is in possession.

2 [E] Andrew Burgevin, legally possessed, sells to Ann Ortega, wife of Antonio Mier of St. Augustine, for $200.00, 100 of the 600 acres sold to Andrew Burgevin by Antonio Hertas. Witnesses: Thomas H. Penn and John A. Cavedo. Before Thomas H. Penn, notary public, and recorded for the alcalde, 6/8/1822.

Ortega, Lazaro                    Con. O 11; DG IV 28

1 [E] claims, through G. W. Perpall, 88 acres on North River and Guana Creek, between the lands of Michael Andrew on the south and Juan Segui on the north; Governor Coppinger's royal title of a grant based on head rights.

[Stitched together 2-9 in Spanish:]

2 - Title page: Florida, Year 1819, Lazaro Ortega Asking Title to 88 acres, etc.,

3 - Tomas Travers yields to Lazaro Ortega, neighbor, on North River

a piece of land which extends from its southern boundary up to the fence that runs east-west on the north which will be the limit of the lands that remain to Tomas Travers on the south of the place called Governor Grant, but the chimneys of the old house that were there belong to Tomas Travers, who intends to give to Lazaro Ortega only the land cultivated up to that time by Tomas Travers' negro, Admon. Travers was not in position at the time to give Ortega a proper title, because of the transfer, 8/22/1806, to Travers' brother.

4 - Lazaro Ortega, unfamiliar with the formalities but having held undisturbed possession, as did the grantor before him, petitions in 1819 for a survey by Andres Burgevin, in default of other surveyor, and also for title. Tomas Travers, a former doctor of the Royal Hospital in St. Augustine was, before signing the enclosed papers, in undisturbed possession of this land, 1/18/1819. Antonio Mier writes for Lazaro Ortega who does not know how to write. Governor Coppinger is favorable, but gives instructions to notify neighbors and obtain oath from Andres Burgevin. Entralgo notifies the latter who signs.

5 - Burgevin certifies plat of 1/30/1819.

6 - Lazaro Ortega, through Antonio Mier, petitions for title, which petition Governor Coppinger grants for the presentation of documents and witnesses.

7 - Lazaro Ortega presents, 6/22/1819, Juan Andreu, illiterate, married, farmer, 50, who testifies to ten years undisturbed possession, raising animals, etc., before Entralgo, as others that follow.

8 - Jose Baya, illiterate, native of St. Augustine, married, farmer, 41, swears the same.

9 - Pablo Sabate, illiterate, married, native of St. Augustine, 61, swears that Lazaro Ortega's occupation and work are well known. Governor Coppinger grants title.

10 [E] Bartolome Pacety swears, 12/24/1825, that Lazaro Ortega has held this land ten years, he having built a house and is still cultivating the soil. Before Fatio and Board of Land Commissioners.

11 [E] Henry Washington's certified plat with Robert Butler's countersignature, 6/20/1836, for 93.14 acres, being in sec. 42, T. 6, R. 29 S&E, and sec. ----, T. 6, R. 30 S&E. Chainmen: Isaac Varnes and John W. Townsend.

[Dossier has Murphy translation of Tomas Travers' grant, of Governor Coppinger's grant of title, of Burgevin's survey and the filing cover of descriptive list, No. 247.]

Pacety, Andrew                    Con. P 1; DG V 405

1 [E] claims 640 acres, a donation on Armstrong Branch, 14 or 15 miles west of St. Augustine. Antonio Canovas, duly sworn, testifies that he knows Andrew Pacety who settled on the tract about the beginning of 1818, has houses, cattle, 2 slaves and is head of a family, and has no other land. Antonio Ponce swears he has been repeatedly on the above claim, and helped Andrew Pacety build a house. Andrew Pacety has raised crops, etc., sworn before Fatio, 7/25/1827.

2 [E] Uncertified and unsigned plat, being 640 acres in Sec. 37, T. 6, R. 28 S&E, confirmed by Congress according to recommendations of Report No. 1, claim No. 1, 1830, by Commissioners of East Florida.

[Six Mile Creek and Mill Creek are shown on the west side of the map.]

Pacety, Andrew                    Con. P 2; DG V 414
St. Augustine

1 [E] claims a tract of "1500"* outside the gates of this city, on the west side of the road, measuring 110 1/6 yards north-south, and in depth east-west the distance from the road to the river St. Sebastian; bounded on the north by lands of Bartolome Lopez, south by lands of Juan Triay, east by the road, west by the river; Governor White's grant of 5/10/1807.

2 [S] Pierre certifies that according to the new arrangement,

---

\* The Mil y quinientas.

made by the engineer in command, at the governor's orders regulating land grants inside of the 1500-yard line, Andrew Pacety was conceded land measured for Pedro L [?]ujada, which extended 110 1/6 English yards in front of the left side of the road coming out of the Land Gate, bordering, etc., as shown above. He was to leave on the south along his border a path one <u>vara</u> [33 inches] wide to serve as a path. Other conditions required that he keep his land cleared, plant no high-growing plants but only garden vegetables, dig no ditches, and construct no house other than a palm hut along the edge of the road or street, measuring nor more than 9 feet wide, 10 feet long, and 10 feet high, which, on order of the commandant, he is to leave and burn, along with his fences, without claim for damages, 5/10/1807. This land Andrew Pacety cultivates with the aid of his father-in-law's slave. Rafael Hernandez, oarsman of the "Launch of the Bar," having been discharged, tried tailoring without much success, then Andrew Pacety allowed him to cultivate a corner of his land on account of the relationship between them. But he left the fences down and Andrew Pacety had to get an injunction from the alcalde of the district to get him out of there, 10/5/1810. Alvarez attests above copy, 11/29/1840.

3 [E] Alvarez' extract from descriptive list, No. 628, attested 12/29/1834.

4 [E] Fatio's summary of above case.

Palmes, Diego                      Con. P 3; DG IV 102

1 [E] James W. Exum certifies plat with Robert Butler's counter-signature for 638.38 acres surveyed for Diego Palmes at the head of Bayou Mulatto, being Sec. 3, T. 1, R. 28 S&W, and Sec. 37, T. 1,

R. 28 N&W. Chainmen: Evans and John Byrd, Jr. Plat shows Marya R. Murrel on the west.

[Jacket notes Governor's Creek, 800 **arpents** claimed.]

Palmes, George and Oliver      Con. P 4; DG IV 221
Savannah, Georgia

1 [E] claim 999 3/4 acres at a place called Turnbull on both sides of Spruce Creek in the Mosquitoes, bounded on the south by land of William Williams; a grant of Governor White as head rights to Robert-McHardy, 7/21/1803, who sold to Paul Dupon, 6/2/1818, who holds the land in trust for George Palmes and Oliver Palmes as will be seen by bond filed in their claim for 245 acres.

[Stitched together 2-10 in Spanish:]

2 - Title page:          Florida,
                           Year 1815,
                 Robert McHardy seeking title
                 to 2,000 acres in Mosquitoes.

3 - Pierra certifies that Governor White granted head rights to McHardy, 7/21/1803, north of the River of Mosquitos on the plantation called Turnbull and on both sides of the so-called Spruce Creek.

4 - Pierra certifies that Governor White allowed McHardy to give up this land in exchange for an equal quantity of land granted Mr. Demoivt Morling on the edge of Tomoca River and now vacant, 9/5/1808.

5 - McHardy mentions these two tracts, the first on Spruce Creek and the second on River Tomoca, bounded on the north by lands of the heirs of Santiago Ormond, east by the river, south by Juan Bunch, west by the public road, which land he has held ten years and cultivated with his slaves. He has complied with conditions and he asks title, 7/1/1815. Governor Estrada asks for witnesses. Juan de Arredondo y Sanfelices also signs.

6 - Entralgo states conditions of grant.

7 - Francisco Pelliser, native of Mahon, married, farmer, 62, swears to conditions fulfilled.

8 - F. M. Arredondo, Jr., married, merchant, 28, swears that McHardy cultivated both tracts.

9 - Gabriel Guillermo Perpall, native of Mahon, married, rancher, 49, swears to constant residence and continued improvements.

10 - Governor Estrada grants title to 2,000 acres, 7/3/1815. Attested by Juan de Arredondo y San Felices.

11 [S] McHardy sells 6/2/1818, the first tract, 999 3/4 acres, to Pablo Dupon for $1,500.00. Witnesses: Jose Mariano Hernandez, Eusebio Maria Gomez, Jose Maria Besquet.

12 [S. Decree slip:] The Board finds title is interfered with by British titles under which Turnbull heirs claim, and forward documents to Congress for determination.

[Jacket is marked:] "Recommended for confirmation by Congress-- not returned. Report 2, No. 15, 1824, DG IV 221, 233." [Again below:] "Valid, but covered by British grants. Report 10, No. 1, 1825. DG IV 287."

Palmes, George F. and Oliver         Con. P 5; DG IV 161
Savannah, Georgia

1 [E] claim 245 acres in St. Diego plains, bounded on the south by lands of John Andrew, east by beach of Santa Lucia, west by vacant pine lands; Governor Coppinger's royal title for service grant to Francisco Medicis who sold to Joseph Delespine [no date], who sold to Gabriel W. Perpall, 12/23/1816, who sold to Joseph Waller, 10/3/1817, who sold to Paul Dupon, 5/27/1818, who holds the land in trust for George and Oliver Palmes.

[Stitched together 2-4 in Spanish:]

2 - Title page:
                              Florida
                              Year 1816

                              Concession made to Francisco Medicis of 245 acres at the Beach called Santa Lucia.

3 - Francis Medicis when he lived with his now dead parents, and when he first married, always enjoyed land gratis [head rights]. He was the first who took up arms at the call against the invaders, served as sergeant of militia, attended to the distribution of rations contributed by neighbors and aided widows and orphans, etc. He asks for land belonging to the house he has recently bought, 2/9/1816. Governor Coppinger states that the government needs this land but that he will grant him land elsewhere.

4 - Francisco Medicis has found vacant lands to the south of the land conceded to the free mulatto Saneo; bounded on the north by Francisco Sanchez and on the east by the beach of Santa Lucia. He petitions for head rights for himself, his wife, 5 children, 2 slaves above 25, and a minor brother under his care, called Antonio Juaneda, who also served in defense of the province, 2/10/1816. On the bottom the Governor asks for the ages of the children. Francisco Medicis states that 3 are above 8, and 2 are under 8. Governor Coppinger grants 245 acres.

    5 [S] Governor Coppinger's royal title to Francisco Medicis. Murphy's copy with Fatio's attest.

    6 [E] William Reynolds certifies [Murphy's handwriting] that Francisco Medicis sold to Joseph Delespine who sold, etc., down to Dupon, 9/3/1824.

    7 [E] McHardy certifies plat of 245 acres surveyed for Joseph

Delespine, 9/12/1816. [The usual McHardy picture.]

8 [E] Gabriel Guillermo Perpall sells to Jose Wales, for $300.00, 245 acres which he bought from Joseph Delespine. Witnesses: Peter Miranda, Arredondo, Reyes, before Entralgo who attests copy.

9 [S] Jose Walles sells to Pablo Dupon for $300.00. Same witnesses. Entralgo attests.

10 [E] Dupon conveys to George and Oliver Palmes, who will pay rent to him. Before John C. Nicoll, N. P. and James Morrison, N. P.

11 [E] Alvarez attests extract from descriptive list, No. 252, 6/2/1845. Attached is copy of McHardy plat.

[Dossier has Murphy translation of Dupon sale.]

Palmes, Pablo               Con. P 6; DG IV 167

1 [E] James W. Exum certified plat with Butler's countersignature, for 637.60 acres on the west margin of Bayou Taxar, confirmed by the West Florida Commissioners and Congress, to Pablo Palmes, being Sec. 49, T. 1, and Sec. 51, T. 2, R. 30 S&W. Frederic Ming and Wesley Inglish, chainmen. 3rd quarter of 1827. Plat shows Jayne Fontenal's land on the northwest, Joseph Maury's on the southeast, and the southwest vacant.

[Jacket notes location as northeast of Indian Pass.]

Papy, Andres                Con. P 7; DG IV 284

1 [E] claims, through B. A. Putnam, 640 acres as a donation, 10 or 12 miles south of St. Augustine on Moses Creek, bounded on the north by land of Francis Mosier, south by creek, east by land of Colonel Murat, west by public land.

2 [E] Before Bernardo Segui, Mayor and J. P. of St. Augustine, appeared Juan Llambias, who swore to Andres Papy's tract and improvements, 6/6/1825.

[Jacket refers to descriptive list, No. 266.]

Papy, Andres                  Con. P 8; DG V 377

1 [E] claims 126 acres at Fort San Diego north of St. Augustine, the east line running along the boundary of Francis Sanchez; Governor White's head rights to Josefa Espinosa. Philip Solano bought of the heirs of Espinosa and sold to Anna Pons, 2/9/1819.

2 [S] Felipe Solana sells to Anna Pons, a widow, 3 _caballerias_ and 26 acres at the plantation called Fort of San Diego, for $126.00, 2/1/1819. One of the witnesses signs for Anna Pons. Witnesses: F. M. Arredondo, Jr., Antonio Girald, Pedro Miranda. Before Entralgo.

3 [E] Andres Papy's receipt from Fatio of Land Commissioners' plat, and certificate of Marrot, 11/18/1824.

[Jacket note: "See Mattair, Lewis, 376 acres for 1 paper". Descriptive list, No. 626.]

Papy, Ann                  Con. P 9; DG V 62

1 [E] widow of Gaspar Papy, claims 200 acres north of the head of Morgan's River and Tomoca Creek, granted to her deceased husband, 6/3/1797.

2 [S] Gaspar Papy petitions for 200 acres for the purpose of agriculture and cattle raising to support his increased family. The tract is located at the mouth of Tomoca and was granted by the British to Mr. Micken. Governor White refers to engineer in command and Berrio approves. Governor White grants; Pierra gives certificate.

3 [S] Pierra's certificate, 6/3/1797.

4 [E] Alvarez attests abstract 6/20/1845, from descriptive list, No. 616.

[Attached is translation of 3.]

5 [E] Fatio summary. Land confirmed to Ann Papy.

Papy, Joseph            Con. P 10; DG IV 284

1 [E] claims 640 acres as a donation, about 4 miles east of Picolata Fort, bounded on the south by Six Mile Creek, north by a small creek called Hunny Branch.

2 [E] Unsigned plat for 640 acres confirmed by Congress, being in Sec. 38, T. 7, R. 28 S&E. Miguel Papy's claim, Sec. 39, lies to the east; Antonio Huertas' claim, Sec. 41, off to the northeast.

3 [E] Joseph Papy swears, before Bernardo Segui, J. P., that he has no other land, Spanish or British.

[Jacket notes descriptive list, No. 264.]

Papy, Miguel            Con. P 11; DG IV 284

1 [E] claims, through G. A. Putnam, 640 acres as a donation, located on Deep Creek about 6 miles from St. Johns River, which he occupied before 2/22/1819. *

2 [E] Bartholomew Solano swears before W. H. Allen that he has long known Miguel Papy who planted a garden and raised some corn for his livestock, etc., 5/26/1825.

3 [E] Miguel Papy swears before Segui, J. P. of St. Johns County, that he never had any other land, 8/6/1825.

4 [E] The Board confirms land to Miguel Papy, 8/16/1825.

---

\* Supra, pp. xlvi-xlvii

5 [E] Unsigned and undated plat of 640 acres confirmed by Congress, being in T. 7, R. 28 S&E.

6 [E] Benjamin Clement certifies plat with Butler's signature, March 1835, 640.80 acres, confirmed to Miguel Papy. Chainmen: Joel Yarnell [?] and John M. McGough.

[Jacket refers to descriptive list, No. 265.]

Paredes, Juana          Con. P 12; DG V 64

1 [E] claims 110 acres on North River at a place known as Marshall's Plantation, bounded on the north by land of Stephen Arnau, west by pine barrens, east by marshes of the river, south by land of James Arnau; Governor White's grant to John Paredes, her late father.

2 [E] Pierra certifies that Juan Paredes petitioned for 110 acres on North River next to land of Jaime Arnau, because the land at Ria [on the estuary of Matanzas at Blood [?] Point of Punta de la Sangre] was found not vacant, and that Governor White granted, 4/17/1807.

3 [S] Juana Paredes, being unable to write, petitions through Jose Mas for a survey by Andres Burgevin, to avoid disputes with neighbors, 6/2/1818. Governor Coppinger grants same date; Entralgo notifies Andrew Burgevin and attests.

4 [E] G. Darling certifies, 9/16/1823, plat of Jane Paredes, 110 acres, granted to Juan Paredes.

5 [E] Antonio Alvarez certifies extract, 6/3/1845, from descriptive list, No. 618.

6 [E. Attached to 5:] Translation of 2.

7 [E. Pasted to 5 and 6:] Translation of 4.

[Dossier contains Fatio's translation of 1 and 2, and decree slip which finds Darling survey immaterial.]

Paredes, Juana                    Con. P 13; DG V 64

1 [E]'claims 69 acres at Alligator Point on the east side of North River, bounded on the north, south and west by the mouth of Guana Creek; Governor Coppinger's royal title for head rights granted to Antonio Caballero, 11/7/1807; title 1/29/1808 and 8/9/1811.

[Stitched together 2-14 in Spanish:]

2 - Title page:                    Florida
                                   Year 1819

                    Juana Paredes, widow of Antonio
                    Caballero, asking title of 69 acres
                    on Punta del Cayman [Alligator Point].

3 - Pierra certifies that Governor White granted the above, 11/7/1807, to Antonio Caballero. On bottom is a note by Entralgo: "No house will be allowed to be erected for the purpose of selling liquor or goods to inhabitants of the vicinity".

4 - Pierra certifies that Antonio Caballero petitioned for 14 acres voluntarily ceded by Mariano Fontan on Alligator Point, and that Governor White granted, 1/29/1808.

5 - Aguilar certifies that Governor Quesada granted a permit to Jose Hernandez Carmona to transfer to Antonio Caballero the 30 acres that he has at Alligator Point, 8/9/1811.

6 - Juana Paredes, illiterate, petitions for title to 69 acres granted her deceased husband, Antonio Caballero, as per enclosed certificate. Governor Coppinger will grant after formalities of right have been established, 1/17/1818.

7 - Entralgo states conditions of grant.

8 - Juan Segui, of Minorca, farmer, about 60, swears to conditions

having been fulfilled, as is well known, but does not sign as he doesn't know how to write.

9 - Antonio Monte de Oca, married, cobbler, 80, swears to the same which he says is well known.

10 - Benito Segui, married, farmer, illiterate, 26, swears Antonio Gaballero built a house and lived there 5 or 6 years until ordered to withdraw to city. All before Entralgo who attests.

11 - Juana Paredes, through Jose Mas, asks survey by Burgevin.

12 - Granted by the Governor.

13 - Burgevin certifies plat.

14 - Juana Paredes petitions for title; Governor Coppinger grants.

15 [S] Governor Coppinger's royal title [4 pp].

[Dossier has extra Burgevin plat and translation, all in Spanish.]

Parker, Needham                  Con. P 14; DG V 662

1 [E] Clements and Exum certify plat of 639.22 acres surveyed for a 640 acre donation confirmed by the West Florida Commissioners and Congress to Needham Parker, being in Sec. 6, T. 5, R. 29 N&W. The land of Miguel Quiggles lies on the northeast boundary. Chainmen: Thomas McClellan and Albert Sebastian. Butler signs, January 1834.

[Dossier has duplicate of 1, not attested.]

Peavatt, Joseph                  Con. P 15; DG IV 285

1 [E] claims, through William Travers, agent of the heirs, 500 acres near the runs [?] of Pablo Creek, bounded on the north by land granted to Robert Payne, the remainder vacant; Governor Tonyn's grant

to Robert Payne who now lives in St. Augustine and did in 1821. Through George Murray, attorney for William Travers.

[Tied together with tape 2 and 3 in English:]
2 - English royal grant of 500 acres to Joseph Peavett near the three runs of Pablo Creek, bounded on the north by land of Robert Payne, south by Robert Bissett, remainder vacant. Signed by Governor Patrick Tonyn, 3/11/1782.

3 - Benjamin Lord certifies plat pursuant to warrant of Governor Tonyn and order of a survey directed to Frederick George Mulcaster, surveyor general, 2/15/1781. The plat shows Mr. Elliott's land on the northwest, Mr. Payne's on the northeast, Bissett's on the south. A dotted line indicates the road to St. Augustine which runs across north-south. Plat is dated 6/22/1781. No. 2 is recorded in Auditor's office by John Forbes, Deputy Auditor General, 9/18/1782.

4 [E] Alvarez certifies extract from descriptive list, No. 368, 1/2/1845.

5 [E. Pasted to 4:] Certified copy of 3 with same date.

[Jacket note: "Confirmed by Commissioners".]

Peavatt, Joseph                Con. P 16; DG IV 285

1 [E] George Murray, attorney for William Travers, agent of heirs of Joseph Peavett, claims 500 acres at Durbin's Swamp at a branch made by Julenton Creek, near land laid out for James Samson. All sides of the land are vacant; a British grant by Governor Tonyn to Joseph Peavett, who held it until the cession.

2 [E] British grant of Governor Tonyn to Joseph Peavett, 500 acres at a branch of Durbin's Swamp and Julianton Creek near land laid out to James Samson. David Yeats records in register's office,

4/5/1783.

    3 [E] Benjamin Lord, a surveyor general, 3/13/1762, certifies plat, etc., [broken].

    4 [E] Alvarez attests extract from descriptive list, No. 369, 1/2/1845.

    5 [E. Pasted to 4:] Duplicate of 3.

Peavett, Joseph, Heirs of      Con. P 17; DG IV 285

    1 [E] claim, through George Murray, 500 acres on branches of Pablo Creek 25 miles northwest of St. Augustine, with the lands of Andrew Turnbull on the northeast, other sides vacant. It was an English grant of Governor Grant to Robert Taylor, 4/29/1771. "The said Payne [not before mentioned] sold to Henry Sowerby, 12/5/1785, who sold to Joseph Peavett who still holds and did in July 1821."

    [Tied together with tape 2-4 in English:]

2 - Grant of Governor James Grant to Robert Payne of 500 acres, etc., 4/29/1771. David Yeats attests and records in back.

3 - James Grant's order of survey to Mulcaster, surveyor general.

4 - Certified plat of Mulcaster.

    5 [E] Robert Payne, 12/5/1780, for 5 shillings paid and one peppercorn if legally demanded, rents to Henry Sowerby the above land for one year to be followed next day by deed of sale.

    6 [E. Torn in two and badly broken:] Robert Payne and Letitia, his wife, sell to Henry Sowerby their land for 100 pounds paid. Seals are made from bits of yellow silk ribbon, 3/4" that is threaded through slits in the paper. On back is receipt of Robert Payne, witnessed by Charles Delap, Justice of Peace, and Angus Kennedy.

7 [E. Slip 4" x 8":] Henry Sowerby promises, 1/24/1781, to give into the hands of Joseph Peavett one tract of land granted to Mr. Payne.

8 [E] Alvarez attests extracts from descriptive list, No. 367, confirmed to Joseph Peavett.

9 [E. Pasted to 8:] A duplicate of 4.

Peavett, Joseph, Heirs of          Con. P 18; DG IV 285

1 [E] William Travers, agent, claims through George Murray, attorney, 250 acres near the three runs, bounded on the north by a branch of Pablo Creek, east by land granted to Robert Payne, west by land granted to Francis Augustus Elliot, south by tract formerly granted to Joseph Peavett, Governor Tonyn's grant to Joseph Peavett who is not in possession and was at the time of the cession. *

[Taped together 2 and 3.]

2 [E] Governor Tonyn's grant to Joseph Peavett, etc.

3 [E] Benjamin Lord, surveyor general, certifies plat pursuant to Governor Tonyn's order, 9/7/1782.

[Pasted together 4-6 in English:]

4 - Alvarez attests extracts from descriptive list, No. 366, 1/2/1845.

5 - Alvarez attests copy of 3.

6 - Alvarez compiled diagram of claims, No. 366, 367 and 368, all in favor of Joseph Peavett.

Pellicer, Francis          Con. P 19; DG V 376

[Cover of protocol no longer attached; only the numbers on pages and the matching weevil holes now show where contents once belonged.]

---

* _Supra_, pp. xlvi - xlvii

1 [E] Title page:  Florida
Year 1818

No. 17, Jan. 24

Concession was made to Francis Pellicer of 2,000 acres in a place called Tomoca.

2 [S] Francis Pellicer says that he now is on the south of the Fort of Matanzas where he was granted 1,100 acres of land which now turns out to be irrigable land and pine forest, not all useful, as Robert McHardy, surveyor newly appointed by the government, can testify. It was here the supplicant lost in the last revolution, all the livestock that he had and was employed in making nightly patrols with the vigilance due the King. Having found in the place called Tomoca some vacant land that borders on the north with land of Jose Arredondo, on the east and west with pine woods, and on the south with vacant land, and which would be useful for his increased family, he petitions for 2,000 acres. On the margin Governor Coppinger grants and orders title sent, 1/24/1818.

3 [S. Incorrectly numbered 2:] Francis Pellicer petitions for survey by Robert McHardy of which Pellicer will pay the costs. Pablo Fontane signs for Francis Pellicer who cannot write. Governor Coppinger is favorable if Robert McHardy will take oaths and the neighbors are notified, 2/4/1818.

4 [S. Incorrectly numbered 3:] McHardy's certified plat of 2,000 acres bounded on the north by Arredondo, east by vacant pine woods, south by heirs of Juan Russell, west by the public road, 3/14/1818.

5 [E] Alvarez' translation of McHardy plat in archives, 11/16/1849.

[The plat shows Smith Creek on the south end.]

Pellicer, Francis              Con. P 20; DG IV 281

1 [E] claims, 1,100 acres at Pellicer's Plantation at Matanzas, bounded on the northeast by marsh, southeast by lands of W. Clarke, southwest by vacant lands; Governor Kindelan's royal title for head rights, 3/30/1815.

[Stitched together 2-11 in Spanish:]

2 - Title page, No. 6                Florida
[Pencil] March 30                    Year 1815

                            Francis Pellicer asking to
                            be sent title, etc.

3 - Francis Pellicer, through his attorney, F. M. Arredondo, Jr., petitions for duplicate copy of his land certificate which he has misleid, and permit for Robert McHardy to survey. On the margin 2 3/4" Governor Kindelan grants the request and Aguilar adds a note that fills the remainder of the margin, all the next page, and one-half of another page. Items below.

4 - Francis Pellicer is now in the state of matrimony with 2 male children, one of 16 and one of 2, 3 daughters, one of 12 and the others of 10, and 2 negro slaves, which is a family that he hires out on monthly salary and needs the land which your predecessor conceded to him, for which you will kindly send him a title. St. Augustine, 9/14/1790. Quesada notes: "Let him produce his documents and title will be provided, 10/4/1790".

5 - Francis Pellicer, who has been cultivating the land and cutting wood, has mislaid the documents but the facts can be proved by the ensign, Josef Hernandez, and other neighbors. It is a favor which he expects to receive from the benignant heart of His Excellency.

Governor Quesada, 10/9/1790, will see that a survey gives to Francis Pellicer the land due his family.

6 - Francis Pellicer petitions for survey by McHardy and asks that he be given copies of his [Francis Pellicer's] previous memorials. Governor White grants requests, 5/21/1808. Aguilar attests copies of the above, 1/17/1815. [End of notes on margin of 3.]

7 - McHardy certified plat, 2/18/1815, of 1,100 acres, surveyed for Francis Pellicer. The middle third of the tract, 13, where the creek runs in on the north, is marked "Savanna". At the north corner a pine woods is labeled "cleared".

8 - F. M. Arredondo, Jr., petitions for consent to produce witnesses and secure title for Francis Pellicer. Governor Kindelan refers the request to the Auditor of War, 3/17/1815. Governor Kindelan and Juan de Arredondo y San Felices sign the order for witnesses. Entralgo notifies Arredondo, Jr. Tomas de Aguilar states conditions of grant.

9 - Joseph Mariano Hernandez, married, merchant, 27, swears the tract is known as Francis Pellicer's and conditions have been fulfilled. Before Entralgo.

10 - Jose Bernardo Segui, married, native, 31, swears the property is known as Francis Pellicer's, etc. Governor Kindelan and Arredondo y San Felices grant title. Entralgo attests all the above documents. [End of protocol.]

12 [E] Governor Kindelan's royal title [3 pp.]

13 [E] Jose S. Sanchez swears that he was on Francis Pellicer's land about 6 years ago, when he and a number of slaves were planting. It looked as if it had been cultivated for years.

14 [E] Clements' certified plat of 1,104.48 acres being in Sec. 29, T. 10, R. 30 S&E. Butler signs, March 1835. Chainmen: John Hagen and John M. McGough.

15 [E] Arthur M. Randolph's certified plat of 1,105.50 acres in the angle of Matanzas River and Pellicer's Creek. "Old Survey" marked approved, 9/30/1830.

[Dossier has duplicate of 15 and duplicate of 1 and Murphy translations of title.]

Pelot, James                    Con. P 21; DG V 379

1 [E] claims 620 acres on Amelia Island, Governor White's grant of head rights to John Francis Pelot, 7/19/1796, confirmed 12/20/1803; cultivated until John Francis Pelot died intestate. James Pelot is in actual possession. Petition made through Farquhar Bethune.

2 [S] Pierra certifies that John Francis Pelot asked how many acres he was entitled to in a place called "Old Fields of the Eagle", on Amelia Island, and Governor White decreed that his family and slaves entitled him to 640 acres, gut without prejudice to others who had made previous claims.

3 [S] George J. F. Clarke certified plat of 620 acres, a part of 640 granted. The plat shows lands of Jorge Atkinson on the north, Antonio Suarez on the southwest, and that part next to a marsh is planted.

4 [E] Farquhar Bethune swears before F. J. Fatio, 7/12/1827, that James Pelot lived on and cultivated this tract from 1805 to his death 3 or 4 years ago; and his heirs are now ready to cultivate it.

[Pasted together in English:]

5 – Alvarez' certified extract from descriptive list, No. 624, and a copy of 3.

[Dossier has another copy of 3 and Fatio's translation of 2.]

Pengree, Rebecca, Heirs of            Con. P 22; DG IV 206

1 [E. Torn down left margin:] The heirs of Rebecca Pengree claim, through Julius Alford, 500 acres adjoining a plantation of 200 acres formerly owned by Mrs. Jones on St. Johns River. The land has never been surveyed. It was Governor White's grant, 5/9/1793, to Rebecca Pengree, which she cultivated until her death, and her son, George Cook, afterwards. His children, who live near Greensborough, Georgia, now make claim.

2 [S] Rebecca Pengree, settler on St. Johns River, was ordered by the government to withdraw before the invaders, from the land she had opposite the St. Johns River, and set fire to all her buildings. She stopped here on Cunningham Creek, which runs towards Julington Creek, where she had 300 acres of plow-land which is not enough for her family and slaves, and the plantation that Mms. Jones possessed in her vicinity being now unoccupied, she petitions for 200 acres as plow-land. Governor White refers the petition to Berrio who is favorable. Granted, and Pierra sent certificate. William Reynolds attests translation.

3 [E] Lodowich Ashley deposes before John B. Strong, judge of the county court, 12/13/1823, that he was well acquainted with Mrs. Rebecca Pengree who died about 20 years ago, leaving George Cook, her son, and Mrs. Eliza Lifley, her daughter, her only heirs-at-law. Mrs. Lifley died some years after her mother, leaving no children, which left George Cook the only heir of Rebecca Pengree and Eliza

Lifley.' George Cook died about 1815 and his wife about 3 months later, leaving these children heirs-at-law by descent, viz., Louisa Rogers, the wife of Josiah Rogers; Eliza Alfred, the wife of Julius C. Alfred; Jane Cook and George Ann Cook. All these are now living in Georgia and are the daughters of this deponent's sister.

4 [E] Alvarez' attested extract from descriptive list, No. 260, and translation of memorial and grant.

[Dossier has translation of 2 and decree slip.]

Pengree, William, Heirs of        Con. P 23; DG IV 160

1 [E] Julius Alford, for heirs of William Pengree, claims 1,000 acres at head of a creek called Nepomuceno and near Doctor's Lake, on a creek about 5 miles away, which have never been surveyed; Governor Quesada's head rights to William Pengree, 1/29/1793. The heirs in possession were finally forced by disturbances in Florida to move to Georgia, and still live there.

2 [S. Chewed by weevils nearly to the point of falling to pieces, and nearly illegible:] William Pengree points out that behind his land on the creek of Nepomucena near Doctor's Lake is vacant land very suitable for the erection of a water saw mill, which apparatus he has half finished on his own land. He petitions for this land to provide lumber for his saw. Governor Quesada refers the project to Marrot, who finds it beneficial to the province and recommends that he go as far as he likes. Governor Quesada directs Marrot to survey the grant and decide later what is comformable to regulations.

3 [E] Alvarez' attested extract from descriptive list, No. 259, 1,000 acres, confirmed to William Pengree. No survey, 12/19/1845.

4 [E. Pasted to 3:] Translation of 2. Marrot has no positive instructions from the above, does not know how much money William Pengree has expended for the mill now set up and for the iron work of another now partly set up on his own land, but recommends 1,000 acres so as not to compel William Pengree to go too far for timber. But he recommends that William Pengree's head rights be not increased for the 3 new slaves he now has, since he did not mention that number when the land was first granted him.

5 [E] Unsigned, certified plat of 1,000 acres confirmed by Congress to William Pengree's heirs, being in T. 45, R. 25 S&E. Plat in Sec. 40 shows Kingsley's claim, Sec. 39, 286.60 acres on east or shore of lake.

6 [E] Board confirms claim made without condition.

[Dossier has Murphy translation of 2, and William Reynolds' attested copy.]

Perchman, John                    Con. P 24

1 [S] John Perchman, Ensign of the Dragoons stationed in this place, petitioned for a 2,000 acre service grant, at Ocklawaha near St. Johns River; Governor Estrada's grant of 12/12/1815. Copy attested by William Reynolds and countersigned by Edgar Macon, district attorney for East Florida.

2 [S] John Perchman petitions for survey by someone competent. Governor Estrada grants promptly, 12/31/1815.

[Taped together 3-11 in English:]

3 - Title page: Land Claim. John Percheman 2,000 acres on the south side of Ocklawaha. Surveyed by Alex McKay.

## Index

  Petition to Spanish government . . . . p 1
  Grant of 2,000 acres . . . . . . . . . p 2
  Petition for survey . . . . . . . . . p 3
  Plat . . . . . . . . . . . . . . . . . p 4
  Decree of superior court . . . . . . . p 4
  Mandate of Supreme Court . . . . . . . p 6
  Certificates . . . . . . . . . . . . . p 8

4 - Translation of 1.

5 - Grant.

6 - Petition for survey.

7 - McHardy's certified plat of 2,000 acres for Lieutenant John Perchman. [No details.]

8 - Superior Court confirms.

9 - Supreme Court, having heard counsel on both sides, confirms, January 1833.

10 - George R. Fairbanks attests above copies, 12/31/1844.

11 - Judge Bronson attests Fairbanks.

[Taped together 12 and 13 in English, on brown paper:]

12 - Superior Court - East Florida.

      Juan Perchman
        vs
      U. S. A.
    Claims 2,000 acres, etc.,
    Statement of this case:

Petitions for confirmation of said tract of land filed in clerk's office of said court, 9/17/1830.

Documents filed and offered in case, to-wit: Memorial and concession to John Perchman, dated 12/12/1817; Aguilar's certified copy of same; petition for order of survey, 12/31/1815; certificate and plat, 8/20/1819; indenture, Perchman to Sanchez, 11/28/1823; answers of attorneys of U. S. A., filed 10/2/1830; replication of claimant filed 10/2/1830; decree of confirmation, 12/14/1830. The court over-ruled objections to attest copies and finds claim valid.

13 - Copies [translations] of all these documents follow [except indenture to Sanchez], all attested by A. Gay, translator. Copy of decree of Supreme Court follows. Decision of John Marshall attested by Thomas Carroll, clerk. All attested by Kingsley B. Gibbs, clerk.

14 [E] Alexander MacKay certifies plat of 2,016.40 acres surveyed to John Perchman as confirmed by Supreme Court, being in T. 12, R. 25 S&E. Chainmen: John Darling and W. P. King [?]. [Not signed by surveyor general Butler.]

[Dossier has extra copy of decree of Superior Court and another copy of mandate of Supreme Court.]

[Jacket notes descriptive list, No. 712.]

Perpall, G. W.                    Con. P 25; DG IV 221

1 [E] claims 1,340 acres west of River St. Johns at a place opposite Rowle's Town; Governor Coppinger's service grant.

[Stitched together 2 and 3 in Spanish:]

2 - Title page:
                              Florida
                              Year 1816
                    Concession made to Don Gabriel Guillermo Perpall of 1,340 acres on margin of North River.

3 - G. W. Perpall has lost 7 horses, carried off by the rebels, and 44 slaves who ran off to the Indians who only returned seven of the oldest slaves for whom he had to pay $50.00 apiece, which completely ruined him and lost to him three successive crops. He

had to flee to some land which some friends kindly let him cultivate, and go on raising horses, cows and hogs. He petitions for a service grant of low land and pine land suitable for growing fodder, containing 1,340 acres, as due him, his wife and children. Governor Coppinger, on margin, asks number in his family. G. W. Perpall replies that he has a wife, 6 children between 14 and 1 year, 17 slaves with him who are between 16 and 50 and 37 in the district of the Indians of whom 25 are of age and 12 are between 1 and 14. Governor Coppinger grants, 2/3/1816, 1,340 acres for himself, his wife and 4 children over 8, since according to his oral declaration:these are not yet 16, and 2 negro slaves above this age and 9 that are in the same case as the children. A certificate will be sent. [End of protocol.]

4 [S] Lands in 3 turn out to have been granted to heirs of Tomas Travers, Travers having acquired them from the late Miguel Yshardy. Consequently Perpall petitions for land on River St. Johns in front of Kolls Town, where there is enough land surrounded by vacant land. Governor Coppinger grants, 2/22/1819.

5 [S] Gabriel Perpall, who was granted 1,340 acres of low land and pine wood on the edge of North River as a reward for his services in defense of the province, points out that this land is only good for pasture and he has no sowing land. He adds that for some time and in the present he is doing a service without any advantage to himself or expense to the royal exchequer, viz., permitting his slaves to work without pay on the fortifications. He also took the troops in small boats when they marched against the insurgents of

Fernandina. He has also lost much in the flight of some of his slaves to the Indians and has as yet not been able to get them back. He petitions for 660 acres in absolute property to complete the number of 2,000 acres in the place known as Encinal Grande (Big Oak Wood), 40 miles northwest of the port of Buena Vista, on the west bank of River St. Johns, the measure of the tract beginning at the north port and following the lines of lands conceded to Jose Albarez [Alvarez], Aguilar and Catalina de Los Hijuelos. Governor Coppinger grants, 12/24/1817.

6 [S] Clarke certifies plat of 1,340 acres of land labeled, "Rich Swamp surveyed for G. W. Perpall, 4/15/1818".

[Pasted together 7 and 8 in English:]

7 - Alvarez certifies extract from descriptive list, No. 279, 5/29/1845.

8 - Copy and translation of 6, dated 5/29/1845.

9 [E] Charles C. Tracy certifies plat of 1,422 acres confirmed by Congress to G. W. Perpall, being in Sec. 41, T. 10, R. 27 S&E. Chainmen: John Manuel and Alexander Solano. Butler's signature, 11/13/1848.

[Dossier has Murphy translation of title with Fatio's attest.]

Perpall, G. W.          Con. P 26; DG IV 160

1 [E] claims, 11/10/1823, 660 acres at [crossed out] a place called Big Hammock, 40 miles west of Buena Vista west of St. Johns River, bounded on the north and northwest by lands of Matias Martines, south and southeast by lands of Catalina de Jesus Hijuelos; the other sides are vacant. Governor Coppinger's service grant.

2 [E] G. W. Perpall petitions for survey by Burgevin, now that General Clarke is absent in service. Governor Coppinger agrees, 6/18/1819.

3 [S] Burgevin certifies plat, etc.

4 [E] On petition of Catalina de Jesus Hijuelos, widow, who is the mother of Francisco de Entralgo, formerly a volunteer in the third batallion of Cuba, who died of wounds received while fighting rebels, Governor Coppinger grants, 12/7/1807, 2,000 acres as a gift, countersigned by Tomas de Aguilar, brevet lieutenant of army serving as secretary, whose mother is grantee, and by Alvarez, who attests translation, 2/3/1843.

5 [E] Governor Coppinger's service grant of 660 acres to G. W. Perpall, 1/12/1818. Alvarez attests translation, 2/3/1843.

[Pasted together 6 and 7 in English:]

6 - Alvarez certifies extract from descriptive list, No. 365, 7/9/1845.

7 - Translation and copy of Burgevin's survey, 7/9/1845.

[Dossier has duplicates of 6 and 7, and Murphy translation of all Spanish with Fatio's attests.]

Perpall, G. W.          Con. P 27; DG IV 253 Rept. 8, No, 4, 1824

1 [E] claims a tract 1 mile square, 640 acres, on River St. Sebastian 1 mile southwest of St. Augustine, bounded on the east by rivers Matanzas and St. Sebastian, south by a little creek called Jula, north by another creek called Gonzalez, west by a pine barren. Judicial sale by Governor Quesada to Thomas Travers who sold to George Taylor whose attorney, F. M. Arredondo, Sr., sold to G. W. Perpall.

2 [E] William Reynolds attests government sale, 3/21/1792, to Thomas Travers, who sold to George Taylor, 8/29/1803, according to

records in archives, 9/7/1824.

3 [E] Decree slip of Board finds facts as in 1, and recommends to Congress for confirmation.

[Jacket notes "descriptive list, No. 361".]

Perpall, G. W.            Con. P 28; DG IV 197

1 [E] claims 600 acres at Matanzas River [Bar], to the south of the orange grove called Buen Retiro, bounded on the north and east by public land, south by land of Joseph M. Hernandez, west by the river; Governor White's concession as head rights to Joseph Bonely, who sold to G. W. Perpall, 12/30/1803.

2 [E. Another memorial, not on a blank:]

He came to the province in 1803 under the hope (induced by the dispatch to France of the U. S. brig Horner, Stephen Decatur, commander) that the province soon would be purchased by the U. S. A. He purchased from Joseph Bonely 600 acres in the same year, 1803, as will be seen from the bill of sale enclosed, which although the ten years tenure was unfinished, the government allowed Joseph Bonely to sell on account of his son's being killed by the Indians and the remainder of his family being carried to the natives [residents of Florida].

3 [E] Decree slip confirms.

[Dossier has translation of Bonely's grant and sale.]

Jacket notes "descriptive list, No. 363".

Perpall, G. W.            Con. P 29; DG IV 198

1 [E] claims 535 acres at the head of Matanzas River at a place known as Sam's Hammock, bounded on the north by the head of the river, west by lands of Joseph M. Hernandez and the late Mr. Fish, south and

east by vacant lands; a royal title as head rights by Governor Kindelan to G. W. Perpall.

2 [S] G. W. Perpall petitions for himself and his sister-in-law, Marianna Sams, and states that before he established himself in this province he bought of Carlos Clarke 5 negroes; of Dona Constanza McFee 4; of Jayme Kerr 7; of Juan Wiggens 1; and there have been born to him 6, which makes 23; and that his sister-in-law's family is composed of 9 whites and 10 negroes, which added to his make 33 of which 9 are between 1 and 8. For the remainder, men and women, G. W. Perpall petitions for 450 acres in Mosquitoes in front of his plantation, bordered on the north by Juan Addison, on the south the River Tomoco which in British times was called La Feria [the Fair], and the other 535 acres in the territory of Matanzas in Sam's Hammock in the place that was conceded to Valentin Fitzpatrick which was not occupied and remained vacant, 8/17/1811. Governor Estrada grants 985 acres, which is the exact number for head rights for whites and slaves, 8/17/1811. A penciled notation on back has "985" followed by "450" over "53[?] 5".

3 [E] Murphy translation attested by Fatio. Governor Kindelan's conditions for tenure being fulfilled, he gives royal title to G. W. Perpall for the 535 acres, 5/24/1815.

4 [E] Decree of board confirms.

[Jacket notes descriptive list, No. 359.]

Perpall, G. W.                    Con. P.30; DG IV 202

1 [E] claims 500 acres on Turnbull's Swamp about 12 miles north of St. Augustine, bounded on the west and northwest by Jose M. Bousquet on the east and northeast by "equivocal" grants, other sides by vacant lands; Governor Kindelan's service grant to John Gonzalez Montesdeoca

for land en Matanzas which was proved to belong to Clarke formerly, and which Governor Coppinger permitted him to exchange for the present land.

2 [S] G. W. Perpall petitions Burgevin to survey land granted him in a place called Turnbull. Governor Coppinger grants, 6/12/1818.

3 [S. Enclosed with 2:] Burgevin's certificate of plat of 500 acres in Turnbull's Swamp bordering on west and northwest with lands of Jose M. Bousquet, bought of Jose de Lespine, which before belonged to Diego Guillermo Lee [By mistake there was a change in the title; the next phrase is hardly Spanish but is perfectly good French as was Burgevin, from Orleans; "Here I see 'west' for 'east'".] The plat shows Six Mile Creek on the south border.

[Stitched together 4-6 in Spanish:]

4 – Title page:                    Florida
    G No. 5                       Year 1816

                        Concession made to Jose M. Bousquet of 780 acres in Matanzas Creek, 4 miles north of the Fort.

5 – List of family and slaves that Juan Gonzalez had:

        Maria Carreras, his wife . . . . . . . . . No age shown
        Juan . . . . . . . . . . . . . . . . . . . 20
        Fernando . . . . . . . . . . . . . . . . . 18
        Ysavel . . . . . . . . . . . . . . . . . . 17
        Susana . . . . . . . . . . . . . . . . . . 16
        24 slaves, aged 8 to 60, nearly all above 17 [all but 2], 8/26/1818, by my father, Juan Gonzalez.

6 – Jose Gonzalez Montesdeoca, who served as soldier in the line, later as an officer or in duties set by the government, petitions for acreage proportionate to his family and slaves, next on the north to lands of Margarita Clarke and on the south the cane brake of Matanzas River. Governor Coppinger grants the 780 acres due as head rights,

9/3/1816.

[Stitched together 7-11 in Spanish:]

7 - Title page:                   Florida
    P. No. 18                   Year 1818

G. W. Perpall asking to be returned 780 acres which he bought from John Gonzalez Montesdeoca, conceded to him by this government, and which turned out to belong to others.

8 - John Gonzalez Montesdeoca sells for $100.00 to G. W. Perpall, 11/6/1817. Witnesses: F. M. Arredondo, Jr., Pedro Miranda, Tomas Saavedra. Entralgo attests copy.

9 - G. W. Perpall having bought the land in the enclosed deed of sale, it turns out to belong to Carlos and Jorge Clarke as inheritance from their deceased mother, Honoria Commins, to whom it had belonged since British times. Perpall petitions that this sale be declared null and that he be given instead 200 acres in Sam's Hammack and the rest in Turnbull's plantation, etc., 4/17/1818. Governor Coppinger grants.

10 - Alvarez certifies extract from descriptive list, No. 270.

11 - Alvarez certifies copy of 3.

[Pasted together 12 and 13 in English:]

12 - Another copy of 10.

13 - Alvarez' copy translated from Burgevin's survey. [See confirmed P. 30, No. 3.]

14 [E] Alvarez attests translation of Governor Coppinger's royal title petitioned by G. W. Perpall in exchange for that bought by error.

15 [E] Plat of land unsigned by deputy or surveyor general, confirmed by Congress to G. W. Perpall, being in T. 6, R. 28 S&E, [266.94

acres] and T. 6, R. 29 S&E [286.78] acres.

[Dossier has Murphy translation of all Spanish with Fatio's attestation.]

Perpall, G. W.    Con. P 31; DG IV 198

1 [E] claims 335 acres at a place called Turnbull about 12 miles northwest of St. Augustine, bounded on the south, east and west by lands of Antonio Huertas, north by Picolata Road; Governor Coppinger's royal title, 1/13/1818, to Ramon de Fuentes, who sold to Antonio Mier, 1/23/1818, who sold to Francis Rovira, 4/3/1818, who sold to Joseph Delespine, 4/4/1818, who sold to Jose M. Bousquet, 4/10/1818, who sold to G. W. Perpall, 11/20/1818, who is now in possession. All in accord with abstract of William Reynolds, enclosed.

2 [E] Reynolds' abstract of above.

[Stitched together 3-14 in Spanish, numbered on right hand pages up to 15, which makes 31 pages:]

3 - Title page:                  Florida
                                 Year 1815

F. No. 14                Ramon de Fuentes asking title of
                         335 acres, etc., of which he bought
                         the land and the improvements from
                         Guillermo Lee.

4 - Ramon de Fuente says that the enclosed evidence proves that he has bought from Diego Guillermo Lee the buildings and other imrpovements on the 335 acres which the government conceded to him. By the royal order, communicated 10/29/1790, by the captain general of Cuba and the Two Floridas, to Governor Quesada, land was to be given to applicants, who took the oath of allegiance, in proportion to their workers, to which Governor Quesada of his own authority added the restrictions that the property could not be alienated until the lapse

of ten years, thus carrying out His Majesty's intention to encourage industry and agriculture and prevent speculation. It is well known that Lee, a sworn vassal, was given 335 acres which he cleared and on which he erected buildings and raised livestock, all still existing, to the value of $800.00, as the writer is satisfied. The ten years of tenure having more than passed, the government will see no inconvenience in giving Lee a title, nor in remitting the transfer of the land, since it is not for speculation. Fuentes signs, 6/16/1815. Governor Estrada directs that this petition be passed to the auditor of war. Governor Estrada and Arredondo y San Felices order the appearance of witnesses [Fees: 16 reales.] Entralgo, interim governor, at the dictamen of the auditor of war, 6/17/1815, notifies Fuentes.

5 [S] Royal order: The introduction of families from Ireland that Your Excellency proposes to me cannot take place on any other terms than those which the King has named to me:

> Every immigrant must pay the Royal Treasury for his transportation and that of his belongings here and must have funds to pay for his subsistence for some time. Every stranger who of his own initiative presents himself to take the oath of allegiance will be granted land free in proportion to the number of his workers. He will not be molested in the matter of religion; though there will be no public cult other than the Catholic. He will be given no help except land, protection and good treatment. Any family can take its property elsewhere with no restrictions, other than the payment of six per cent export duty on its value. He will be obliged to take up arms only in case of invasion.

Limit yourself to these provisions. God guide Your Excellency many years. Havana, 10/19/1790. Luis de Las Casas to Senor Don Juan Nepomuceno de Quesada. This is a copy of the original from the secretary's office temporarily in my charge. Kindly forward a copy of the government notary. Don Domingo Rodriguez de Leon, St. Augustine, 7/15/1791. Manuel Rengil.

6 - The statement of conditions of grant.

7 - Deed of sale: Francis Rovira of this city, attorney of Diego Guillermo Lee, now in Havana, sells to Ramon de Fuentes buildings, fences, groves and other improvements on the land, 335 acres for $800.00 paid. Witnesses present: Jose Mariano Hernandez, Gabriel Guillermo Perpall, Fernando de la Maza Arredondo, Jr. Before Entralgo, *interim* government notary.

8 - Aguilar certifies, 3/14/1812, that on the memorial of Diego Guillermo Lee, 1/30/ult., asking to be granted 400 acres at Turnbull about 12 miles distant where Felipe Roberto Yonge had a cow-pen which is now vacant, Governor Estrada granted 335 acres, the quota for Lee, his wife and 11 slaves.

9 - Francisco Rovira, attorney of Diego G. Lee, asks the government for permit for sale he has contracted with Ramon de Fuentes for the improvements on 335 acres granted him. Governor Estrada orders the request passed to the auditor of war. Governor Estrada and Arredondo y San Felices ask to see power of attorney. Fee: 12 *reales*.

10 - Diego Guillermo Lee, power [4 pp.] to Francisco Rovira. Witnesses: Juan de Entralgo, Bernardino Sanchez and Juan Xavier de Arrambide. Before Jose de Zubizarreta, notary *pro tem* of government. The sale is permitted as Entralgo attests.

11 - Ramon de Fuentes having been permitted the sale by the Auditor of War, who has since been ill and has gone to Havana and so cannot legalize it, petitions to have the transaction regularized by the notary of the government. Governor Coppinger agrees, 1/7/1818.

12 - Ramon de Fuentes presents Francisco Ferreyra, married, planter,

25, who swears that Lee was complying with conditions prescribed and had built his cow-pen when the insurrection and invasion obliged him to withdraw with his slaves.

13 - Felipe Solano, married, 29, saw the improvements and cow-pen made by Lee, and the building erected by the slaves.

14 - Fernando de la Maza Arredondo, Jr., married, 29, swears he had several times visited the plantation and seen the improvements made before Lee was obliged to withdraw his slaves. Governor Coppinger will order title sent, Entralgo notifies Ramon de Fuentes.

[Pasted together 15-16 in English:]

15 - Alvarez' attested translation of Governor Coppinger's grant to Ramon de Fuentes.

16 - Alvarez' attested translation of Burgevin's attestation of plat to Jose Maria Bousquet which he bought of Jose Delespine. [Plat attested by Fatio is crossed out.]

17 [E] Alvarez' attested translation of Governor Coppinger's title to Ramon de Fuentes.

18 [E] Alvarez' attested extract from descriptive list, No. 362, 355 acres, confirmed to G. W. Perpall.

19 [E] Alvarez' certified translation of Burgevin's certified plat, land of Jose Maria Bousquet bought of Jose Delespine.

20 [E] Board confirms on the evidence.

21 [E] Unsigned plat in conformity with Report 1, claim 50, 1825. Confirmed by Congress to G. W. Perpall, being in T. 6, R. 28 S&E.

[Dossier has Murphy translation of all Spanish documents with Fatio's attest and another of Alvarez' certified extracts from descriptive list, No. 362.]

Perpall, G. W.    Con. P. 32; DG IV 202

1 [E] claims 280 acres at Sam's Hammock, head of Matanzas River, bounded on the southeast by vacant lands, southwest by George J. F. Clarke and Jesse Fish; southeast by lands of G. W. Perpall. Sold by John Gonzalez Montesdeoca who received 780 acres as a service grant in 1816. Governor Kindelan gave title but survey showed the land belonged to the Clarke family. Governor Coppinger permitted survey. Land in actual possession of the claimant.

[Pasted together 2-4 in English:]

2 - Antonio Alvarez certifies extract from descriptive list, No. 277, 5/8/1845.

3 - Alvarez certifies translation of G. W. Perpall's memorial that land granted on service grant to John Gonzalez Montesdeoca, who sold to G. W. Perpall as per deed enclosed, turned out to belong to Carlos and George Clarke as inheritance from their mother, Honoria Comings, who had it from English times, whereupon G. W. Perpall petitioned that duplicate of Montesdeoca be marked null by the secretary and that G. W. Perpall be granted 280 acres at Sam's Hammack at the head of the Matanzas River and 500 acres at Turnbull Plantation about 12 miles north of St. Augustine, bounded on the north and east by lands granted to Diego Guillermo Lee. Governor Coppinger grants, 4/17/1818. Alvarez attests, 5/28/1845. [Note in pencil on back:] Sam's Hammack tract surveyed 300.72 acres, Sec. 45, T. 11, R. 31 S&E, and in ink above "change of location, etc."

4 - Alvarez' copy of certified plat of 280 acres confirmed to G. W.

Perpall.

[Jacket notes in ink: "Same papers as No. 476"; and in pencil: "See bundle No. 70 for one paper in this claim".]

Perpall, G. W.   Con. P 33; DG IV 199

1 [E] claims 150 acres on River Halifax opposite Mount Oswald, bounded on the east by Sea Beach, west by the river, on other sides by vacant lands. Governor Kindelan's grant as head rights; now in actual possession of the claimant.

[Stitched together 2-9 in Spanish:]

2 - Title page:                Florida
                               Year 1815

P. No. 7        G. W. Perpall asking title to 1,900
                acres at Mosquitoes in a district
                called Mount Oswald, and 150 on its
                beach in front.

3 - Juan Purcell plat [20" x 16"] torn and stuck together with slips of paper; no certification. In upper right hand corner is the title:

Plat which denotes the form of Mount Hoswell [Oswald], situated on the Halifax and Tomoca Rivers, belonging to land conceded to G. W. Perpall, contains 1,900 acres. St. Augustine, 10/20/1803.

Plat shows the peninsula of Mount Oswald between the two rivers. The flow of currents is shown by arrows. In upper left hand corner is legend: Landing on point, and houses near it, land near is cultivated. A trench between the two rivers bounds it. Piney woods and Mount Oswald are indicated.

4 - Pierra's certificate of Governor White's grant of land in proportion to the number of workers G. W. Perpall may have.

5 - Another Pierra certificate, 9/27/1803. Governor White limits the

land conceded to 150 acres, quota of G. W. Perpall, who asked for 300 acres for his wife's aunt, Susannah Doud, widow of Seth Doud, and 4 negroes.

5b - G. W. Perpall, on 7/21/1803, was conceded 1,900 acres in accord with certificate and plat enclosed.

6 - G. W. Perpall, who was granted 1,900 acres at Mount Oswald between the rivers Alipax [Halifax] and Tomoca, bounded on the south by land since granted to Enrique Yonge, who on 9/27/ petitioned for 300 acres for his sister-in-law, Susana Doud, who was only given 150 acres, bounded on the east by the beach, north and south by vacant lands, and west by the river, and this lady having died, found himself with sufficient laborers to cultivate the land and took charge; and these lands are included in the accompanying plan marked with three little houses which are found there [marked on plan; on east shore of Halifax River.] Having cultivated them continuously he petitions with the usual formalities for title to the 2,000, 20 and 50 acres. St. Augustine, 3/9/1815. Attest - "20 doesn't count". Governor Kindelan refers petition to auditor of war; the governor and Arredondo y San Felices ask for conditions of grant, which Entralgo states in the next two pages.

7 - Jose Mariano Hernandez, married, neighbor, 27, swears before Arredondo and Entralgo that he has been there several times, saw the plantation of Mount Oswald, and found the land opposite on the beach cultivated, improved, etc.

8 - F. M. Arredondo, Jr., married, native, 28, has been sent there various times on commissions for his father and has seen conditions that deserves a title.

9 - Juan Huertas, married, farmer, 25, swears to conditions fulfilled. Governor Kindelan and Arredondo grant title, 5/24/1815, as Entralgo attests.

10 [E] Alvarez certifies translation of Governor Kindelan's title, 11/13/1845.

11 [E. On paper 20" x 16", actual writing covering a space of 7" x 4";] Randolph certifies plat of 131.17 acres confirmed by Congress to G. W. Perpall, being in Sec. 41, T. 13, R. 26 S&E.

[Dossier has Murphy translation of all Spanish documents with Fatio's attestation and decree slip of board confirming.]

Perpall, G. W.      Con. P 34; DG V 65

1 [E] claims 100 acres at Little Matanzas Bar, land called Buen Retiro, situated opposite land of Francisco Pellicer.

2 [S] Pierra certifies that Juan Daly petitioned for 100 acres at Barra Chica on Matanzas, next to Franco Pellicer, giving up the 200 acres that he had on River Nassau, and that Governor White granted the land to Maria Daly, widow of the deceased, 3/9/1808.

3 [S] Maria Daly, widow, sells, 6/10/1808, to G. W. Perpall for $120 in hand the land granted by the government on 3/14/1799 and gives him her certificate that he may prove title when 10 years is up. Entralgo signs for Maria Daly who cannot write.

4 [E] Board confirms.

[Dossier has translation of 2 and 3. Jacket refers to descriptive list, No. 620.]

Perpall, G. W.      Con. P 35; DG V 66

1 [E] claims on regular blank for U. S. Commissioners: [For

more complete details see 2 E.]

2 [E] G. W. Perpall claims through William Reynolds, 11/10/1824: 20 acres about 1 1/2 miles north of the Castle of St. Augustine in front of the stockade, bounded on the east by Capuaca Road, north by an old road which comes out of Capuaca Road, west by the St. Nicholas - St. Diego Road, south [not described]: Governor White's head rights, 8/13/1800, to John Capo who sold to Jose Sanchez as per translation of bill of sale enclosed, whose widow and executor, 6/12/1820, sold to G. W. Perpall. Title confirmed to her by Governor Coppinger, 6/10/1818.

3 [S] Juan Capo points out that 2 miles distant from the Hornwork [bastion] on the west of the road that goes to the ranch of Capuaca and north of lands of the late Juan Sanchez is a piece of land about 20 acres that seems cultivated by nobody and not used by anyone in the service of the King, but which will suffice to maintain his wife and nurseling child. He petitions for this land, 8/20/1800. Governor White grants and Pierra sends certificate, 8/31/1800.

4 [S] Governor Coppinger's title to Jose Sanchez who bought of John Capo, 6/10/1810, as per deed enclosed by Christina Hill, widow of Jose Sanchez, 6/10/1818. Entralgo attests.

5 [E] Burgevin certifies plat, 3/1/1820, of 20 acres 1 1/2 miles north of St. Augustine on River of the Fair and Capuaca Road, surveyed for the widow and heirs of Jose Sanchez. The plat shows the highway to Capuaca on the east, the old trail on the north is the road to San Nicolas and San Diego, along the beach next to the River San Sebastian and of the Fair. [Ferry ?]

6 [S] Christina Hill sells to G. W. Perpall for $100.00.

Witnesses: Pedro Miranda, Jose Lubian, Bernardo Reyes. Entralgo attests.

7 [E] Alvarez certifies extract from descriptive list, No. 621.

8 [E and S] William Reynolds certifies extract, 9/15/1824, from original will of Jose Sanchez, St. Augustine, 9/21/1824: "And I declare that I am married to Christina Hill, from which we have legitimate children, Francisco, Jose, Ramon, Santiago, Venancio, Maria Fermina and Maria Florancia. And I name as my executors and custodians of property first and above mentioned, my wife, Christina Hill, the second, G. W. Perpall to whom I give my power of attorney."

[Dossier has decree slip of board and translation of all Spanish documents.]

Perpall, G. W.     Con. P 36; DG IV 243

1 [E] claims, through William Reynolds, 16 acres about 1 mile north of the Town Gate, bounded on the north by lands of the late Jose Sanchez, east by Capuaca Road, south by lands formerly belonging to Peter Triay, west by St. Nicolas Road. Governor White's head rights, 2/16/1815, and Governor Coppinger's title, 6/19/1818, both to Diego Carreras, who sold to G. W. Perpall, 4/23/1819, who is now in possession.

[Stitched together 2-4 in Spanish:]

2 - Title page:                        Florida
                                       Year 1818

  C. No. 25            G. W. Perpall as attorney of Diego
                       Carreras asking title of 16 acres
                       that the government conceded to him
                       about 2 miles north of this place
                       in the district called Chaparral.

3 - Diego Carreras as shown by enclosed certificate was given land on 10/4/1796 and allowed to establish himself with his family in

Mosquitoes on the north where was a Catholic church. He cultivated the land for the first two years, but having suffered some misfortune, and finding it impossible to cultivate this land with only two negroes, he begs to turn in this tract and receive in exchange 16 acres now vacant about 2 miles to the north of this place at a district called Chaparral on the San Sebastian River, bounded on the north with land conceded to Juan Capo, east by highway that goes to Capuaca, south by another road, and west by margin of said river, which is sufficient for the cultivation of the two negroes, and conforms to chapter 6 of the new regulations for settlers. Jose Bernardo Reyes writes at the request of Diego Carreras, 2/6/1805. Governor White grants. Aguilar attests copy.

4 - G. W. Perpall with power of attorney from Diego Carreras petitions for title since he has fulfilled conditions and asks title without further formality on account of the small acreage. On margin Governor Coppinger grants, 6/10/1818.

5 [E] Murphy translation of deed of sale [missing], Diego Carreras to G. W. Perpall for $100.00. Witnesses: Patricio Lynch, Andres Burgevin, Pedro Miranda, before Juan de Entralgo who attests copy. Fatio attests translation.

6 [E] Alvarez certifies extract, 12/9/1834, from descriptive list, No. 251.

7 [E] Murphy translation of Burgevin survey of 2/15/1819.

8 [E] Board confirms. Many of these English papers call the [Tamoka] river De La Feria, "The Ferry River."

[Dossier has translation by Murphy of all Spanish documents.]

Perpall, G. W.                    Con. P 38; DG IV 198

1 [E] claims 8 1/2 acres about 1 mile north of the Gate of St. Augustine, bounded on the north by land lately belonging to Diego Carreras, south and west by St. Nicholas road, east by Capuaca Road; Governor White's title to Pedro Triay who sold to Lucas Munuz from whom G. W. Perpall purchased as shown by receipt No. 14.

2 [S] Pierra certifies that Pedro Triay petitioned for Martin Pellicer's land on account of Martin Pellicer having sold it, without the government's permission, to Manuel Bendicho; and Governor White ordered Martin Pellicer to return the land certificate issued him by the secretary's office, and granted it to Pedro Triay, but warned him that unless the land is cultivated he will lose it, and no other land will be granted him elsewhere in the future, 9/30/1805.

3 [E] Murphy translation of receipts marked "B & C". "A" is missing.

      Extract B: Pedro Triay received of Lucas Munuz $20.00. Havana, 13th January, 1820.

      Extract C: Received from G. W. Perpall $20.00 for a piece of land in the northwest corner of the 1,500 yards (*), which is said to contain 25 acres, promising a deed when required, 2/20/1820. Written by Anthelm Gay for Lewis Munuz who cannot write. Witness: Mateo Somellar.

4 [E] Alvarez certifies abstract, 12/9/1834, of papers in archive "No. 360. G. W. Perpall, 8 1/2 acres, concession dated 9/30/1806. No survey."

[Dossier has decree slip of board and translation of 2.]

---

* The Mil y quinientas.

Perpall, G. W.                    Con. P 39; DG IV 198

1 [E] claims a small island of 1 acre in Matanzas River opposite the orange grove of Bueno Retiro; Governor Coppinger's royal grant as head rights, 1/15/1818.

2 [S] G. W. Perpall petitions for a small Key of about 1 acre, at highwater mark, in the Matanzas River in front of his plantation and northwest of the orange grove, which isle is of use only as G. W. Perpall uses it, for raising pigs, being only a pasture of mangles [a water weed]. He petitions for royal title which Governor Coppinger concedes 12/15/1817.

3 [E] Murphy translation of Governor Coppinger's title attested by Entralgo and by Fatio.

4 [E] Alvarez certifies extract from descriptive list, No. 364, 1 acre to G. W. Perpall, 5/30/1845.

5 [E. Pasted to 4:] Alvarez' attested translation of 3.

Petty, Sarah                      Con. P 40; DG IV 211

1 [E] claims, through John B. Strong, 8 caballerias and 2 acres on Julington Creek. One line borders on land of Alexander Creighton. Title, a Marrot-Eastlake certified plat of 1793. George Long having died, his property was left to his heirs, Christina Long, Mathew Long, Joseph Long and Samuel Long, who sold to Sarah Petty on 11/26/1821, as shown by deed enclosed and attached to survey.

2 [E] Joseph Summerall swears before John B. Strong, judge of county court, that Sarah Petty is the only heir and daughter of John Houston, who in his lifetime owned two tracts of land on St. Marys River of about 200 acres each, the first being 1 or 2 miles above the

mouth of Little St. Marys at Loftin's Bluff where he had a house and lived. He began his settlement about 1788 or 1789 and occupied the land until killed by the Indians in 1793. The other tract is about 18 or 20 miles by land above the last mentioned place. Houston lived there at the time of the British, and from about 1783 to 1789 when the Indians became troublesome and he moved to the other tract. After the Indian troubles he cultivated both tracts. The last tract was called Hickory Grove, but he had houses at both places. Joseph Summerall lived at the time at Trader's Hill and often visited both places. Joseph Summerall also knows another place claimed by Sarah Petty on St. Johns River, about 150 acres, called Bueno Vista, which was granted to Thomas Rogers, who sold to Elizabeth Houston, who was the mother of Sarah Petty. Elizabeth Houston cultivated the tract about 6 years, 1806-1812, when she moved further down the river and died. Joseph Summerall also knows a tract of 250 to 260 acres where Sarah Petty now lives with her family of negroes. This tract she bought in 1821 of the heirs of George Long who had lived there for 20 or 30 years. George Long had four children--Mathew, Joseph, Margaret and Jane, 12/23/1823.

[Pasted together 3-4 in Spanish:]

3 - Heirs of George Long sell to Sarah Petty for $800.00 cash the house and lands where they live. Witnesses: Joseph Summerall, Moses Bowden, James Hall, 11/26[?]/1821.

4 - Marrot-Dupont certified plat.

5 [S] David Thomas' certified plat of 291.37 acres confirmed by Congress to Sarah Petty, being in Sec. 24, T. 4, R. 26, and Sec. 19, T. 4, R. 27 S&E, June 1833. Chainmen: R. W. Green and William O'Neall.

[Dossier has translation of 4 and decree slip.]

Petty, Sarah                    Con. P 41; DG IV 207

1 [E] The only heir of John Houston, deceased, claims, through John B. Strong, 6 caballerias [200 acres] on River St. Marys, surveyed to her father by Marrot-Eastlake in 1792. Her father lived there until murdered by the Indians and the others left in fear. The place has since been occupied by Hobkirk and others, 9/26/1828. The tract adjoins lands of the John Forrester.

2 [S] Marrot-Eastlake's certified plat, 3/30/1792.

3 [S] Samuel Smith deposes before Fairbanks, J. P., 12/7/1823, that he knew John Houston who about 1789 to 1793 lived on the farther side of the river and had two separate houses on the river, --one at a bluff a little above the mouth of Little St. Marys and the other about 20 miles up,--land that was claimed by George Petty in behalf of his wife.

[Pasted together 4 and 5 in English:]

4 - Antonio Alvarez' certified extract from descriptive list, No. 273, 3/5/1845.

5 - Alvarez' translation of 2.

[Dossier has Murphy translation of 2 and decree slip.]

Petty, Sarah                    Con. P 42; DG IV 206

1 [E] claims, through John B. Strong, 200 acres on River St. Marys, a Marrot-Eastlake survey to John Houston, whose heir is Sarah Petty.

2 [S] Marrot's certified plat.

3 [E] Sarah Faulk Petty deposes before Samuel Fairbanks, Justice of the Peace, 12/10/1823, that she was well acquainted with John Houston in 1793, who lived at Lofton's Bluff about 3 miles above the mouth

of Little St. Marys River on the southern bank, and that he occupied a place on the same side about 20 miles above Hickory Grove, which two tracts of land she lived on for 8 years. She stated that she and Houston obtained the land from the Spanish government and George Petty claimed in her behalf.

[Pasted together 4 and 5 in English:]

4 - Alvarez' certified extract from descriptive list, No. 274, 2/27/1845.

5 - Translation of 2. [Board confirms 2 and 3. Dossier has translation of 2.]

Petty, Sarah             Con. P 43; DG IV 206

1 [E] claims, 8/20/1823, through John B. Strong, 150 acres, bounds not known, never surveyed, on St. Johns River near Buena Vista, which she got as only heir to her mother, Elizabeth Houston, who bought of Thomas Rodgers, 11/4/1805, who had it from the Spanish government. She held it until driven out by the troubles in 1812.

[Stuck together with seals, 2 and 3:]

2 [E] "Received of Mrs. Houston, his houses and chene [china?] orange trees and all other improvements and an order to Mr. Lewis for seisin [possession] of four or five shoats for my house and other improvements laying near Buen Bisto [Buena Vista] by the little orange grove; when the above mentioned order is paid will be in full received by me." Thomas Rodgers, 10/4/1805.

3 [S] Pierra certifies, 9/8/1804, that Thomas Rodgers petitioned for 100 acres for himself and 2 negroes which he claimed to have, but Governor White granted only 50 acres, since he found that Thomas

Rodgers had no slaves.

    4 [E] Decree slip confirms 50 acres. [Note on back of 3 shows T. Rodgers and E. Houston exchanged land. Descriptive list, No. 263.]

    [Dossier contains Thomas Murphy's translation of 3.]

Philibert, Pedro           Con. P 44; DG IV 102

    1 [E] Register's Office, Tallahassee. Claim of Philibert and Dominguez in Sec. 7, T. 1, R. 28 S&W; Sec. 4, T. 1, R. 29 S&W; Sec. 2, T. 1, R. 29 N&W, containing 678.40 acres on Bayou Mulatto, was reported by the commissioners of West Florida in report A. No. 37, and confirmed by Congress; a patent will be issued to Pedro Philibert.

    2 [E] Exum's certified plat, 4th quarter 1827, signed by Robert Butler. Chainmen: Enos Evans and John Byrd. Plat [mutilated] shows Bayou Mulatto on the north, Escambia Bay and Indian Bayou on the south; Antonio Pol on the east and vacant lands on the west.

Philibert, Pedro           Con. P 45; DG IV 106

    1 [E] certificate of Register's Office, Tallahassee. Pedro Philibert claims from Manuel Rodriguez 676.94 acres on Bayou Mulatto, north side in Sec. 35, T. 1, R. 29 N&W.

    3 [E] Clements' certified plat with Butler's signature, 2/18/1828, of 676.94 acres confirmed to Philibert, in Sec. 35, T. 1, R. 29 N&W. Plat shows north line vacant, east partly vacant and lands of Lorenzo Bacum [?], south Bayou Mulatto, west Henry Wilson, northwest vacant lands.

Philips, Joseph, Heirs of,     Con. P 46; DG IV 103

    1 [E] James W. Exum certifies plat of 456.20 acres on the margin of Pensacola Bay, confirmed by commissioners and Congress to Joseph

Philips' heirs, being at the mouth of Bayou Taxar, in Sec. 5, T. 2, R. 29 S&W. The plat shows Joseph Antonio Miralla at the northeast, the Bay at the southeast, the Bayou west. The plat is countersigned by Butler. Chainmen: Frederic Ming and Wesley Inglish.

[Jacket notes 400 arpen* claimed. Manuel Gonzalez, claimant.]

Pickett, Seymour          Con. P 47, DG V 69

1 [E] claims 640 acres, a donation grant, on Rains Branch, which is a part of Trout Creek into which it empties. The tract was settled and improved since 1819. [The writing is in Fatio's hand.]

2 [E. First two lines in Fatio's hand, remainder in Charles Downing's:] Charles W. Clarke swears before the Board in Session that about 15 years ago he surveyed Sibbald's tract on which Seymour Pickett has lived for 11 or 12 years. Pickett has 8 negroes, a white family of 8 and has no English or Spanish grant elsewhere. Seymour Pickett swears the same. Both before Charles Downing, 10/28/1827.

3 [E. Fatio's writing:] William Silcock swears that he knows Seymour Pickett, who is head of a family and over 21, has a place on the South Prong of Six Mile Creek, occupied since before 2/22/1819,** and claims no land elsewhere. William Carter attests above. Before the Board in Session, 5/18/1825.

4 [E] Seymour Pickett deposes that the claim of 350 acres confirmed to him on the river a little west of Mosquitoes, number 103 on abstract No. 1 of the Report of the Commissioners of East Florida, and acted on by Congress was placed on file before the Board without

---

\* An arpen was about .84 of an acre.
\*\* For terms of the "Donation Act" see pp. xlvi-xlvii.

his knowledge or consent, that he has never had any title or claim to said grant but whatever right or title he may have by the confirmation above he relinquishes. The claim was found and presented without his knowledge. He had a claim before the cession, but abandoned it. He asks that his donation claim be confirmed to him. Before Charles Downing, 12/27/1827.

5 [E] Henry Washington's certified plat with Robert Butler's signature, January 1834, 640 acres confirmed to Seymour Pickett, being in T. 1, R. 25, T. 1, R. 26, T. 2, R. 25, and T. 2, R. 26 S&E. The plat shows Lane's Branch *alias* Six Mile Creek at the north end. King's Road cuts the northeast corner.

6 [E] Unsigned and uncertified plat shows Sibbald's claim to the north and east and claim of Lane to the northeast.

[Jacket notes: Descriptive list, No. 622, illegal. Seymour Pickett has other lands, see 48 and 49.]

Pickett, Seymour                    Con. P 48; DG IV 212

1 [E] claims, through John B. Strong, 350 acres at New Smyrna in Mosquitoes, bounded by the canal, Governor White's head rights, held and cultivated by Seymour Pickett until houses were all burned and inhabitants fled in 1808. After the cession he again took possession and put Jeremiah Ives in as tenant. St. Augustine, 8/16/1823. Since making out the above, a survey has been found. The land is bounded on the north by Robert Shippard, east by Mosquito River, south by the land of John Addison, west by vacant land.

2 [S. On green paper:] Seymour Pickett wishes to dedicate himself to agriculture and petitions for 350 acres on the shore of Hillsborough *rio* beginning at the canal or *zanja*. Governor White

grants the quota according to the number of laborers, 9/3/1803. Pierra sent certificate.

3 [E] Translation of 2 in unknown hand, attested by F. J. Fatio.

4 [E. On back of 3:] Murphy translation of Purcell's certification of plat for 350 acres to Seymour Pickett, 5/20/1804. Attested by Fatio.

[Dossier has William Reynolds' copy of 2 and decree slip. Jacket notes descriptive list, No. 269.]

Pickett, Seymour          Con. P 49; DG IV 280

1 [E. Upper corners torn off:] claims through John B. Strong, 250 acres at a place called Hodguin's Plantation, Governor Kindelan's grant of head rights to Reuben Hogan, who sold to Seymour Pickett. [On same paper 2 and 3.]

2 [E] Reuben Hogan acknowledges before D. S. H. Miller, acting judge, receipt of $200.00 from Seymour Pickett for 250 acres sold to Pickett.

3 [S] Copy of Governor Kindelan's royal title to Reuben Hogan of 9 caballerias of land at Hodguin's, according to Marrot-Eastlake plat [missing]. Entralgo attests copy, 5/26/1815.

[Dossier has Murphy translation of 3 with Fatio's attest of same and confirmation slip. Descriptive list, No. 268.]

Pintado, Vicente Sebastian        Con. P 50

[This claim has two jackets, numbered 46 and 50. No. 46 shows 2,110.06 acres confirmed by the U. S. Commissioners for West Florida, as referred to in DG IV 157 and discussed at length in DG IV 118, 119. The claim was found illegal under an old Roman law. The jacket of No. 50 is marked confirmed, 6 lots on Pensacola, in the space between Seville Square and the Bay; 2,110.06 (acres) confirmed; 10,000 arpens in different places including 19 <u>arpens</u> adjoining Pensacola on the west.]

1 [E] Certificate of register's office, Tallahassee, signed G. W. Ward, that Sec. 17, T. 1, R. 29 S&W, Sec. 3, T. 2, R. 29 S&W, Sec. 33, T. 1, R. 30 S&W and Sec. 1, T. 2, R. 30 S&W, containing 2,110.06 acres are confirmed to Vicente Sebastian Pintado. [A penciled estimate seems to reduce this to 2,070.81 acres.]

2 [E] Unsigned, undated plat of 1817, of 19 <u>arpanas</u> [<u>arpens</u>] surveyed to Vicente Sebastian Pintado. The plat shows the rivulet of the washerwomen from its mouth on Pensacola Bay to Pedro Riggio's lot, and the tannery on the edge of Forbes' property. Another rivulet of the washerwomen on the west is the boundary of the land of Brigadier St. Maxent. Dimensions are in English feet and inches, the scale used for city lots.

3 [E] James W. Exum's certified plat of 1825 with Butler's signature. Chainmen: Frederic Ming and Wesley Inglish. Plat shows Bayou Texar on the southwest, called Indian Pass, Lorenzo on the northwest, Vetrian [?] on the east, Joseph M. Miralla on the southeast, the heirs of Joseph Philips on the west.

Playm, Andrew     Con. P 51; DG IV 205

1 [E] claims, through John B. Strong, 500 acres at Doctor's Lake on St. Johns River, formerly occupied by Christopher Nelly during the British occupation and never surveyed; Governor Quesada's grant as head rights, 2/10/1791. It was occupied by Andrew Playm until the revolution of 1794 when all inhabitants were ordered to the east side of the river, and gunboats destroyed all improvements, 10/10/1823.

2 [S] Andrew Pleym petitions for 500 acres for self, 15 negroes, 3 horses, 2 plows and various other farming tools, 2/8/1791. Governor Quesada grants.

3 [E] Joseph Summerall deposes before Strong that he is well acquainted with Andrew Pleym and the tract of land on an island in Doctor's Lake. Andrew Pleym settled there about 1789 and lived there until disturbances called Wagner's War in 1794. Andrew Pleym built a house and had about 20 acres under cultivation, 12/24/1823.

4 [S] Copy of 2, certified by William Reynolds, 7/28/1823.

5 [E] Translation of 2 certified by Reynolds, 7/28/1825. This is again certified by Pedro Lynch, whose name is crossed out by Fatio who signs below, 2/5/1824.

6 [E] Alvarez attests extract from descriptive list, No. 270, 12/19/1844.

7 [E. Pasted to 5.] Translation of 2.

8 [E] Unsigned and uncertified plat of land confirmed by Congress to heirs of Andrew Pleym, being in T. 4, and T. 26 S&E. [Attached to 7 by a very rusty clip is a blue print of plat.]

Plummer, James    Con. P 52; DG IV 281

1 [E] claims, through Clarke, 300 acres north of Julington Creek at St. Johns River, bounded on the north and east by Robert Prichard; Governor Coppinger's grant as head rights according to Clarke's survey

2 [S] Clarke's certified plat alleging "disposition of S. S. [His Excellency] of 10/20/1817."* Signed 7/18/1819.

3 [E] David Thomas, deputy surveyor, certifies plat of 281.51 acres confirmed by Congress to James Plummer, being in Secs. 21 and

---

* Supra, p. lv.

22, T. 4, R. 27 S&E, June 1833. Chainmen: R. W. Green and William O'Neill.

[Dossier has another duplicate of Clarke's plat, a Murphy translation of same and decree slip in Murphy's hand, 11/4/1825.]

Plummer, Prudence          Con. P 53; DG IV 278

1 [E] Prudence Plummer, widow of Daniel Plummer, deceased, claims through John Rodman, 350 acres at a place called Montpellier, east of St. Johns River and bordering lands of Isaac Bowden and Aron Travers; head rights of 1792 to Samuel Eastlake, who did not comply with conditions. Governor White granted it to Prudence Plummer in whose possession it has been ever since.

2 [S] Marrot-Eastlake's certified plat, 1/6/1792, of 10 caballerias and 17 acres conceded to Samuel Eastlake for self, wife and 2 slaves. William Reynolds attests, 9/12/1823.

3 [S] Jose de Ortega, lawyer of the royal counsel and of His Majesty's dominions in the Indies, lieutenant governor, auditor of war, and assessor general of this city and the Province, and charged with the command during the illness of Governor White, having seen the claims made by Juan Salom as husband of Ana Eastlake against Prudence Plummer, widow of Daniel Plummer, represented by Juan Gianopoly, trying to dislodge Prudence Plummer from the plantation she is cultivating, claiming that the land is his, having been granted to his father-in-law, Samuel Eastlake, and claiming that it descended to his wife as her property, His Excellency says that Juan Salom has not proved his claim to the land called Montpellier, for such land was not transmissible until after ten years of uninterrupted tenure which she has proved and he has not, and she deserves protection. Besides, Prudence Plummer has promised a certain gratification in

maize to be left undisturbed. Although the Governor finds in Prudence Plummer's favor, she is condemned to pay, in token of gratitude, to the widow of Eastlake, if she still lives, or in case of her death to the heirs including the wife of Juan Salom, 50 bushels of maize of the next harvest or its equivalent in cash, and she is assessed the costs of this trial. Before Zubizarreta, 9/7/1800, who attests action and notifies Juan Gianopoly through Juan Salom who found him absent in the country. William Reynolds attests copy, 9/12/1823.

4 [E] David Thomas certifies plat, May 1833, 292.70 acres confirmed by Congress to Prudence Plummer. Chainmen: R. W. Green and Augustus Tibbits.

[Dossier has translation of all Spanish documents.]

Pol, Antonio                    Con. P 54; DG IV 102

1 [E] James W. Exum's certified plat of 645.50 acres confirmed to Antonio Pol by Congress, being on the southern margin of Bayou Mulatto, Sec. 39, T. 1, R. 28; Sec. 1, T. 1, R. 28, and Sec. 1, T. 1, R. 29 S&W. Signed by Robert Butler. The plat shows Maria R. Murrell on the east and south; Pedro Philibert on the west.

[Jacket notes 800 arpens claimed.]

Pol, Josefa                     Con. P 55; DG IV 105

1 [E] Clements-Exum certified plat of 676.98 acres confirmed by Congress to Josefa Pol, being Sec. 37, T. 2, R. 31 S&W. Chainmen: James M. Sawyers and Andrew A. Crawford. The plat shows Santiago Coleman on the west side with all other sides vacant.

[Dossier has duplicate of 1.]

Pons, Antonio, Widow and Heirs of    Con. P 56; DG V 65

1 [E] claim, through Richard Murray, 175 acres at the mouth of

Halifax River south of St. Augustine, bounded on the north by vacant land, south by district known as Mosquitoes or New Smyrna, east by the ocean, west by the river; granted 10/11/1803, to Antonio Pons.

2 [S. weevil eaten on edges:] Antonio Pons has heard there is vacant land at Mosquitoes at the Orange Grove near the Bar, and petitions for 400 acres for himself and his wife and 7 children, aged 2 to 14 [shown in list on next page]. Francis Marcen signs for Antonio Pons who cannot write. Governor White concedes 175 acres in accord with new regulations. Pierra sends certificate.

3 [S] Robert McHardy's certified plat of 5/20/1819.

4 [S] Governor Coppinger's service grant [$3\frac{1}{2}$ pp.] of 5/25/1819.

5 [E] Joseph Baya swears before W. H. Allen, 12/24/1824, that ke knows Antonio Pons, who built a house and occupied the land until the Indians drove him off.

[fastened together 6-13:in English:]

5 - Title page:                       Florida
                                    Year 1819

                                Benita Usina soliciting title of absolute ownership of property conceded to her deceased husband [Antonio Pons].

7 - Translations of Pierra's certificate.

8 - Bartolome de Castro y Ferrer certifies to the governor that Antonio Pons occupied the land granted him until driven out; he served in the militia in 1812 and was assassinated by colored troops of the battalion one night when he was in the besieging lines, and his widow in entitled to more land. Governor Coppinger grants the 175 acres.

9 - McHardy is named to make the survey and accepts; Entralgo attests.

10 - McHardy's certified plat.

11 - McHardy's plat.

12 - Translation of title.

13 - Claim to U. S. Commissioners. On the back the surveyor general attests copy.

14 [E] Pasted together.] Alvarez' certified translation of 2 and 9.

15 [E] A. M. Randolph's certified plat of 320 acres confirmed by Congress to Antonio Pons, being in T. 16, R. 34 S&E.

[Dossier has translation of 2 and 7.]

Pons, Mathias, Heirs of          Con. P 57; DG IV 280

1 [E] claim, through Francis Marin, 400 acres on River Matanzas at a place called Cassa Pula, bounded on the north by lands of Fernando Fallary [?], east by the river, south by lands of Pedro Choot [?], west by vacant lands; a royal title, 9/17/1814, based on head rights; Governor Kindelan's grant to Mathias Pons, who departed this life leaving Antonia Pons, wife of Francis Marin, Agaty Pons, Francis Pons and Peter Pons, his children and heirs.

[Stitched together 2-10 in Spanish:]

2 - Title page:
                         Florida
                         Year 1814

                       Mathias Pons asking title to 400 acres granted him on River Matanzas.

3 - Manuel Rengil, interim government secretary, certified that Mathias Pons, 11/25/1791, petitioned for a tract that bordered on the south with lands that belonged in the time of the English to Moultrie, about 5 miles from here; on the west it borders Matanzas River. Governor

Quesada granted until surveyor should arrive to allot his quota, 12/10/1794.

4 - Pierra certified that Mathias Pons petitioned for 12 acres that Jose Pedro de Munzo had in a place called Moultrie, which Munzo did not cultivate, but had given to a free negro, and Governor White decreed that since it is well known that Jose Pedro de Munzo does not cultivate this land or have it done by his slaves, 12 of the 18 acres should be granted to Mathias Pons and the remaining 6 acres to the above mentioned negro, 7/6/1805.

5 - John Purcell's certified plat of 400 acres conceded to Mathias Pons at a place called Casa Pulla on River Matanzas, bounded on the north by land of Don Ferdinand, east by the river, south by Pedro Chuet, west by vacant lands, 3/9/1809.

6 - Mathias Pons wrote that in July of 1805, the predecessor of His Excellency had conceded to him 12 acres, 18 of which Jose Peso de Burgo [is not Jose Pedro de Munzo intended?] had owned for some time but which he had turned over to a free mulatto, but neither cultivated it. Now the negro refused to vacate, insisted that he is cultivating the land and is patching up a dilapidated wooden shack he has there. Mathias Pons petitioned for the negro to be ejected, 10/24/1806. Pierra attested that the negro was ordered to vacate inside of three months.

7 - Mathias Pons having complied with all requirements of the government for the tracts of 400 acres and 12 acres for more than ten years, petitioned for a title. Francisco Pons signed for his father. Governor Kindelan referred the letter to the auditor of war and the two demanded witnesses. Entralgo attested the above action and

listed conditions of the grant.

8 - Fernando de la Maza Arredondo, Jr., swore before Arredondo y San Felices that Mathias Pons had complied with conditions.

9 - Bernardo Segui swore the same.

10 - Jose Bernardo Reyes swore the same. All on 9/15/1814. Governor Kindelan and Arredondo granted title as Entralgo attested.

11 [S] Governor Kindelan's title [3½ pp.] to Mathias Pons, 9/10/1816.

12 [E] Clements' certified plat to Mathias Pons confirmed by Congress, 397.22 acres, being in Sec. 39, T. 8, R. 30 S&E. Chainmen: John Hagan and I. [J?] M. McGough. Butler signs, March 1835.

[Dossier has translation of 11 and decree slip.]

Pons, Peter             Con. P 58; DG IV 280

1 [E] claims, through Clarke, 875 acres in Mill's Swamp on Nassau River, Governor Coppinger's service grant of 7/4/1817.

[Stitched together 2-5 in Spanish:]

2 - Title page:                    Florida
                                   Year 1817

P. No. 14              Concession in favor of Pedro
                       Pons of 875 acres on the Point of
                       River Nassau.

3 - List of slaves, with ages, of Peter Pons, 5/22/1817, 27 slaves from 18 to 40 years of age.

4 - Peter Pons, as a reward for his services as lieutenant in the urban militia to which Governor Kindelan appointed him, petitions for title to land to which he is entitled for 4 whites, all of age, and 27 slaves on point of River Nassau at Mill's Swamp, bounded on the south by land of Franco Fatio, north by the Swamp, east by vacant land, west by Simo Pierett. Fernandina, 5/22/1817. On the margin Governor Coppinger

instructs the petitioner to qualify and promised that the land will be provided.

5 - Francisco Pons, who "lends his voice and song" for Peter Pons, now absent in Fernandina, encloses testimonials asked for and requests their return. On the bottom Governor Coppinger, 6/4/1817, acknowledges and returns the certificates of the former commandant of Fernandina, the brevet captain, Francisco Rivera, and the captain of urban militia, Jose de la Maza Arredondo, and concedes the 875 acres asked.

6 [S] Governor Coppinger's royal title [2½ pp.], 6/4/1817. Entralgo attests.

7 [S] Clarke's certified plat of 9/8/1817. Plat shows on the north vacant lands, east the lands of Nabet [?] Davis, south the lands of F. L. Fatio, west those of Seymour Pickett.

[Pasted together 8 and 9 in English:]

8 - Alvarez certifies extract from descriptive list, No. 258. No survey.

9 - Certified copy of 7.

[Dossier has translation of title by Thomas Murphy,* and decree slip.]

Potts, Henry                              Con. P 59; DG IV 105

1 [E] Clements-Exum certify plat of 679.19 acres [800 arpens] confirmed to Henry Potts by Congress, being Sec. 22, T. 5, R. 30 N&W. Robert Butler, surveyor general, signs, January 1834. Chainmen:

---

* Thomas Murphy was an extra clerk employed by the Board of Commissioners for East Florida.--Supra, pp. xlviii, xlix.

Thomas McClelland, Albert Sebastian, James M. Sawyers, Andrew A. Crawford. Plat shows all sides vacant except for the Escambia River on the south.

[Jacket names Charles Beeler as claimant. Dossier contains duplicate of 1.]

Prevatt, Joseph            Con. P 60

1 [E] claims, through Clarke, 400 acres at Turner's Swamp; Governor Coppinger's grant as head rights.

2 [S] Jorge J. F. Clarke certifies plat, alleging "disposition of S. S. [His Excellency] of 10/20/1818."* No details.

3 [E. and S.] Plat by Thomas T. Woods, pasted to Clarke's certification, in Spanish, same as in 2, for 400 acres. Surrounded by vacant land. No details.

4 [E] R. B. Ker certifies, 1st quarter of 1831, a plat of 400 acres, confirmed by Congress to Joseph Prevatt, being in Sec. 29, T. 4, R. 24 N&E. Chainmen: Daniel Wells, Jr., and John Handley. No details.

[Dossier has Murphy's translation of No. 2 attested by Fatio, and decree of the board dated, 11/4/1825. Jacket notes: "Descriptive list, No. 253."]

Prevatt, Thomas           Con. P 61; DG IV 568, 650

1 [E] claims, through Clarke, 550 acres on St. Marys River, Governor Coppinger's grant as head rights, according to Clarke's document.

2 [S] Jorge J. F. Clarke certifies plat, 5/14/1813, alleging

---

* The date Clarke usually gave in such connection was 10/20/1817.-- Supra, p. lv.

"disposition of His Excellency [S. S.] of 10/20/1817.* Plat shows lands of Will Hogans in the west.

3 [E] Thomas T. Woods certifies plat, 5/14/1818, which shows below a plantation, a swamp marked "impassabel" [sic]. Sworn chain bearers: James T. Prevatt and William Hogans.

[4 and 5 pasted together in English:]

4 - Antonio Alvarez certifies extract from descriptive list, No. 254.

5 - Antonio Alvarez certifies translation of No. 2.

6 [E] Decree of the board.

[Dossier contains translation of 2 certified by Fatio.]

Priest, Gabriel          Con. P 62; DG IV 161, 213

1 [E] claims, 5/21/1823, through John M. Fontane, 500 acres on Black Creek, bounded on the west by lands of Henry Yonge; Governor Estrada's service grant to Gabriel Priest, who will file plats by Clarke and Burgevin whenever they are required.

2 [S] Juan M. Fontane petitions for 500 acres as a service grant, for his unpaid services in the rebellion of 1812 and 1813. Governor Estrada grants, 1/5/1816.

3 [S] Jorge J. F. Clarke certifies plat, 10/10/1819, of 500 acres, granted, 1/7/1816. The plat shows the land in the bend of the river. The land of Enrique Yonge is on the southwest.

4 [E] Antonio Alvarez certifies, 12/19/1844, extract from descriptive list, No. 275.

5 [E] Antonio Alvarez certifies translation of No. 3.

[Dossier has William Reynolds' copy of 2 and Fatio's certified translation of same.]

Prieto, Felipe          Con. P 63; DG IV 102

---

* See preceding footnote.

1 [E. Printed blank form filled in.] Register's Office, Tallahassee, certificate No. 99 of plat of survey deposited in the name of Felipe Priesto, who is entitled to a patent to Sec. 56, T. 2, R. 30 S&W, 811.19 acres, 3 miles west of Pensacola. [Pencil note on back says:] "Interferes with Juan Domingues, A, No. 16, Sec. 34."

2 [E] Clements and Exum certify, 4th quarter of 1828, a plat of 640.69 acres; confirmed by Congress to F. Prieto, being Sec. 56, etc., as shown in 1. Chain bearers: John M. Norris, John Gayler, Frederic S. Ming and James S. Ming. Robert Butler approves. Plat shows West Florida; Juan Domingues is on the northeast, the other boundaries are vacant lands.

[Dossier has duplicate of 2.]

Pringle, Abraham            Con. P 64; DG IV 117

1 [E] Clements and Exum certify, January 1834, a plat of 640.69 acres in West Florida, confirmed by Congress as a donation grant, being Sec. 19, T. 5, R. 30 N&W, and Sec. 38, T. 5, R. 31 N&W. The plat shows Escambia River on the south and Charles Barone on the southwest. Chainmen: James M. Sawyers and Andrew A. Crawford. Robert Butler approves.

[Dossier has duplicate of 1.]

Pritchard, Eleanor          Con. P 65; DG V 379

1 [E] claims 270 acres on the east side of St. Johns River, at a place called Beauclark's Point, bounded on the north by Robert Cowen's land, south by Mrs. Plummer's land, east by vacant land and west by the river. Governor White's grant as head rights, 11/15/1815. James Wall [?] signs for his wife.

2 [E] Another claim, also on U. S. commissioners' printed blank, of heirs of Robert Pritchard, through John B. Strong, for 270 acres;

Governor's White's grant based on head rights to Robert Pritchard; since his death claimed by Eleanor Pritchard.

3 [S] Roberto Pritchard petitions, 2/22/1800, for title to land next to that conceded to Guillermo Bowden, about 5 miles up from San Nicolas. About 5 years ago he was located on River San Juan, in the place called St. Nicolas whence on account of not enjoying good health, nor his family, he moved to the land he now occupies, and prepared ground for seed; and he did all this without a permit of the government. The Governor, your predecessor, told him, he "could not be bothered now" being busy with the revolution. Governor White refers the petition to the engineer in command. Berrio sees no inconvenience and Governor White grants land to him until a new survey, which will assign his quota. Pierra sent certificate.

4 [S] Pierra certifies, 2/26/1800, that Governor White conceded land at Buckler's Bluff. Note: By decree of 10/15/1808 the land corresponds to the interested parties, his children and his slaves, 270 acres.

5 [E] Translation of 4.

6 [E. Fatio's holograph translation:] Eleanor Pritchard, in order to avoid future contention, petitions through Arredondo for survey, to be made by Purcell, of the land she is cultivating. Governor White asks statement of the number in her family, including their ages. E. Pritchard writes she has 4 children over eight years and 7 negroes, of whom 5 are over sixteen and 2 are eight. Governor White orders compliance with preceding decree, 2/23/1808. Certificate of Nathaniel Hall, St. Johns, 10/1/1803, that family of late Robert Pritchard in September 1800, consisted of: Deceased,

42 years; wife, 32; 4 children, oldest 15, youngest 8; and 8 negroes from 1 to 35 [3 under 16]. Before me, William Lawrence. There are several individuals who can certify that the family of Robert Pritchard is as Nathaniel Hall stated, 10/1/1808. Governor White asks, 10/4/1808, what family Eleanor Pritchard has now. William Lawrence lists, 10/24/1808, the family of E. Pritchard as follows: Widow, 39 years of age, married to Dr. Hall; 4 children, three to eighteen; 5 negroes over sixteen, 3 from eight to sixteen, and 1 aged six. Governor White orders Purcell to survey the land. Fatio certifies true copy.

7 [E] Purcell certifies plat, ordered, 10/7/1803; done, 2/8/1809.

8 [E] Joseph Summerall and Joseph Hagan depose, 6/19/1824, before Samuel Fairbanks, J. P., that R. Pritchard took a tract of 275 acres in 1795 and lived there, where his widow still lives as wife of James Hall.

9 [E] Daniel Thomas certifies, May 1833, a plat of 265.87 acres confirmed by Congress to Eleanor Pritchard, being in Secs. 31 and 32, T. 3, R. 27 S&E. Chainmen: R. W. Green and Augustus Tibbits.

10 [E] Another plat, unsigned and undated, shows other lands in the bend of the river belonging to P. Plummer, Hannah Kehler and R. Pritchard's heirs.

[Jacket calls Buckler's Point, "Beaucler's". Descriptive list, No. 625.]

Pritchard, Robert, Heirs of      Con. P 66; DG IV 278

1 [E] James Hall and Eleanor Hall, his wife, formerly the wife of Robert Pritchard, deceased; John Creighton and Mary Creighton,

daughter of said R. Pritchard; Ann Stallings, widow of Elias Stallings and daughter of said R. Pritchard; and Robert and Amelia Pritchard, children of said R. Pritchard, are all citizens of the U. S. A. James Hall and Eleanor, his wife, were residents in Florida and your/other memorialists were in the states of Georgia and South Carolina at the time of the cession of Florida. J. Hall, E. Hall and Ann Stallings are now actual residents of East Florida, and the others are residents of the U. S. A. All the above mentioned persons claim, 10/23/1823, through John Rodman, their attorney, 450 acres in Jacksonville, comprising the town of Jacksonville on the west side of the River St. Johns, in Duval County, formerly called the Ferry of St. Nicholas, which said tract is part of a grant of the Spanish government which Governor Quesada made as head rights, 1/3/1791, to Robert Pritchard. Soon after the grant a regular survey was made but it was lost in the trouble of 1811 and 1812; however, lines can be proved by witnesses now residing on the tract. Robert Pritchard took possession in 1791, planted, and put up buildings. Agents of the heirs remained in possession until ousted by the troubles of 1811 and 1812; and are now kept out of possession by different persons on the premises.

2 [S] R. Pritchard has been told by the surveyor that the land he holds at Pass of San Nicolas should be set aside for the King, and he petitions for as much as 650 acres on the west side of St. Johns River, near the creek of the Cowford, which he has under cultivation; he has a settlement there, with his wife, 3 children, 7 negroes, 35 head of cattle, 30 hogs and various farm implements. Governor Quesada demands a report from Marrot. Marrot replies,

12/30/1791, for R. Pritchard to remain in possession, as the King does not want the land. William Reynolds certifies true copy.

3 [E] Joseph Summerall deposes, 6/19/1824, before George R. Fairbanks, J. P., that he knew R. Pritchard who was settled on and cultivated 650 acres on both sides of the river at old St. Nicolas, now in possession of Isaac Hendricks.

4 [E] Joseph Hogans deposes before Fairbanks, in same terms, at same date.

5 [E] John Jones deposes, 6/19/1824, before Fairbanks, that 20 years ago he was well acquainted with R. Pritchard, who settled a tract of land now held by Zechariah Hogans.

6 [E] Joseph Hagens deposes, 6/19/1824, before Fairbanks, that in 1803 or 1804 he did know John Joseph Lain, who cultivated, for R. Pritchard, the tract granted to him for head rights and which is now in possession of Lewis Z. Hogans.

7 [E] James Plummer deposes, 6/22/1824, before Fairbanks, that 3 or 4 months ago Isaac Hendricks took out of the Spanish office two papers and carried them to George J. F. Clarke who picked out the pages belonging to Hendricks; Plummer carried the other paper back to the office, not knowing what it was.

8 [E] Daniel Hogans deposes, 6/23/1824, before Fairbanks that about 18 or 20 years ago he called at a place on the other side of St. Johns River, near Jacksonville; that a man named Lain lived there, who said he was put there by Robert Pritchard; and that there was a small crop of corn and one or two small buildings on the place; he adds that about 20 years ago his father showed him a tree,

which was a corner of Pritchard's land which answered with Van Evens' [?] late plat and survey which he saw in Jacksonville last April.

9 [E] David Scurry, illiterate, deposes, 6/24/1824, before Fairbanks, that in 1818 he was in company with Isaac Hendrix, who told him he had taken two plats out of the Spanish office of Pritchard and carried them to George J. F. Clarke who gave him one for the land this side of the river where said Hendrix lives; the other papers he put back in the office; and that he had traced out his lines by Pritchard's plats, and found everything as he had been told; and found the stump of the corner tree near the garrison where the soldiers had cut down a short leaf pine, and said he would hew a light wood post and set it at the corner. Hendrix wished to know if American law would take it from him, if he had more land than the plat called for. The plat called for 215 acres but Hendrix thought it was near 300 acres and told Scurry that he had all his papers in his own name and could go on and build in safety as Dr. Stiles told him to do, since Stiles had more sense than half the men in Florida.

[Pasted together 10-11 in English:]

10 - Plat of 450 acres to Robert Pritchard, on fly leaf of old note book. Reverso is labeled, "Pritchard survey. Plummer, Scurry, Daniel Hogans."

11 - Decree of the Board finds claim of Pritchard's heirs valid.

12 [E] Antonio Alvarez certifies extract from descriptive list, No. 271.

13 [E] Antonio Alvarez certifies translation of 2.

[Dossier has Murphy's certified translation of 2.]

Pritchard, Robert                Con. P 67; DG V 378

1 [E] claims, through James Hall, 250 acres on the east side of St. Johns River at a place called Goodham's Lake, about 32 miles from St. Augustine; Governor Quesada's grant as head rights to Thomas Bowden, who was in possession of the land at the cession.

2 [S] Maria Morlen petitions, 5/4/1803, for the copy of the original survey made by Marrot when the land was given to her deceased husband, Thomas Bowden. Entralgo signs for M. Morlen who cannot write. On the margin Governor Ortega approves and signs with his rubric, a decorated capital L. Below Zubizarreta adds his rubric; below is copy of the Marrot-Eastlake certified plat that covers 3 pp. [see No. 3.]

3 [S] Marrot-Eastlake's original certified plat of 7 caballerias and 17 acres, surveyed, 10/19/1791, for T. Bowden.

4 [E] David Thomas certifies plat of 247.11 acres confirmed by Congress to the heirs of R. Pritchard, surveyed, May 1833, being in Secs. 29, 30, 32, T. 3, R. 27 S&E.

5 [E] Unsigned and undated plat. Surroundings show lands of Eleanor Pritchard on the southwest, of Hannah Nohler on the west, of B. Whitmore on the northeast, and B. Scurry on the east.

[Dossier has Murphy's translation of 2 certified by Fatio.]

Proctor, Antonio                Con. P 68; DG IV 260

1 [E] claims, through John Drysdale, absolute title to 185 acres, situated about 5 miles from St. Augustine at the Orange Grove; Governor Coppinger's grant, 3/8/1816, according to documents in the archives. The lands are bounded on the east by those of Philip Edinburgh, a free man of color.

[Stitched together 2-4 in Spanish:]

2 - Title page:    Florida
                   Year 1816

P. No. 11    Concession was made to the free
             mulatto, Antonio Proctor.

3 - Antonio Proctor, mulatto, and instructed in the Indian language to draw, who has a numerous family that count 7, petitions for land proportionate to his family, in the uncultivated Orange Grove, about 5 miles from St. Augustine. Juan Oderiz signs for A. Proctor who cannot write. Governor Coppinger refers, 2/17/1816, the above to the Auditor of War.

4 - Juan de Arredondo y San Felices [Auditor] explains, 2/24/1876, that this man is not one of the ordinary mulattoes of the place but knows the Indian language perfectly; that when the place was attacked by the revolutionists aided by the savages he did much to pacify the province; that he deserves the land proportionate to his family. Governor Coppinger asks to know the number in Antonio Proctor's family. Entralgo asks A. Proctor, and reports as follows: Wife, 1 son seventeen years of age, and 4 who are between eight and fourteen. Governor Coppinger grants 185 acres.

5 [S] Royal title [3 pp.] granted by Governor Coppinger to A. Proctor. Entralgo, government notary pro tem, attests, 3/8/1816. Fatio certifies true copy.

6 [S] Burgevin certifies, 12/18/1818, plat of 180 acres on the other side of the River of the Ferry.

[Dossier has translation of 5, certified by Fatio. Descriptive list, No. 256.]

## ERRATA

Perpall, G. W.     Con. P 37; DG IV 252

1 [E] claims 15 or more acres on Barataria Island at Little Matanzas Bar; Governor Coppinger's grant to Joseph Hughes, who sold to G. W. Perpall, 1/27/1818.

2 [S] Jose Hughes, old inhabitant from the time of the British occupation, got from Governor White the concession of an island of about 10 acres, of no value for agriculture, where he built a store house. He had to go to his son's house, about 5 miles south, on account of illness, when he returned he found his house without doors or windows. He knows who ruined it but cannot accuse them publicly. Having lived here more than 10 years, he petitions for title; Governor Coppinger grants and will have title sent, 1/24/1818.

3 [E. Thomas Murphy's translation of deed not found elsewhere.] Jose Hughes sells to G. W. Perpall his island of about 10 acres for $100. Witnesses: F. M. Arredondo, Jr., Francis Richards and Pedro Miranda. Juan de Entralgo attests and then Francisco Jose Fatio.

[Pasted together 4-5 in English:]

4 - Antonio Alvarez' certified extract, 5/9/1845, from descriptive list, No. 278--Gabriel W. Perpall--15 acres.

5 - Attached to 4 is translation of 2.

[Dossier has confirmation slip of board and translation of 2 by Thomas Murphy.]

Quigles, Migel                    Con. Q 1; DG IV 102

1 [E] Benjamin Clements certifies, 2/18/1828, plat of 66.89 acres being in sec. 3, T. 5, R. 29 N&W, and sec. 27, T. 6, R. 29 N&W, for Migel Quigles. Butler, surveyor general, signs.

2 [E] Tallahassee Land Office certificate No. 10, for plat of 669.89 acres on Escambia River, being in sec. 3, T. 5, R. 29 N&W, and sec. 27, T. 6, R. 29 N&W, issued, 9/20/1831, to Migel Quigles.

[Dossier contains duplicate of 1.]

Rain, Joseph             Con. R 1; DG IV 245
and William Bailey

1 [E] claim, through Bellamy, 1,000 acres on Trout Creek where the public road leading from St. Augustine to the State of Georgia crosses into Duval County in the Territory of Florida. The grant was made, 12/19/1772, by the English government to Frederick Rolfe who sold to Benjamin Dodd. [Both documents are lost.] In the deed of lease and release between Dodd and Arthur Gordon for several tracts of land is one belonging to this tract; here also is the deed, 1799, of conveyance from John Haley, marshal, to Peter Bagley in consequence of a judgment obtained by Bagley against Harried Precilla Gordon. Peter Bagley's heirs sold, in 1818, the 2 tracts of 500 acres each at Trout Creek to Joseph Rain and William Bailey, Camden, Georgia.

2 [E] Deed, 8/13/1777: Benjamin Dodd sells 250 acres at the head of Trout Creek on the west side of St. Johns River; 1,000 acres also on Trout Creek, bounded on the east and west by John Burnell's land; and 1,000 acres on the southern branch of Trout Creek, bounded on the north and west by John Burnell, east by William Barker and south by Lutterloh, all for 5 shillings cash to Arthur Gordon. On back: Sealed and delivered in the presence of Rice Williams, Jr., and James Radan[?].

3 [E] Deed of lease and release, 8/14/1777, between Benjamin Dodd, provost marshal of the province of East Florida in America, and Arthur Gordon for the 2,250 acres at Trout Creek, lately belonging to Frederic Rolfe. Witnesses: James Madam and William Rice, Jr.,

4 [E] Deed [very badly torn:] John Haley, marshal of his Brittanic Majesty, conveys, 8/30/1779, to Peter Baglie [Bagley] for the sum of 150 pounds, the three tracts of land of 250, 1000, and 1000 acres at Trout Creek, in consequence of a judgment obtained by Bagley against Harriet P. Gordon, administratrix of Arthur Gordon, for 467 poinds 3 shillings and 5 pence. Witnesses: John Haley and William Mass.

5 [E] John Funk certifies, 2/15/1773, plat for 1,000 acres at Trout Creek about 46 miles northwest of St. Augustine, adjacent to a 250-acre tract of John Burnet who sold to Mr. Rolfe and bounded on the west by a 500-acre tract also belonging to J. Burnet. Benjamin Lord, surveyor, certifies true copy.

6 [S] Marrot and Dupont certify, 4/6/1793, plat of 30 <u>caballerias</u> at the Rolfe Plantation for Timotheo Hollingsworth as guardian of Francisco, Carlota, Margarita and Ysabel Bagley.

7 [E] Deed: Camden County, Georgia, 11/26/1818, John Hollingsworth sells to Joseph Rain and William Bailey for $500 cash 500 acres [half of a 1,000-acre tract situated between the Nassau and St. Johns Rivers, embracing the head of Trout Creek]. Witnesses: Isaac Crews and James Campbelle. Belton A. Copp, notary public, attests signatures.

8 [E] Deed: Camden County, Georgia, 12/12/1818, Elizabeth Bayley sells 500 acres [half of the 1,000-acre tract situated between the Nassau and St. Johns Rivers, embracing the head of Trout Creek[ for $1,000. Witnesses: Mary Gumley and Lewis Gumby. Belton A. Copp attests signatures.

9 [E] Antonio Alvarez' extract, 11/16/1844, from descriptive list,

No. 285, J. Bain and W. Bailey, 1,000 acres, British grant, 12/19/1772.

[Dossier contains 2 translations of 6.]

Ramirez, Salvador                    Con. R 2; DG IV 102

1 [E] Benjamin and J. B. Clements and J. W. Exum certify, 4th quarter of 1831, plat of 336 acres, being sec. 27, T. 1, R. 30 N&W, and sec. 53, T. 1, R. 30 S&W, for Salvador Ramirez. Chainmen: Thomas McClelland and Albert Sabaster [Sebastian ?]. Butler approves, January 1834.

Rawls, Cotton                        Con. R 3; DG V 411

1 [E] claims 630 acres near the head of the South Prong of Trout Creek, a donation grant of which he has been in possession since 1820.

2 [E] James McCormic deposes, 5/18/1825, before the Board in Session that he has known Cotton Rawls, who is over the age of 21; head of a family; he has occupied the 640 acres since 1821 until about 18 months ago when William Carter took possession of and cultivated it; Cotton Rawls has not any claim on any other land in this territory.

3 [E] George Willis certifies, September 1831, a plat of 640 acres, being sec. 38, T. 1, R. 25 S&E, for Cotton Rawls. Butler approves, January 1834.

Reyes, Domingo                       Con. R 4; DG V 57, 60

1 [E] claims, through Isaac N. Cox, 2,000 acres on the Halifax River, 6 or 7 miles from Spring Garden, a plantation belonging to John Williams; Governor Coppinger's grant.

[Bound together 2-6 in Spanish:]

2 - Domingo Reyes, inspector and overseer and inspector pro tem of

the royal and military hospital, Nuestra Senora Guadulupe, petitions, 2/12/1816, for 2,000 acres about 6 or 7 miles east of "Sprin Gardin" plantation belonging to John Williams and about 20 miles from William Williams' plantation known as Williams' Place. He, Reyes, rendered services during the 1812 revolt in defense of the city. Governor Coppinger grants, 2/16/1816.

3 - Domingo Reyes petitions, 2/5/1821, to have the 2,000 acres surveyed by Andrew Burgevin in order to be able to obtain the title to the land. Governor Coppinger grants. Entralgo attests and notifies Domingo Reyes and Andrew Burgevin who countersigns.

4 - Andrew Burgevin certifies, 4/5/1821, a plat for 2,000 acres for Domingo Reyes.

5 - Domingo Reyes petitions, 5/5/1821, for title to 2,000 acres which Governor Coppihger Coppinger grants.

6 - Unfinished plat for 2,000 acres, being in sec. 38, T. 16, R. 3 S&E, for Domingo Reyes.

7 [E] Alvarez' extract, 7/1/1845, from descriptive list, No. 630, Domingo Reyes, 2,000 acres.

[Dossier contains copy and translation of 2 and 2 translations of 4.]

Reyes, Jose B.                                      Con. R 5; DG IV 238, 239

1 [E] claims 200 acres on Moultrie Creek to the south of St. Augustine, bounded on the south by said creek, and east by lands of Carlos Gobert, Governor Coppinger's grant to Bartolome Castro y Ferrer who sold, 7/21/1818, to Jose B. Reyes.

[Bound together 2-6 in Spanish:]

2 - Pierra certifies, 12/7/1799, that upon petition of Bartolome de Castro y Ferrer for 200 acres on Mutlri [Moultrie] Creek south of

St. Augustine, which formerly belonged to the Gerardo tract, Govern[o] White granted without injury to a third party and until a new surve[y] when he will be granted his quota.

3 - Bartolome Castro y Ferrer petitions, 6/23/1818, to present the formation necessary for acquiring title to the 200 acres above, gra[nt]ed him in 1799. Governor Coppinger grants. Entralgo attests and notifies Castro y Ferrer.

4 - Entralgo lists conditions necessary to the delivery of title.

5 - Fernando de la Maza Arredondo, Jr., married, 30, deposes, 6/6/1818, before Entralgo that as his own plantation is beisde the 200 acres of Ferrer he has been able to see the land under cultivation several years and the owner making all the necessary improvements.

6-- Pedro Miranda, married, 45, also deposes that Ferrer has improv[ed] and cultivated with his slaves the 200 acres in question.

7 - Juan Huertas, married, 28, also deposes, confirming the above. Governor Coppinger grants. Entralgo attests and notifies Bartolome Castro Y Ferrer.

7 [E] Bartolome Castro y Ferrer petitions, 12/17/1799, for 200 acres on Mutri [Moultrie] Creek, south of St. Augustine, which formerly belonged to the Gerardo tract. Governor White requests informa[tion] from Berrio, commandant of engineers, who reports favorably. Governor White grants, Fierra issues certificate. William Reynolds certifies true copy, 4/7/1824.

8 [S] Unfinished plat of 200 acres, bounded on the south by Ca[ñada] de Multry [Moultrie Creek] and east by lands of Carlos Coobert [Gobert?].

9 [S] Royal title to 200 acres at Moultry Creek granted, 6/6 1818, by Governor Coppinger to Bartolome Castro y Ferrer.

10 [S] Deed: Bartolome Castro y Ferrer sells, 7/2/1818, 200 acres on Multry Creek south of St. Augustine to Jose B. Reyes for $500.00. Witnesses: Fernando M. Arredondo, Pedro Miranda and Eusebio Maria Gomez. Entralgo certifies and attests true copy.

11 [E] Benjamin and J. B. Clements certify plat of 198.46 acres on Moultre Creek, being in sec. 37, T. 8, R. 29 S&W, for Jose B. Reyes. Chainmen: John Hagan and John M. McGough.

[Dossier contains a copy of 7 and 1 translation each of 9 and 10.]

Richard, Francis            Coh. R 6; DG V 73

1 [E] claims, through Clarke, 16,000 acres on Potsborugh Creek and Cedar Swamp, which tract is to the east of and about one mile distant from McQueen's Mills. Governor Coppinger's grant.

2 [S] Francisco Richard petitions, 5/11/1817, for a tract of 5 miles at Potsbourgh Creek, bounded by a place called Strawberry Hill, and the same amount at Cedar Swamp about a mile from McQueen's Mills. He wishes to build a water saw mill.

[Bound together 3-9 in English:]

3 - Governor Coppinger grants, 6/4/1817, 5 miles for a water saw mill on Pottsburgh Creek and license for the construction of it, on condition that the grant will be considered null so long as the machinery for the mill is not set. When the condition is met the petitioner is to have the privilege to use the pines and any other trees on this tract as well as on another equivalent tract granted to him at Cedar Swamp. Aguilar certifies true copy. Anthelm Gey certifies, 6/18/1832, true translation.

4 - Burgevin certifies, 11/26/1824, plat of 1,600 acres [part of 16,000 acres granted to Francisco Richard] at Cedar Swamp about 3 or

4 miles from St. Johns Bluff.

5 - Burgevin certifies, 11/1/1824, plat of 17,610 acres for Francisco Richard. "From this tract must be deducted the following tracts":

| | | |
|---|---|---|
| Tract bought by Francisco Richard | 650 | Acres |
| "      "      "      "      " | 350 | " |
| "      "      "      "      " | 200 | " |
| "      granted to     "      " | 250 | " |
| "      belonging to John B. Richard | 250 | " |
| "      bought by M. G. Hendricks | 200 | " |
| "      belonging to Peter Bagley | 200 | " |
| "      belonging to the estate of Mrs. R. Hogans | 395 | " |
| "      of land found to be in excess of the above tract | 215 | " |
| "      of land covered with water | 500 | " |
| | 3,210 | " |

Remaining, 14,400 acres.

6 - Decree of the superior court, 5/26/1832, finds claim of Francisco Richard for 2 tracts, 4 and 5 above, valid.

7 - Mandate of the U. S. Supreme Court, second Monday of January term 1834, delivered by John Marshall, Chief Justice, to the superior court to have further proceedings and to have a new survey made of plat 5 above, for 14,400 acres not previously granted, no more nor less.

8 - Further decree, 8/5/1834, of the superior court of East Florida, July term 1834, ordering the new survey to be made as demanded by the U. S. Supreme Court. George R. Fairbanks certifies, 12/19/1844, true copy of the proceedings. Judge Bronson certifies Fairbanks' signature.

9 - Decree of the district court of the United States for the northern District of Florida, April term 1852, confirming the grant of 16,000 acres to Francisco Richard after the presentation of the new plat for the further proceedings commanded by the Supreme Court.

[Dossier contains a translation of 2 and copies of 3, 4, 5, 6, 7 and 8. An old jacket with no number contains receipt signed by John Rodman for certain documents from Antonio Alvarez from the archives, these documents being: Copy and translation of concession and 2 original surveys and plats, one for 1,400 acres and the other for 1,000 acres.]

Richard, Francis                              Con. R 7; DG V 380

1 [E] claims, through Antonio Alvarez, 1,025 acres on the west side of Lake George about 7 miles from Dryton's [Drayton's] Island at a Hammoc near Big Spring; Governor Coppinger's grant, 1/10/1818.

2 [S] Pierra certifies, 1/9/1804, that upon petition of Luis Francisco Richard, Jr., for 50 acres on Matanzas River extending from north of Juan Bautista Ferrya's place to that of DuPont's, Governor Coppinger granted same.

3 [S] Francisco Richard, Jr., through Esteban Arnau, petitions, 1/7/1812, for 1,025 acres, 875 of it on the west side of Lake George, about 7 miles from Dryton's Island at a Hammoc near Big Spring, and the remaining 150 acres at the same place, to be given to him in exchange for an equal amount of acres that he possesses in Matanzas territory. Governor Coppinger grants, 1/10/1818.

4 [E] Burgevin certifies, 8/22/1826, plat of 1,025 acres including a small island in a cove on the west side of Lake George opposite the western coast of Dryton or Kingley [sic] Island north of the mouth of the Big Salt Spring, for Francis Richard.

5 [E] Uncompleted and torn plat dated, January 1850, for 1,060.05 acres being in sec. 40, T. 13, R. 26 S & E, for Francis Richard; showing also an island on the St. Johns River, called Florence McLean's Isla, or Hog Island.

[Dossier contains 2 translations of 3 and a copy each of 3 and 4.]

Richard, Francis   Con. R 8; DG V 376

1 [E] claims, through Antonio Alvarez, 650 acres at Dudley on the east of St. Johns River and on the north of Potsburgh, bounded on the north and east by lands of Francis Richard, south by Potsburg Creek and St. Johns Creek; Governor Quesada's grant, 12/2/1795, to Samuel Russell who sold, 2/21/1822, to the claimant who is in actual possession.

2 [S] Samuel Rusell petitions, 7/18/1819, for a certified copy of the document of concession of the above 650 acres, made to him on 12/2/1795, as he has lost the original. Governor Coppinger grants the request, 7/27/1819.

3 [S] Samuel Russell petitions, 12/1/1795, for the quota corresponding to himself, his wife, 2 sons and 7 negro slaves, at a place called Dudles [Dudley's] at the mouth of Potsbourgh on St. Johns River. Governor Quesada grants, 12/2/1795, without injury to a third party until the new survey when his quota will be measured to him. Aguilar certifies true copy, 7/27/1819.

4 [S] Clarke certifies, 1/14/1820, plat of 650 acres for Samuel Russell.

5 [S] Samuel Russell petitions, 6/5/1821, to have 650 acres surveyed by Clarke. Governor Coppinger grants.

6 [E] John R. Hogan deposes, 8/6/1827, before Samuel Fairbanks that Samuel Russell had lived, with his wife, 2 sons and 7 slaves, at the entrance to the mouth of Potsburg Creek, on the north side, since 1795 and that he has had 10 years of uninterrupted possession and

cultivation.

7 [E] David Thomas certifies, June 1833, a plat of 484.57 acres on the east side of St. Johns River and north of Big Pottsburgh Creek, being in secs. 15, 16, 21 and 22, T. 2, R. 27 S & E, for Francis Richard. Chainmen: R. P. Green and William O'Neill.

8 [E] Fatio's abstract of the case.

Richard, Francis                     Con. R 9; DG IV 427

1 [E] claims, through Clarke, 466 acres at Branchester on St. Johns River; Governor Kindelan grants, 3/20/1815, to claimant who is in actual possession.

[Bound together 2-12 in Spanish:]

2 - Fierra certifies, 1/9/1801, that upon petition of Francis Richard for all the land that the rebel Guillermo Jones formerly possessed in the year 1792 located on the south side of St. Johns River and bounded on the south by lands of the late Widow Hogans, north by Tole Ponce, and east by pine lands of Francisco Facio, asking for 755 acres at Punta de Ysabel between Ponce's and Facio's lands, Governor White granted same.

3 - Marrot and Eastlake certify, 5/1/1792, a plat of 6 caballerias and 30 acres at Fargue, being part of what corresponds to head rights of Guillermo Ponce.

4 - Marrot and Eastlake certify, 1/23/1792, plat of 14 caballerias at Branchester, being part of what corresponds to Guillermo Torres who has a family of 22 persons as follows: husband, wife, 7 children and 13 negroes.

5 - Francis Richard petitions, 3/17/1815, for permission to present testimonials of his having fulfilled all conditions necessary to

obtain title to the land. Governor Kindelan requests information from the war autidor; permission is granted and Arredondo countersigns. Entralgo attests and notifies Francis Richard.

6 - Entralgo lists conditions necessary to obtain title.

7 - Jose de la Maza Arredondo deposes, 3/17/1815, before Juan Arredondo y San Felices, 29, married, that it is well known that Franci Richard had cultivated uninterruptedly, for more than 10 years, the land granted, 1/9/1801, to him, which had formerly belonged to the rebel, Guillermo Jones; and that on Punta Ysabel he has also fenced built and made other improvements, fulfilling thus the conditions necessary to the title.

8 - Fernando de la Maza Arredondo, Jr., 28, married, deposes before Arredondo confirming above.

9 - Juan Gaiger, married, tanner, also deposes confirming 7 above.

10 - Governor Kindelan grants, 3/18/1815. Arredondo countersigns; Entralgo attests and notifies Francis Richard.

11 - Clarke certifies, 3/1/1812, plat of 110 acres on the east bank of St. Johns River about a mile distant from the former Santa Esabe detachment, for Francis Richard, Sr.

12 - Francis Richard, Jr., as representative of his father, present 1/26/1818, the above plat and petitions for title. Governor Coppinger grants. Entralgo attests and notifies Francis Richard.

13 [S] Royal title to 466 acres at the plantation called Branchester granted by Governor Kindelan, 3/20/1815, to Francis Richard

14 [E] Alvarez' extract, 12/28/1844, from descriptive list, No 280, Francis Richard, 466 [446 acres according to descriptive list, No. 280].

[Dossier contains a translation each of 4 and 14.]

Richard, Francis                    Con. R 10; DG V 58, 66

1 [E] claims 350 acres at Strawberry Hill, or at Francis Goodwin's plantation south of St. Johns River; Governor Coppinger's grant of 4/17/1817, to Reuben Hogans.

[Bound together 2-8 in Spanish:]

2 - Pierra certifies, 6/20/1798, that upon petition of Reuben Hogan for a tract of land known as Strabare Hill on Francisco Goodwin's plantation on the south bank of St. Johns River, it was granted to him.

3 - Ruben Hogan, through Miguel Papy, petitions, 4/14/1817, for permit to present witnesses as to his having fulfilled all conditions required for a royal title to the 350 acres granted him at Strabare Hill. Governor Coppinger grants. Entralgo attests.

4 - Entralgo lists, 4/15/1817, conditions required for the royal title.

5 - Gasper Papy, married, 64, deposes, 4/16/1817, before Governor Coppinger that it is true that Ruben Hogan possessed the 350 acres formerly belonging by concession to Francisco Goodwin, which land Hogan has cleared, cultivated and improved for many years; he has also raised cattle.

6 - Juan Bautista Collins Pardo, from New Orleans, widow [widower] 60, deposes confirming 5 above.

7 - Daniel Swancy [Sweney], single, 30, also deposes confirming 5 above.

8 - Governor Coppinger grants, 4/17/1817. Entralgo attests and notifies Ruben Hogans.

9 [S] Royal title to 350 acres at Strabare Hill granted, 4/17/1817, to Ruben Hogan. Entralgo attests and certifies true copy.

10 - [E] Unfinished plat for 350 acres, being in sec. 56, T. 3,

R. 27 S & E, for Francis Richards.

11 [E] Alvarez' extract, 12/28/1844, from descriptive list, No. 633, Francis Richard, 350 acres.

[Dossier contains 1 translation of 9.]

Richard, Francis            Con. R 11; DG V 66

1 [E] claims, through Antonio Alvarez, 250 acres on St. Johns River near the Cowford at Red Bay Hammock, on Arroyo Bog, about half a mile from the mouth of Boggy Branch, bounded on the south by lands of himself, and east by William Richard. Governor Coppinger's grant.

2 [S] Francis Richard, Jr., petitions, 11/5/1817, for 250 acres on San Nicolas at the place known as Monte de Laurel Colorado [Red Bay Hammoc] on Arroyo Bog, bounded on the north by the banks of St. Johns River and south by lands of the heirs of J. Richard. Governor Coppinger grants, 11/17/1817. Aguilar attests and certifies copy.

3 [S] D. S. H. Miller certifies, 3/22/1819, for Francis Richard, a plat of 250 acres on Red Bay Hammoc on Boggy Branch, about half a mile from its mouth.

4 [E] Unfinished plat of 250 acres, being in T. 2, R. 27 S & W, for Francis Richard.

5 [E] Decree of the board confirming the claim, accompanied by Fatio's abstract.

6 [E] Alvarez' extract, 12/27/1844, from descriptive list, No. 632, Francis Richard, 250 acres.

[Dossier contains 1 copy and 1 translation of 3.]

Richard, Francis            Con. R 12; DG IV 294

1 [E] claims, through Clarke, 230 acres at "Pargue" on St. Johns

River; Governor Kindelan's grant, 3/20/1815.

   2 [S] Royal title to 230 acres at the Fargue Plantation granted to Francis Richard by Governor Kindelan, 3/20/1815. This land formerly belonged to Guillermo Jones. Entralgo attested and certified true copy.

   3 [E] David Thomas certifies, June 1833, a plat of 284.17 acres east of St. Johns River in sec. 33, T. 1, and secs. 4 and 5, T. 2, R. 27 S & E, for Francis Richard. Chainmen: R. W. Green and William O'Neill.

   4 [E] Unfinished plat of 276.46 acres, being in T. 2, R. 27 S & E, for Francis Richard.

   [Dossier contains 1 translation of 2.]

Richard, Francis            Con. R 13; DG V 58, 66

   1 [E] claims, through Alvarez, 200 acres on the east side of St. Johns River, at the head of Pottsburgh's Creek known as Tyger Hole; Governor Coppinger's concession, 6/12/1817, to Lewis Zacharias Hogans, who sold to Francis Richard.

   2 [S] Luis Zacarias Hogans, sergeant of the provincial militia formed for the defense and conservation of St. Johns River and San Nicolas, petitions, 6/12/1817, for the quota that corresponds to himself and his 5 slaves, all older than 16 years, on Pottsburgh Creek about 5 miles from St. Johns River. Governor Coppinger grants 200 acres. Aguilar attests and certifies true copy.

   3 [S] Clarke certifies, 6/26/1818, plat for 200 acres for Luis Zacharias Hogans.

   4 [E] Antonio Alvarez' extract, 12/27/1844, from descriptive list, No. 631, Francis Richard, 200 acres.

5 [E] Decree of the Board confirming the grant accompanied by Fatio's abstract.

[Dossier contains a copy and a translation of 3.]

Richard, Francis, Sr.            Con. R 14; DG IV 280, 430

1 [E] claims, through Clarke, 110 acres on St. Johns River at Point Santa Esabela; Governor Coppinger's grant, 1/9/1801.

2 [E] Pierra certifies, 1/9/1801, that upon petition of Francis Richard for the land surveyed on two occasions for the rebel, William Jones, on the south side of St. Johns River, bounded on the south by lands of the deceased widow of Hogans, north by Jose Fonce and east by Francisco Facio; also 755 acres at Point Sante Isabel below the lands of said Fonce and Facio, Governor White granted same. William Reynolds certifies true copy. Fatio certifies correct translation.

3 [S] Clarke certifies, 3/1/1812, plat of 110 acres on the east side of St. Johns River about a mile and a half from Santa Esbila Point, for Francis Richards.

4 [S] Royal title to 110 acres described above, granted, 1/27/1818, by Governor Coppinger to Francis Richards.

5 [E] David Thomas certified, June 1833, plat of 157.91 acres, east of St. Johns River in secs. 4 and 9, T. 2, R. 27 S & E, for Francis Richard. Chainmen: R. W. Green and William O'Neil.

6 [E] Unfinished plat for 157.91 acres, being in T. 2, R. 27 S & E, for Francis Richard.

[Dossier contains a copy of 3 and a translation of 4.]

Richard, John B., Heirs of            Con. R 15; DG V 376

1 [E] Rebecca Jones, formerly the wife of John B. Richard, and

her husband, David B. Jones, together with the children of Rebecca Jones and her first husband, viz., John B. Richard, Jr., and Betsey Ann Richard Brown and her husband, Thomas Brown, claim, through Belton A. Copp, 230 acres at he head of North Bay Creek, north of Edward Turner's plantation.

2 [S] Juan Bautista Richard petitions, 10/19/1803, for 250 acres on the south side of St. Johns River at the head of Potsborogh Creek and north of Edward Turner's plantation. Governor White grants him 230 acres as the quota corresponding to himself, his wife and 6 slaves. Pierra attests. Fatio certifies true copy.

3 [S] Pierra's certificate of memorial and grant.

4 [E] Daniel S. Hart, 29, deposes, 10/19/1824, before Judge Doggot of Duval County Court, that Rebecca Jones is his sister, that David G. Jones is now dead and that Rebecca Jones was formerly John B. Richard's wife. He also knows Betsey Ann Brown and Thomas Brown, her husband, and that Betsey Ann and John B. Richard, Jr., are children of John B. Richard and are his heirs. John B. Richard settled in 1803 on the land in question and lived there until his death in 1811. After his death, Rebecca, his wife, came back.

5 [E] Daniel S. Hart deposes, October 1825, that he knew John B. Richard, who settled the place at Potsburg Creek between 1801 and 1805, and died in 1810; that Rebecca Jones was J. B. Richard's wife at the time of his death; and that William and Elizabeth, also a widow, are the only living children of John B. Richard.

6 [E] Alvarez' extract, 12/24/1844, from descriptive list, No. 634, John B. Richard, 230 acres.

7 [E] Unfinished plat of 250 acres, being in T. 2, R. 27 S & E, for John B. Richard.

[Dossier contains 2 translations of 3.]

Riobo, Thomas P.                Con. R 16; DG IV 103

1 [E] Benjamin Clements certifies, 2/8/1828, plat of 705.66 acres, being in sec. 42, T. 1, R. 28 N&W, for Thomas P. Rioboo [sic]. Butler approves.

Riz, James, et al.                Con. R 17; DG IV 256

1 [E] James and Tryphena Riz, co-heirs surviving their late father, William Riz, claim through James Riz, their attorney-in-fact, 640 acres at Picolata on St. Johns River, bounded on the west by said river, and north and south by lands of Edward M. Wanton; a donation grant to their father who was in actual possession of it at the time of the cession of this territory to the United States. Their father, their mother, sister, Mr. George Colee and several negroes occupied and cultivated this land from April 1821 to December 1821, when upon the death of their father and mother, and because of illness in the family, they were obliged to retire to the city.

2 [E] George Colee deposes, 9/9/1824, before E. B. Gould, J. P., in St. Johns County, that he worked for William Riz, father of the claimant, from December 1820 until his death, October 1821; that William Riz and his wife, on account of sickness, were forced to retire to the city.

3 [E] Horatio S. Dexter, having seen Colee's deposition, deposes confirming it, adding that he was in the habit of visiting Riz at Picolata where he saw him clearing and improving the land and

planting fruit trees with his slaves. The Riz family consisted of 6 whites and 10 to 12 negroes.

4 [E] James Hall deposes, 6/14/1825, that he was acquainted with Lewis Quibent previous to 1818, who purchased 400 acres at Cedar Head near Picotala [sic]; that around Christmas, 1821, he and Colonel Smith of New York visited at the plantation of William Riz where they saw George Colee and Tryphena Riz who were ill and it was understood would have to be removed from the place; that due to this state of affairs the deponent and said Smith left the house and encamped about 200 yards from the Riz home from which place they could see the small log house at Quibert [Quibent?] on Mr. Wanton's old field. Besides his house at the landing, Quibert was building a house at Cedar Head, where it still remains.

Robinson, Eliza                         Con. R 18

1 [E] claims, through her husband, Silvester Robinson, [and later through her attorney, John Robinson], 105 acres at Stockade, about a mile and half from St. Augustine, bounded on the south by lands of James Gujot and west by St. Sebastian River; Governor White's grant of 3/5/1803 to Pedro Capo, who sold through Miranda to Edward S. Robinson for his mother, Eliza, on 11/9/1821, the deed of conveyance having been recorded on 12/8/1821: a certified copy of Capo's memorial and Governor White's grant; Pedro Miranda's memorial and Governor Coppinger's decree confirming it; power-of-attorney from Pedro Capo to Pedro Miranda authorizing a sale of land and survey of plat.

2 [S] Power-of-attorney given to Pedro Miranda by Pedro Capo to solicit for the royal title to the Estacada de las dos Millas [Two

Mile Stockade] and then to sell it at the price he considers most convenient. Domingo Acosta signs for Pedro Acosta who cannot write. Witnesses: Reymon de Arriba, Juan Cercopoli, Andrez Lopez, Jose Bergello, James L. Lewis, 5/19/1820.

3 [S] Pedro Miranda petitions, 3/14/1821, for a certified copy of Pedro Capo's petition for the 105 acres at Estacada and the decree granting this land which he has bought from Capo.

4 [S] Pedro Capo petitions, 2/28/1803, for 105 acres about one-half mile from the hornabegue [hornwork] at Stockade, north of the plantation of Pedro Estopa. Governor White requests, 3/4/1803, information from Engineer Parcelo who reports, 3/5/1803, favorably. Governor White grants; Aguilar attests and certifies true copy.

5 [E] Deed, 9/9/1821: Pedro Miranda, as agent or attorney-in-fact of Pedro Capo, sells to Eliza Robinson 105 acres for $131.25 cash.

6 [E] Peter Lynch certifies, 9/30/1821, plat of the 105 acres which he bought from Pedro Miranda for Edward S. Robinson.

7 [E] Alvarez' extract, 1/13/1834, of the proceedings of the Board confirming the 105 acres to Edward Robinson.

[Dossier contains translations of 2, 3 and 4 and a copy of 6.]

Robion, Charles                    Con. R 19

1 [E] claims 750 acres west of Matanzas River south of St. Augustine, bounded on the north by lands of Jaime Falany, south by Fernando Arredondo, and east by Matanzas River; Governor Coppinger's grant, 3/18/1816, and royal title to Pedro Miranda who sold to Robira [Robion].

2 [S] Royal title to the above 790 acres granted, 7/17/1816, by Governor Coppinger to Pedro Miranda. Estralgo attests. William Reynolds certifies true copy.

3 [E] Benjamin and J. B. Clements certify plat of 787.76 acres, being in sec. 41, T. 8, R. 30 S & E, for Charles Robion. Chainmen: John Fogan and John M. McGough.

4 [E] The decree of the Board confirming the grant has an abstract by Fatio.

Rodriguez, Domingo                     Con. R 20; DG V 413

1 [E] Clarke certifies, 2/2/1817, for Domingo Rodriguez, plat of lot No. 6 Square 3, measuring 17 varas front and 34 varas depth, bounded on the north by the lot of Mateo Ferradas, east by Jose Candelario, south by Gardines Street and west by David Garvin.

2 [S] Francisca Aguilar, widow, petitions, 5/26/1819, for title to the above lot for her son, Domingo Rodriges, absent in Habana, Cuba. This lot in Fernandina was granted to him as shown by the accompanying certificate and he has improved the lot. Governor Coppinger grants.

3 [E] Fatio's abstract of the claim.

[Dossier contains copy of 2.]

Rodriguez, Nicholas                    Con. R 21; DG V 420

1 [S] Lorenzo Rodriguez petitions, 2/15/1793, for 300 acres north of Anastasia Island at Cano de la Escolta [Creek of the Guard], as he has several slaves which he intends to use in agriculture. Governor Quesada grants, 2/16/1793, until a new survey can be made, without injury to a third party, and on condition that petitioner

will not allow fire which may endanger the woods of the island.

2 [S] Lorenzo Rodriguez, through Sebastian Berzactrize, petitions 8/27/1801, for certified copy of the document granting him the above 300 acres, as he has misplaced the original. Governor White complies; Pierra attests.

[Bound together 3-11 in Spanish:]

3 - Travers certifies, 9/16/1804, for Lorenzo Rodriguez, a plat of 100 acres on Anastasia Island, bounded on the south by the road going to the Tower, east by the quarry, north by the beach and west by marshes.

4 - Pierra certifies, 8/27/1801, that upon Lorenzo Rodriguez' petition for 300 acres at Cano de la Escolta, Governor Quesada granted the land.

5 - Lorenzo Rodriguez petitions, through Manuel Fernandez Bendicho, 8/12/1804, to have the 300 acres surveyed by Juan Travers. Governor White consents.

6 - Lorenzo Rodriguez, through M. F. Bendicho, petitions, 11/19/1804, to present testimonials of his having inhabited, cultivated and improved for more than 10 years the 300 acres. Governor White grants. Ortega countersigns; Zubizarreta attests.

7 - Zubizarreta lists conditions necessary to the grant, 1/8/1805.

8 - Juan Rodriguez, of Seville, Spain, married, 41, deposes before Ortega that Lorenzo Rodriguez has been established for more than 12 years on the land in question, which at first he called Buena Vista. He has fenced, cultivated, built and added other improvements, although he does not gain much because the land is not good.

9 - Antonio Palma, from Cadiz, Spain, married, 42, deposes confirming 8 above.

10 - Francisco Rovira, from Orihuela, bachelor, deposes confirming 8 and 9 above.

11 - Governor White grants; Ortega countersigns; Zubizarreta attests and notifies Lorenzo Rodriguez.

12 [E] Royal title to 100 acres granted, 1/9/1805, by Governor White to Lorenzo Rodriguez. Zubizarreta attests. Alvarez certifies true translation, 6/3/1845.

13 [E] Alvarez' extract, 6/3/1845, from descriptive list, No. 644, Nicholas Rodriguez, 300 acres.

[Dossier contains translation of 1.]

Rodriguez, Santos            Con. R 22; DG V 376

[Bound together 1-4 in Spanish:]

1 - Clarke certifies, 4/6/1818, plat of 2,000 acres on the north side of Dunn's Lake, for Santos Rodriguez to whom they were granted on 1/24/1818.

2 - S. Rodriguez petitions, 12/22/1817, for 2,000 acres east of St. Johns River at the place called Donsleck, bounded on the south by Montocar, north by the Businel [Eusebio Bushnell] saw mill, east by pine lands and west by St. Johns River. He rendered many services during the 1812, revolution. Governor Coppinger grants, 12/24/1818.

3 - Royal title to 2,000 acres east of St. Johns River, granted, 6/10/1818, by Governor Coppinger to Santos Rodriguez. Entralgo attests and certifies true copy.

4 - Santos Rodriguez petitions, 8/4/1818, to have the boundaries of the land rectified and recorded, since a mistake has been made. The new and correct boundaries and situation are: The land is situated

about 12 miles east of St. Johns River, bounded on the south by Dunn's Lake, north and west by vacant pine lands and east by lands of Fernando de la Maza Arredondo; Governor Coppinger's grant, 8/4/1818.

5 [E] NOTE: There is a small clip of paper as follows: "N. 638------ 1828 - Report 1, No. 36. Santos Rodriguez, 2,000 acres. This claim was by mistake included in the descriptive list of confirmed land claims. It is now, with other claims, in the possession of the register and receiver for re-examination according to an act of Congress."

[Dossier contains 1 copy and 1 translation of 1.]

Rodriguez, Teresa                 Con. R 23; DG IV 283

1 [E] Teresa Rodriguez, widow of Miguel Marcos, claims through John Simonton, 5,500 acres at Big Spring on the creek running from the west and emptying into St. Johns River about 2 miles north of Long Lake; Governor Estrada's grant, 10/18/1815, to Miguel Marcos.

2 [S] Miguel Marcos, Sargento y Teniente de premio del Real Cuerpo de Artilleria [first sergeant and sub-lieutenant by brevet of the corps of royal artillery], detached in this city, petitions, 10/18/1815, for the 5,500 acres above mentioned. He has rendered service to the crown for more than 40 years, especially in the revolt of 1812, and now he has many children to rear. Governor Estrada grants.

3 [S] Clarke certifies, 5/2/1821, for Miguel Marcos, a plat of acres at Big Spring, west of Languna Larga along St. Johns River.

4 [E] Alvarez' extract, 6/30/1845, from descriptive list, No. 629, Teresa Rodriguez, 5,500 acres.

5 [E] The decree of the board considers the claim valid and recommends it, December 16, to Congress for confirmation.

[Dossier contains a copy and 2 translations of 2.]

Rogero, Antonio     Con. R 24; DG IV 297

1 [E] claims a lot measuring on the front north and south 59 varas inglesas, without and to the north of St. Augustine on the west side of the road leading from the City Gate, bounded on the north by lands of Juan Triay, east by said road and west by St. Sebastian River; Governor White's grant to Augustin Santana, 8/8/1810.

2 [S] Margarita Prat, widow of Augustin Santana, soldado de destacamento de Artilleria nacional [soldier of the national artillery detachment] petitioned, 7/27/1820, to transfer the title of 59.6 acres to Antonieta Villa, widow, who has children and slaves with whom she will be able to cultivate the land, whereas she, Margarita Prat, is unable to do so. Governor Coppinger grants, 7/27/1820.

3 [S] Tomas de Aguilar, official of the secretary of this government, in the absence of Juan de Pierra, Teniente de grenaderos del 3º batallion de Cuba [lieutenant of grenadiers of the 3rd batallion of Cuba], certifies that upon petition of Augustin Santana for the above mentioned lot, within the 1,500 varas of the fortifications, formerly belonging to Jose Peso de Burgos, Governor White granted under the conditions stated by the commandant of engineers, viz., petitioner must clear it, and in matters of defense relinquish it without protest when asked by the government to do so.

4 [E] Fatio's abstract of claim.

5 [E] Alvarez' extract, 12/29/1834, from descriptive list, No. 643, Antonio Rogero, 59 1/6 yards.

Rose, James                              Con. R 25; DG V 376

1 [E] claims, through Clarke, 25 acres in Pevett's Swamp about 4 miles westward from St. Augustine which place had formerly been cultivated by a colored man called Clark. Governor White's grant.

2 [S] Jim Ros, black, free, who has served sentence, and upon being freed married Teresa Fish, also free, petitions through Jose de Zabalia, 7/11/1810, for 100 acres at Pevet Swamp, south of the lands of Jose Clark, also black and free. Governor White requests information from Bartolome Castro y Ferrer for Ros' conduct during his sentence, and from Robert Yonge, under whom Ros has worked. Alvarez certifies copy, 11/28/1840.

3 [S] Jim Ros petitions, 8/21/1810, for the above mentioned 100 acres. Governor White again requests the above information.

4 [S] Bartolome Castro y Ferrer, 9/15/1810, reports favorably concerning the conduct of Ros during his sentence, from 4/2/1806 to 7/27/1807, and Governor White grants 25 acres. Antonio Alvarez certifies true copy, 11/28/1840.

5 [S] Aguilar certifies, 8/15/1810, that upon petition of Ros for 100 acres, Governor White granted 25 acres.

6 [E] Charles W. Clarke deposes, 11/10/1827, before Fatio that he knows of the land in question, formerly cultivated by a colored man named Clarke, who lived there many years, and that Ros later took possession of it, built a cabin, planted trees and raised crops.

7 [E] Francis Phillip Sanchez deposes, 11/20/1827, that Ros, head of a family, took possession of the above tract about 13 years ago, since which time he has cultivated and built houses on it.

8 [E] Benjamin and J. B. Clements' certified plat of 25 acres on Pevet Swamp and lying north of a survey in the name of Daniel Halbert, being in sec. 46, T. 7, R. 29 S & E, for James Ros. Chainmen: John M. McGough and John Hagan. Robert Butler approves, March 1835.

9 [E] Fatio's abstract of the claim.

Ross, Francis J., et al.     Con. R 26 [See descriptive list, No. 763]

[Bound together 1-3 in English:]

1 - Phillip Dell petitions, 2/10/1801, for 800 acres, his quota, corresponding to himself, his family and slaves, on St. Johns River at the plantation abandoned by Francisco Richard and that adjoining it, also abandoned. Governor White requests information from the commandant of engineers, 2/11/1801.

2 - Pedro Dias Berrio reports favorably to the granting of this land upon conditions that petitioner should leave it upon request of the government if it were necessary for the defense of the territory. Governor White grants; Pierre certifies copy. Sanchez, translator and interpreter of superior court, certifies true translation.

3 - By a decree the superior court, 11/16/1840, finds this claim valid, and Joseph B. Lancaster is appointed to locate and survey this land. Fairbanks certifies true copy, 12/20/1844. Judge Bronson vouches for Fairbanks' signature.

[Dossier contains a copy each of 1, 2 and 3.]

Rouse, James     Con. R 27; DG IV 299

1 [E] claims, through Bellamy, 640 acres on St. Marys River in Nassau County, East Florida, as a donation grant. He has not received a title either from the Spanish or from the British government.

2 [E] J. D. Hart deposes, 6/26/1827, before Fatio, that he is acquainted with James Rouse, who has had possession of the above tract of land since March 1819, has cultivated it and built houses on it, and has never received any title to any other land.

Rua, Juan de la            Con. R 28; DG IV 102

1 [E] James R. Donelson's certified plat of 672.97 acres on Escambia River, being in secs. 2 and 3, T. 2, R. 31 N&W, and in secs. 34 and 35, T. 3, R. 31 N&W, for Juan de la Rua. Chainmen: Robert Mosely and William Washington. Robert Butler approves.

2 [E] Certificate No. 16 of the register's office, Tallahassee, 9/20/1831, for plat of 672.97 acres, sec. 40, T. 2, R. 31 N&W, on Escambia River for John de la Rua, under Ignacio Barrios.

[Dossier contains 2 copies of 1.]

Ruiz, John            Con. R 29; DG IV 102

1 [E] James R. Donelson's certified plat of 536.08 acres being in secs. 23, 25 and 26, T. 4, R. 31 N&W, for John Ruiz. Chainmen: Robert Moseley and William Washington. Robert Butler approves.

2 [E] Certificate No. 11 of the register's office, Tallahassee, for plat of 536.08 acres, sec. 38, T. 4, R. 31 N&W, on Escambia River, for John Ruez, on his own right.

[Dossier contains 1 copy of 1.]

Rushing, John G.            Con. R 30

1 [E] claims, through Gibbs, attorney-in-fact, 200 acres on the north side of St. Johns River; Governor Estrada's grant, 11/27/1815.

2 [S] Juan G. Rushing with his wife, Isabela Fondine, 5 children, and 7 slaves, petitions, 10/1/1815, for 500 acres consisting

of a tongue of land north of St. Johns River between Great and Little Dunn's Creeks, beginning at the confluence of said creeks and running all the length of the Clapboard Creek to its mouth. Governor Estrada requests, 10/27/1815, information from the military and political commandant of St. Johns River concerning the conduct, property and ages of the children and slaves of Rushing.

3 [S] Thomas Llorente reports, 11/21/1815, that Rushing has 5 children from 2 to 9 years of age; 1 negro slave with 3 children at Jaime Smith's, others at Jaime McHardy's and still another at Jorge Clarke's. He has them thus scattered because he has not land of his own for them to work. The information concerning Rushing's character is excellent. Governor Estrada grants 205 acres, 11/27/1815; Aguilar certifies true copy.

4 [S] Clarke certifies, 2/1/1817, plat of 125 acres on Dunn's Lake as part of the 205 acres granted north of St. Johns River for Juan G. Rushing.

5 [S] Clarke's certified plat, 2/8/1817, of 60 acres at Clapboard Creek north of St. Johns River for John G. Rushing, which together with the above 125 acres makes the 205 granted him, 11/27/1817.

6 [S] Clarke certifies plat, 2/1/1818, for the 125 acres at Dunn's Lake for John G. Rushing.

7 [E] Alvarez' extract, 11/29/1844, from descriptive list, No. 284, John G. Rushing, 200 acres.

[Dossier contains a copy of 1 and 2 translations of 2, 3, 4, and 1 of 5.]

# INDEX TO PERSONAL NAMES
(Page numbers refer to Introduction; other references to claims)

Abreu, --, Spanish notary, M 38
Acosta, Domingo, K 14
Adams, John Quincy, pp. viii, xliii
Addison, John/Juan, M 27; P 29, 48
Aguilar, Francisca, R 20
Aguilar, Juan A. de, N 10
Aguilar, Tomas de, p. lvi; K 3, 11-13, 18; L 4, 7, 10, 31, 32; M 25, 27; P 13, 20, 25, 26; R 8, 13, 24, 25
Albion, a slave belonging to Angus Clark, M 22
Alfred, Eliza Cook, P 22
Alfred/Alford, Julius C., P 22
Allen, William Henry, pp. xlix, 1; L 3, 5; M 38, 49; P 11, 56
Alvarez, Andres, L 9
Alvarez, Antonio, pp. vi, vii, viii, ix, x, xii, xiii, xxxix; K 7, 8, 10, 13, 17, 18, 19, 24; L 2, 3, 4, 6, 7, 8, 11, 12, 14, 21, 22, 24, 29, 30, 31; M 20, 21, 23, 24, 40; N 6; P 15, 22, 36, 62; R 4, 7, 18, 24, 30
Alvarez/Albarez, Jose, L 4; P 25
Alvarez, Phillip/Phelipe/Felipe, L 9
Andreu, Jose, K 3
Andreu, Michael/Miguel, K 3; O 11
Andrew/Andreu, John/Juan, K 12; L 9; O 11; P 5
Andrew, Thomas, O 5, 6
Apodaca, Juan Ruiz de, pp. xxiv, lv, lxii
Armstrong, Benjamin, M 48
Arnau, Francisco, L 9
Arnau, James/Jamie, P 12
Arnau, Stephen/Esteban, M 26; P 12; R 7
Arnold, John, K 10
Arrambide, Juan Xavier de, P 31
Arredondo, Fernando de la Maza, Jr. and Sr., p. xlv; M 9

Arredondo, Fernando de la Maza, Jr., L 11, 12, 30; M 13, 18, 21, 32, 34; O 9; P 4, 8, 20, 33, 37, 57; R 5, 9
Arredondo, Fernando de la Maza, Sr., L 12; M 12, 29; P 27
Arredondo, Joseph M./Jose de la Maza, M 18, 43; P 19; R 9
Arredondo y San Felices, Juan de la Maza, K 3, 12-14; M 18, 32; P 4, 20, 31, 57; R 9
Artacho, Maria A., K 4
Ashley, Lodowich, P 22
Ashley, widow, M 25
Ashton, John, K 11, 13, 19
Atkinson, Andrew, M 32
Atkinson, George/Jorge, P 21
Avice, Julian, M 20
Ayala, Manuel, L 12
Ayres, Benjamin, M 42

Bacun, Lorenza, P 45
Bagley, Carlota, R 1
Bagley, Margarita, R 1
Bagley, Peter, R 1, 6
Bagley, Ysabel, R 1
Bailey, Lewis, L 5
Bailey, William, R 1
Balderas, Antonio, p. lv
Barcelo, Nicolas, L 8; M 13
Barker, William, R 1
Barone, Charles, P 64
Barr, D. H., O 2
Bauson/Bouysson, William/Guillermo, M 41
Baya, Joseph/Jose, L 27; O 11; P 56
Beeler, Charles, P 59
Bell, Marmaduke, M 24
Bellamy, Abraham, L 2, 8, 29; M 11; R 1
Bendicho, Manuel Fernandez, R 21
Benitez y Galvez, Bartolome, M 6
Bennett, Robert, O 9

Bergallo, Joseph, M 48
Berrio, Pedro Diaz, L 1, 21, 22;
  M 33, 38; O 6; P 9, 22, 26
Berzaztrize, Sebastian, R 21
BetHune, Farquhar, M 17, 40, 41,
  42, 48, 49; O 5, 6; P 21
Betts, Samuel, M 48
Bisbee, H., Jr., p. xiii
Bissett/Bisset/Biset, Robert,
  M 26; P 15
Black, Alexander, M 18; see also
  McDowell & Black
Black, Honoria, M 21
Black, Margarita, M 21
Blackstone, William, p. xviii
Blair, William W., pp. xxxix,
  xlvii
Blunt, Reding, K 16
Boney, Jose, K 21
Bosquet/Bousquet, Jose Maria,
  K 14; P 30, 31
Bowden, John M., O 2
Bowden/Borden, Isaac, Jr., N 7
Bowden, Isaac, Sr., N 7
Bowden/Bowdin, Maria, N 7
Bowden, Moses, K 11
Bowden, Thomas, P 67
Bradford, Robert H., see Drummond
  & Bradford
Brady, Joseph, K 2
Briggs, Cyrus, L 8
Broadaway, Diller [Delia?], L 5
Bronson, Isaac H., L 10, 11; P 24;
  R 6, 26
Broward/Browfard, Charles, L 1,
  8
Broward/Boward, John, L 8
Brown, Betsey Ann, R 15
Brown, J., M 41, 43
Brown, Thomas, R 15
Browne, Montfort, p. lxi
Bryan, Langley, M 40
Bunch, John, M 28; P 4
Burch, Guillermo, M 34
Burdecat, Louis de, p. lv
Burgevin, Andres, K 3, 15, 19;
  L 9, 11, 12, 13; M 12, 18,
  19, 20, 21, 26; N 1; O 10, 11;
  P 26, 30, 36; R 4, 6, 7
Burgevin, Carolina, M 20

Burgevin, Constantino, M 20
Burgo, Jose Peso de, M 9; R 24
Burke, John, L 15, 17
Burnell/Burnett (*), Eliza, M 6
Burnell, John, R 1
Burr, David A./H., L 4, 32
Butler, Robert, p. lv; K 2, 6,
  14; L 1, 11, 14, 15, 16, 17,
  23, 24, 26, 28, 32; M 1, 2,
  12, 22, 29, 32, 36; N 5, 12,
  14; P 3, 6, 20, 25, 44, 54;
  R 2, 16, 28, 29
Byrd, John, Jr., P 3, 44

Caballero, Antonio, P 13
Cain, Elizabeth, see Kane
Call, Richard Keith, pp. vi, xv,
  xxvii, xlix, liii
Callava, Jose Maria, p. lxiii
Calvet, Buenaventura, L 12
Campbelle, James, R 1
Campos, Pedro, M 17
Caniche/Camiche/Corniche, Paul
  M., O 2
Canovas, Antonio, P 1
Capo, John/Juan, M 24; P 35, 36
Capo, Pedro, R 18
Carmona, Jose Hernandez, P 13
Carney, William, L 30, 31;
  O 6, 7
Caro, Joseph E., pp. viii, ix,
  x, xi; K 5
Carreras, Diego, P 36, 38
Carroll, William Thomas, L 12,
  32; P 24
Carter, Isaac, L 1
Cartilla, Manuel, K 20
Casas, Luis de las, P 31
Castro y Ferrer, Bartolome de,
  N 4; P 56; R 5, 25
Cashen, James/Santiago, M 11,
  43
Cashen, Susana, M 35, 43
Catron, John, L 32
Cavedo, John/Juan A., M 34; O 10
Chapin, S. B., p. iii
Chester, Peter, p. lxi
Chifan, Joseph, K 18
Chocochate Indians, L 12

---

*Shown in American State Papers as Burnett.--DG, IV, 278; G&S, IV,
602.

Christopher, William, L 32
Clark, Angus, M 22, 25
Clark, Jose, R 25
Clarke, Archibald, K 14
Clarke, Charles W., L 1; M 7, 28b; N 1, 2; P 29
Clarke, George J. F., pp. xxiii, xxiv, xxvi, xxvii, xlv, lv, lxv; K 8, 11, 13, 14, 16, 17, 21, 22, 23; L 4, 5, 6, 7, 10, 12, 20, 25, 29, 30, 31, 32, 41; M 51; N 1, 2, 3, 6; P 31, 26, 30, 52, 60; R 8, 12, 13, 22
Clarke, Margarita, P 30
Clarke, Roberto, M 13
Clay, Henry, p. viii
Clements, Benjamin, K 2, 4, 5; L 23, 28; M 1, 3, 4; N 5, 14; P 14, 20, 44, 57; R 2, 5, 19, 25
Clements, J. B., L 23, 28; M 1, 3, 4; N 5, 11, 14; P 15, 20, 44, 57; R 2, 5, 19, 25
Clinch, Duncan L., N 2
Coit, Diego F., K 14
Colee, George, R 17
Coleman, Santiago, P 55
Coll, Dona Aqueda, L 9
Collel, Francisco, p. lxiii
Collins, Juan Bautista, N 7
Commins, Honoria, P 30
Cook, Daniel P., p. vi
Cook, George, N 7; P 22
Cook, George Ann, P 22
Cook, Jane, P 22
Copp, Belton A., N 2; R 1, 14
Coppinger, Jose, pp. xxvii, lv, lxii; K 8, 11, 14, 16, 17, 19, 20, 21, 22, 24; L 5, 9, 11, 12, 13, 14, 20, 31, 32; M 9, 20, 26, 31, 40, 50; N 6, 8; O 9, 11; P 5, 13, 19, 25, 30, 32, 37, 39, 56, 60; R 4, 7, 10, 18, 22, 24
Cornell, Thomas F., N 1, 2, 3
Corniche, Paul, see Caniche
Cowan/Cowin, Robert, K 9; N 7; P 65
Cowan/Cowin, Susan, N 7
Cox, Isaac N., L 12
Crawford, Andrew A., M 3, 4, 16; P 55, 59, 64

Crawford, William H., pp. xxv, xliii
Creighton, Alexander/Alejandro, M 22; P 40
Creighton, John/Juan, K 9; M 22; P 66
Creighton, Mary, P 66
Crespo, Blas, M 39
Crews, Isaac, R 1
Crispo, Manuel, O 2
Cromer, Eusebio Maria, L 31
Crosby, Sara, M 22
Crosby, Thomas, M 22
Cyrus, a slave belonging to Angus Clark, M 22

Daly, John/Juan, P 34
Daly, Maria, P 34
Darley, James, p. ii
Darling, Gamaliel, M 59; P 12
Darling, John, P 24
Davis, Hugh P., K 3
Davis, Jonathan, p. lxv
Davis, T. Frederick, p. xxxvii
DeBrahm, William Gerard, p. lxv
Decatur, Stephen, P 28
DeLaire, James, p. lxv
Delany, Daniel, M 32
Delap, Charles, P 17
Delespine/Lespine, Joseph/Jose de, P 5, 30
Dell/Dil, Jose, M 13
DeSoto, see Soto
Dewees/Devees, Philip/Felipe, L 14; M 13; R 26
Dexter, Horatio S., M 5; O 1; R 17
Dil, Jose, see Dell
Dodd/Dood, Benjamin, R 1
Dominguez, Manuel, P 44, 45
Donelson, James R., M 2, 10; R 28, 29
Dorr, Francisco, M 40
Douglas, Thomas, L 14
Downing, Charles, p. xlix; L 10; O 9; P 47
Drake, C. I., K 2
Drayton, William, p. lvii
Drummond, William, L 3, 4
Drummond & Bradford, L 32
Drysdale, John, L 23; M 6, 18, 19; P 67

Dublin, a slave, M 22
DuBoso, John, K 3
DuBoso, Margaret, K 3
Dupon, Paul/Pablo, M 20, 21, 56;
 P 5
Dupont, Bike, M 38
Dupont/Dupon, Josiah/Josias,
 p. lxv; K 10; L 2; M 9, 29
Durnford, Elias, pp. lxi, lxv

Eastlake, Ana, P 53
Eastlake, Samuel, p. lxv; K 10,
 14, 18; L 3, 18, 22; M 29; N 7;
 O 4; P 40, 49, 53; R 9
Edinburgh, Philip, P 63
Eliot/Elliott, John, pp. lxi, lxii
Elliot, Francis Augustus, P 18
Ellis, Thomas C., N 4
Entralgo, Juan Blas de, K 10, 11,
 12, 13, 14, 15, 17, 20, 24;
 L 12, 13, 31; M 18, 28a, 32, 40,
 52; N 4; P 8, 20, 31, 37, 57;
 R 5, 10, 19, 22
Escoderos, Leslie, M 22
Eslick, Dr., surveyor, p. lxv
Espinosa, Andrea, Jr., M 12
Espinosa, Andrea, Sr., M 12
Espinosa, Diego, M 12
Espinosa, Diego Juan Jose, M 12
Espinosa, Fania, M 12
Espinosa, Josefa de la Encarna-
 cion, M 12; P 8
Espinosa, Sebastian, M 12
Estacholy, Domingo, K 14, 21
Estacholy, Franicsco, K 20
Estrada y Torro, Juan Jose de,
 pp. xxiv, lxii; K 3, 12, 13,
 22; L 4, 7, 14, 30; M 5, 18,
 26, 28a, 31, 53; P 4, 24, 30,
 62; R 23, 30
Evans, Enos, P 44
Evans, Jesse, M 4
Exum, James W., L 6; 26, 28; M 1,
 4, 51; N 5, 12, 15; O 8; P 6,
 15, 46, 50, 59; R 2

Facio, Francisco Felipe, Jr., M 22;
 R 14
Facio, Francisco Felipe, Sr., M 22
Fairbanks, George R., K 24; L 10,
 11, 12; M 27; P 24, 66; R 6, 26
Fairbanks, Samuel, K 5; P 42; R 8
Falaney, Jaime, M 54; R 19

Fallary, Fernando, P 57
Fate, John/Jan/Jean Eduard, M 13,
 32
Fatio, Felipe, M 22
Fatio, Francisco Jose, pp. xxxix,
 xliv, xlix; K 3, 10, 14, 24;
 L 1, 2, 7, 12, 13, 14; M 27,
 28b; P 21, 33, 47; R 11, 14,
 20, 25
Faulk, John, K 9
Fenwick, Joseph/Jose, L 4; M 48
Fernandez, Domingo, L 31; M 11
Ferreyra, Francisco, P 31
Ferreyra, Juan Bautista, R 7
Fish, Jesse, p. xiv
Fish, Teresa, R 25
Fitzpatrick, Valentine, P 29
Fleming, George/Jorge, L 9; M 22;
 N 4
Fleming, Joseph/Jose, M 30
Floyd, Davis, pp. xxxix, xl, xlvii,
 xlviii, xlix; M 26, 41, 48
Folch/Vicente y Folch, Juan
 p. lxiii
Fondine, Isabela, R 30
Fontan, Mariano, P 13
Fontane, John M., P 62
Forbes, James Grant, p. vi
Forbes, John/Juan, M 9; P 15
Forraster/Forrester, Juan, K 9;
 M 22; P 41

Fuentes, Ramon de, P 31
Fujada, Pedro, L 25
Funk, Jonathan, p. lxv
Furman, Charles M., N 1

Gage, E. V., p. i
Galvez, see Benitez y Galves
Garcia, Rafael, L 12
Gavilan, Dolores, M 12
Garvin, William/Guillermo, M 5,
 40; N 1, 2, 3
Gay, Anthelm/Antelem/Anthelam/
 Antelm/Attelm, p. vi; L 10,
 11; M 27
Gayler, John, P 63
Geiger/Gaiger/Gayler, John/Juan,
 K 12; M 18, 26; R 9
Gelabert, Francisco de Paula,
 p. lxiii
Gianopoly/Gianopole, George/
 Jorge, M 59

Gianopoly, John/Juan, L 9; M 59; P 53
Gibbs, George, K 9, 10, 11, 12, 13, 14, 15, 16, 17, 19, 20, 21, 22, 23; L 11; N 6, 8; R 30
Gibbs, Kingsley B., L 10
Gibson, Edward R., pp. vii, viii; M 23, 24
Gill (*), Teofilo, M 6
Gill/Hills, Theresa, see Theresa Marshall
Gillett, Emma M., L 32
Ginaudy, Miguel de, M 22
Giraldo/Giralde/Girald, Antonio, M 26; P 8
Girt, James M., see McGirt
Gobert, Carlos, R 5
Gomez, Eusebio Maria, p. xlv; K 21; R 5
Gomez, Tomas, L 12
Gonzales, Fernando, P 30
Gonzales, Juan, P 30
Gonzales, Mateo Manrique, see Manrique
Gonzales, Susana, P 30
Gonzales, Ysavel, P 30
Gonzalez, Manuel, P 46
Gonzalez, Maria Carreras, P 30
Gonzalez, Mathew, M 49
Gonzalez, Santiago, M 47, 49
Goodwin, Francis/Francisco, R 10
Gordon, Arthur, R 1
Gordon, Harriet Precilla, R 1
Gordon, John, p. xiv
Goss, J. H., p. xiii
Gould, Elias B., R 17
Grair, Tomey, M 25
Grant, James, p. lxi; L 22; M 24, 45; P 17
Greeks, colonists, see New Smyrna
Green, James, K 7; L 5, 24, 12, 14
Guez, Francisco, M 26
Guiber, G., K 19
Guillet, Julia, M 20
Gujot, James, R 18
Gumby, Lewis, R 1
Gumley/Gumby, Mary, R 1

Hagan/Hogan, John, P 20; R 5, 19
Hagens, John, M 47
Hagens, Joseph, L 3; P 66
Hainsman, Barbara, see Hindsman
Hale, William, N 1
Haley, John, R 1
Hall, Eleanor, P. 66; see also Eleanor Pritchard
Hall, James/Santiago, N 7; P 66, 67; R 17
Hall, John, p. liv
Hall, William, M 43
Hamilton, Alexander, pp. xxv, xxvi, xxxvii, xxxix, xl, xli, xliii, xliv, xlv, xlvi; O 9
Handley, John, L 24; M 31; P 60
Hanham, I. R., N 9
Hanson, John M., K 15; M 44
Harrison, Samuel, L 1; M 42
Harrison, Tipton B., p. xxxvii
Hart, Daniel S., R 15
Hart, J. D., R 27
Hartley, William, K 19; L 22
Hayword, Elijah, N 14
Heintsman, Anthony, see Hindsman
Henderson, --, M 34
Hendricks, Isaac, P 66
Herman, Richard B., N 4
Hernandez, Joseph/Jose Marion/Mariano, p. xlv; K 11, 21; M 12, 18; P 20, 29, 31, 33
Hernandez, Rafael, P 2
Hernandez & Chauviteau, L 12
Hertas, Antonio, see Huertas
Hesell, James, K 3
Hesell, Thomas M., K 3
Hibben, James, Jr., N 1
Hibberson & Yonge, K 11, 22
Higginbottom, Burrows, K 13, 16
Higginbottom, Ysabela, K 13, 16
Hijuelos, Catalina de Jesus, P 26
Hill, Ana Maria, M 6
Hill, Cristina, M 12; P 35
Hill, Juan, M 6
Hill, Juana, M 6
Hill, Louise Biles, p. lix
Hill (**), Maria, M 6
Hill (***), Maria, M 12

---

*Shown in American State Papers as Lodowick Hills.--DG, IV, 278; G&S IV, 602.
**Daughter of Theresa Marshall.
***Nee Maria de la Sanchez.

Hill, Maria del Carmen, K 15
Hill/Hills, Theresa, see Marshall
Hill, Ysabela, M 6
Hindsman/Heintsman/Hainsman, Anthony, M 45
Hindsman/Heintsman/Hainsman, Barbara, M 45
Hobkirk, G., K 16; P 41
Hogan, John, see Hagan
Hogan, Reuben, P 49
Hogan/Hogans, widow, R 6, 9
Hogans, Daniel, P 66
Hogans, Lewis Zacarias, P 66; R 13
Holcombe, Robert/Roberto, K 14
Hollingsworth, John, K 18; R 1
Hollingsworth, Timothy, K 18; M 29, 30; R 1
Hollingsworth, William, K 18
Hollomon, Harmon, L 5
Hollomon, Hinchey, L 5
Holzendorff, Juan, M 32
Houston, Elizabeth, P 43
Houston, John, P 40, 41, 42
Hovey, Charles/Carlos, M 15
Huerta, John/Juan, M 18
Huertas/Hertas, Antonio, L 9, 11; O 10; P 10, 30
Huges, Joseph, see Hughes
Hughes/Huges/Yus, Joseph/Jose, M 37; P 38
Huguon, Lewis, pp. xli, xlix
Hull, Ambrose/Ambrosio, K 10; M 8
Hunter, Morris, p. xxxviii
Hutchison, Robert/Roberto, K 13

Inglish, Wesley, K 6; L 26; M 1, 51; N 11; P 46, 50
Innerarity, John/Juan, K 2
Italians, colonists see New Smyrna
Ives, Jeremiah, P 48

Jack, a slave, M 22
Jack, Pedro, N 142
Jackson, Andrew, p. viii
Joaneda, Jose, M 12
Joaneda, Magdalena, M 12
Johnson, William, L 15
Johnstone, George, p lxi
Jones, Mrs., landowner, P 22

Jones, John, P 66
Jones, Margarita, M 25
Jones, Rebecca, R 15
Jones, William/Guillermo, R 9; 12, 14
Juaneda, Antonio, P 5

Kane/Cain, Anne, K 18
Kane/Cain, Elizabeth/Isabel/Ysavel, K 18
Kane/Cain, Elizabeth, Jr., K 18
Kane/Cain, Margaret, K 18
Kane, William/Guillermo, K 18
Kehr, John D., K 1
Kelker, Jacob, K 2
Kennedy, Angus, P 17
Ker, R. B., L 5, 24; M 31
Kerr, Jayme, P 29
Kershaw, John, K 3
Keyser/Kiser, Joseph C., K 3, 4, 5, 6
Kindelan y Oregon, Sebastian de, K 11, 12, 13; M 18, 27, 32, 41; N 1, 7; P 20, 29, 32, 49, 57; R 9, 12
King, Charles R., L 32
King, Thomas, K 7, 8
King, W. P., P 24
Kingsley, Anna M./Ana Madgigine K 9
Kingsley, Zephaniah, K 9, 10, 11, 12, 13, 14, 15, 16, 17, 18, 19, 20, 21, 22, 23; M 52
Kunen, Marian/Mary, K 24

Lain, John Joseph, P 66
Lamb, Thomas, L 1
Lancaster, Joseph, pp. xxxix, xlii; R 26
Lane, William, L 2
Lang, Isaac, L 3
Lang, Richard, N 6
Larcey, Joseph, L 4
Lasseter, Reuben, L 5
Law, Edmund, p. vii
Lawrence, John Henry, p. xlii; O 9
Lawrence, William/Guillermo, K 18; L 30; M 29, 32
Leath, Hartwell, L 6
Lecount/LeCoun, John/Juan, L 7
Ledwith, Garret, L 8
Lee, Amos, K 14

Lee, Guillermo Diego, P 31, 32
Leonardi/Leonardy, Antonia, L 9
Leonardi/Leonardy, Bartolome, L 9
Leonardi/Leonardy, Josefa Clorinda, L 9
Leonardi/Leonardy, Juan, L 9
Leonardi/Leonardy, Roque/Rocco, L 9
Leonardy/Leonardi, Maria, L 9
Lesley, Eliza Cook, see Lifley Isabel
Leslie/Lesley, Eliza/Isabel Cook, see Lifley/Lesley
Leslie, Flora, L 10
Leslie/Lifley, Juan, K 10
Lespine, Jose de, see Joseph Delespine
Levy, Moses E., L 10, 11, 12, 13; M 11
Lewis, Frankee, L 15
Lewis, James L., R 18
Lewis, Jonathan, L 16
Lewis, Mary, L 17
Lewis, Polly/Tolly, L 17
Lewis, Surl, L 15
Lifley/Lesley, Eliza/Isabel Cook, K 10; P 22
Llambias, Geronimo, p. viii
Llambias, Juan, P 7
Llorente, Thomas, K 9; R 30; see also Lorente
Lofton, John/Juan, Jr., L 18, 19, 20, 21, 22
Lofton, John/Juan, Sr., L 18, 19, 21, 22
Lofton, William/Guillermo, L 18, 19, 20, 21, 22
Long, Christina, P 40
Long, George/Jorge, L 20, 23; M 47; P 40
Long, Jesse, L 24
Long, Joseph, P 40
Long, Mathew, P 40
Long, Samuel, P 40
Lopez, Bartolome, L 24; P 2
Lopez, Francisco, L 26
Lopez, Justo, K 1
Lopez, Manuel, L 30
Lord, Benjamin, p. ixiii; P 15 18
Lorente, Jose, M 32; see also Llorente

Lorenzo, John/Juan, L 27
Love, Alexander, L 28
Love, Charles, L 29
Lowe/Low, John/Juan, landowner on Bell's Creek, L 30, 31, 32
Lowe, John, p. xxxix
Lowe, John W., L 32
Lubian, Jose, P 35
Luckett, Craven P., p. xxxviii
Lynch/Linch, Patrick/Patricio, pp. vii, xliii; K 24; M 13, 20; N 4; P 36
Lynch, Peter/Pedro, P 51; R 18

McClelland/McClellan, Thomas, M 4; P 14, 59; R 2
McClure, John, K 23
McCormic, James, R 3
McCullock, Joseph/Jose, M 22
McCully, William, M 15
McDavid, Joel A., M 16
McDonald, Randolph, M 22
McDonell/McDonald, Ferdinand D., M 17
McDougal/McDugal, M 26
McDowell/McDowall & Black, M 18, 19, 20, 21
McDowell, Alexander/Alejandro, M 22
McDowell, Andrew, M 18, 19; see also McDowell & Black
McFee, Constance/Constancia/ Constanza, M 22; P 29
McGirt, Daniel, L 31; N 7
McGirt, Jacob/Jacobo, L 30
McGirt/McGirtt/McGirth/Girt, James/ Jaime M., M 23, 24, 25
McGough, John M., L 23; M 37, 38; R 5, 19
McGregor, Gregor, p. xxiv
McHardy, Caroline Esabel/Isabel Williams, M 26
McHardy, Robert/Roberto, p. lxv; K 24; M 19, 20, 26, 27, 28a; N 1; O 9; P 4, 5, 19, 56
McHarthi, --, arbitrator in land dispute, L 14
McHenry, William, M 17
McIntosh, J. M., K 10
McIntosh, John/Juan Houston, p. xlv; K 14; L 32; M 28b; 28c, 29, 30
McIntosh/McYntosh, Maria, see Maria Mills

McKay/McKeys, Alexander, L 11, 12
Mackay, George, L 15, 16, 17
McMurren/McMarrin, Frederic, M 31
Macon, Edgar, pp. xxxvii, xxxix, P 24
McQueen/McQuin, John/Juan, K 14, 20; M 29, 31, 32, 33; P 20
McYowell, John M., M 7
Madam, James, R 1
Maestra/Mestre, Louis, M 1
Malagosa, Juan, M 2
Malloy, Daniel, M 3
Manning, Drury, M 4
Manrique, Mateo Gonzales, p. lxiii
Manton, --, overseer for George Sibbald, K 12
Manucy, John, M 29
Marcos, Miguel, R 23
Marin, Francis, M 5; P 57
Marrot, Pedro, pp. xxi, xxiii, xxiv, lxv; K 10, 14, 18; L 2, 3, 9, 18, 19, 22; M 9, 22, 23, 24, 29; N 7; O 4; P 23, 40, 49, 53; R 1, 8, 9
Marshall, John, P 24
Marshall, Manuel, M 45
Marshall, Theresa, M 6
Martin, George W., M 7
Martin, Henry B., M 8
Martin, M., L 32
Martinely, Geronima, M 9
Martinely, James/Jayme, K 13
Martines/Martinez, Matias, P 26
Mas, Jose, P 13
Mason, Littleberry, M 10
Masot, Jose, p. lxii
Mattair/Mattain, Lewis/Louis/Luis, L 31; M 11, 12
Maury, Joseph, P 6
Maxey, Peter, M 13
Maxey, Robert Clark, M 13, 32
Mazells/Mozell/Mozells, John, M 14
Meazles, --, hired farm laborer in E. Fla., L 6
Meers, Margarita, M 35
Meers, Samuel, M 35
Mestre, Antonio, M 37
Mestre, Bartolome, M 37, 38
Mestre, John/Juan, M 39
Mestre, Mariana, M 38
Mestre, Pedro, M 24, 36
Mialls/Mills, Francis, M 34
Midicis, Francis/Francisco, M 12, 34; P 5

Middleton, John, M 40, 41, 42, 43
Mier, Antonio, L 14; O 10, 11
Miles, Francis, K 15; M 44, 45
Miller, David Solomon Hill, p. lxv; K 18; R 11
Miller, Francis/Francisco, K 15
Mills, Maria McIntosh, M 47, 48, 49
Mills, William/Guillermo, M 47, 48, 49
Minchin, Christopher, M 50
Ming, Frederick L., K., K 6; L 26; M 51; N 4, 11, 12, 14; P 46, 50, 63
Ming, James S., M 1; N 1, 11; P 63
Ming, S. L., M 1
Minorcans, colonists, see New Smyrna
Mins, Jose, M 47
Miralla, Jose Antonio, M 51; P 46
Miralla, Joseph M., P 50
Miranda, Francis Xavier, M 12
Miranda, Pedro, K 15, 20, 21; L 11, 13; M 9, 12, 20, 52, 53, 54, 55; P 8, 30, 35, 36, 37; R 5, 18, 19
Mitchel, Octavius, M 56
Mitchel, Robert, M 56
Mitchell, Andrew, M 2
Mitchell, Thomas, L 15, 17
Mizels, Jehu, L 6
Molina, Antonio, M 57
Mollere, Maria D., M 58
Monro/Monrro, Maria/Marria, M 7
Monroe, James, p. xliii
Monte de Oca, Antonio, P 13
Montero/Montes, Antonio, M 59
Montes de Oca, Juan Gonzales, P 30, 32
Morales, Bartolome, p. lxi; K 14; L 21
Morales, Francisco, K 14, 22; M 40
Morales, Juan Ventura, pp. xxviii, lxiii
Morlen, Maria, P 67
Morling, Demoivt, P 4
Mosely, Robert, M 2, 10; R 28, 29
Mosier, Francis, P 7
Moultrie/Moultry, John, p. lxi
Mozells, John, see Mazells
Mulcaster, Frederick George, p. lxv; P 15, 17

Munen, Frederick M., M 11
Munoz, Lucas, P 38
Munzo, Jose Pedro de, P 57
Murat, Achille, P 7
Murphy, Thomas, pp. vii, xlviii,
　xlix; K 1, 10, 11, 12, 13, 14,
　15, 17, 20, 24; L 2, 3; N 4;
　P 30, 33, 36, 37
Murray, George, pp. xlviii, xlix;
　L 13; P 16, 17, 18
Murray, Richard, P 56
Murrell, Maria R., P 54

Napier, Thomas, N 1, 2, 3, 4
Nelly, Christopher, P 51
Nelson, William, N 6
Newton, Jesse, K 8
Nobles, Hannah, N 7, 8
Noda, Joseph/Jose de, N 9, 10
Noriega, Joseph, N 11, 12, 13,
　14, 15
Norris, John M., P 63
Norris, Ralph W., L 10

Okekeoaka Indians, L 12
Oliver, John, O 1
Oliveros, Raphael, O 2
O'Neal, Henry, M 4; O 3
O'Neal/O'Neilly, Margaret, O 4,
　5, 6
O'Neal, William, O 7
O'Neill, Arthur/Arturo, p. lxiii
　L 20; M 30; R 8, 12
O'Neilly [O'Neal?], Asa, O 4
O'Neilly [O'Neal?], Ebrero, O 4
O'Neilly [O'Neal?], Margarita, O 4
Ordozgoity, Vincent, O 8
Oregon, Sebastian de, see Kinde-
　lan y Oregon
Ormond, Emanuel, O 9
Ormond, James/Santiago, K 24;
　M 28a; O 9; P 4
Ormond, Mrs. Russell [James?],
　K 24; O 9
Ortega, Ann, O 10
Ortega, Jose de, p. lxii; K 10, 20;
　M 29; N 7; O 4; P 53; R 21
Ortega, Lazero, K 3; L 14; O 11
Ortega, Sebastian, K 20
Overton, Samuel R., pp. xxxiv,
　xxxviii, xxxix
Owel, Joel F., see Yowell

Pacetty, Domingo, L 32
Pacety, Andrew, P 1, 2
Paint, T., L 16
Pall, Teresa, L 9
Palma, Antonio, R 21
Palmes, Diego, P 3
Palmes, George, P 4, 5
Palmes, Oliver/Oliveros, P 4, 5
Pangua, Benito de, K 13, 22; L 31;
　M 11, 31
Pania/Pancia/Pancer/Pancier,
　Antonio, p. lix
Panton, Leslie Co., K 10; L 11,
　12; M 5, 27
Papy, Andres, O 2; P 7, 8
Papy, Ann, P 9
Papy, Gaspar, P 9; R 10
Papy, Miguel, P 10, 11; R 10
Pardo, Juan Bautista Collins,
　R 10
Paredes, John, P 12
Paredes, Juana, P 12, 13
Parker, Needham, P 14
Pate, Juan E., K 18
Payne, Letitia, P 17
Payne, Robert, L 11; P 15, 17, 18
Peavatt, Joseph, P 15, 16, 17, 18
Pegui, a slave, M 22
Pellicer/Pelliser, Francis/Fran-
　cisco, M 38, 47; P 19, 20, 34
Pellicer, Santiago, M 20
Pelot, James, P 21
Pelot, John Francis, P 21
Pengree/Pangree, Rebecca, K 10;
　P 22
Pengree, William, K 10, 18; P 23
Penn, Thomas H., M 34; O 10
Percheman, Juan, K 24; P 24
Perchet, Juan N., p. lxv
Perez, Nicolas, N 10
Perpall, Gabriell William/Guiller-
　mo, M 22, 32, 47; N 1; O 11;
　P 5, 25, 27, 29, 33, 37, 38, 39
Petty, Sarah, P 40, 41, 42
Philibert, Pedro, P 44, 45, 54
Phillips, Joseph, P 46, 51
Picket, Seymore/Seymour, L 1; P 47,
　48, 49
Pierra, Juan de, K 12, 20; L 1, 8,
　21, 22, 25, 30; M 28a, 28b; N 7,
　9; P 4, 8, 12, 34, 56, 65; R 9
　10, 14, 24, 26

Pillion, Francisco, M 18
Pintado, Vicente Sebastian, p. lxv; P 50
Pleym, Andrew, P 51
Plummer, Daniel, P 53
Plummer, James, P 66
Plummer, Prudence, P 53
Pol, Antonio, P 54
Pol, Josefa, P 55
Ponce, Antonio, P 1
Ponce, Jose, R 14
Ponce, Tole, R 9
Pons, Agaty, P 57
Pons, Anna, P 8
Pons, Antonia, P 57
Pons, Antonio, P 56
Pons, Asa, O 4
Pons, Francis/Francisco, P 57
Pons, Mathias, P 57
Pons, Peter, P 57, 58
Ponton, Cayetano, L 12
Potts, Henry, P 59
Preston, James P., p. xxxviii
Prevatt, Joseph E., L 24; P 60 61
Priest, Gabriel, P 62
Prieto, Felipe, P 62
Pringle, Abraham, P 64
Pritchard, Amelia, P 66
Pritchard, Eleanor, P 65; see also Eleanor Hall
Pritchard/Prichard, Robert, P 52, 65, 66, 67
Proctor, Antonio, P 68
Puente, Fernando de la, K 20
Puentés, Juan, L 9
Purcell/Porcel, John/Juan, pp. xxiii, xxiv, lxv; L 30; M 33; O 5; P 57
Putnam, Benjamin A., pp. ix, xiii; L 12, 32; M 5, 17; P 7, 11

Quesada y Arrocha, Juan Nepomuceno, pp. xx, xxxi, lxv; K 13; L 9; M 6; 9, 22, 23, 24, 25, 30; N 2; P 13, 20, 31, 57; R 21
Quibent, Lewis, R 17
Quigles, Migel, P 14; Q 1
Quintana, Jose Gregorio, K 12, 18; M 12, 17

Radan, James/Jame, R 1
Rain, Cornelius, L 22

Rain, Joseph, L 22; R 1
Ramirez, Alexander/Alexandro, p. lxiii
Ramirez, Salvador, R 2
Randall, Thomas, p. vi
Randall, William, p. lxv
Randolph, Arthur, K 9; L 11; M 5, 17, 28a; O 9; P 20, 33
Rawls, Cotton, R 3
Reggio, Pedro, p. lxv
Reid, Robert Raymond, L 14
Rengil, Manuel, M 25; P 31, 57
Rengil, Miguel, M 22, 38
Reyes, Mrs., of St. Augustine, p. viii
Reyes, Domingo, R 4
Reyes, John, M 28a
Reyes, Jose Bernardo, K 3, 15, 21; M 21; P 57; R 5
Reyes, William/Guillermo, L 11, 15
Reynolds, William, pp. vii, viii, xxxix, xliii; K 1, 10, 12, 14, 15; L 1, 2, 3, 12, 27; M 21, 29, 32, 52, 53; P 5, 22, 24, 27, 31, 35, 53, 66; R 14, 19
Ribero, Francisco, M 40
Ricardo, Lewis, M 34
Rice, William, Jr., R 1
Richard, Francis/Francisco, K 15; P 37
Richard, John B., R 6, 15
Riddle, James, p. vi
Riggio, Pedro, P 50
Riobo/Rioboo, Thomas P., R 16
Ripley, Fileon, K 3
Rivas, Paul, K 6
Riz, James [attorney], R 17
Riz, James [landowner], R 17
Riz, Tryphena, R 17
Robinson, Edward S., R 18
Robinson, Eliza, R 18
Robinson, Jeremy, p. vi
Robinson, Silvester, R 18
Robion/Robira, Charles, R 19
Robles, Juan Jose, M 39
Rodgers, Thomas, P 43
Rodman, John, K 3; M 26, 27, 28a; O 7; P 66
Rodriguez/Rodriges, Domingo, R 20
Rodriguez, Juan, R 21
Rodriguez, Lorenzo, R 21
Rodriguez, Nicholas, R 21

Rodriguez, Teresa, R 23
Rodriquez de Leon, Domingo, K 13
Rodriquez, Isabel/Ysabel, K 20
Rodriquez, Jose Francisco, L 9
Rodriquez/Rodrigues, Santos, L 9; M 12; R 22
Rogero, Antonio, R 24
Rogers, Josiah, P 22
Rogers, Louisa, P 22
Rogers, Louisa Cook, P 22
Rolfe, Frederick, R 1
Rolfe, George, p. lxv
Rolle, Denys, p. xvi
Romas, Bernard, p. lxv
Romero, Manuel, K 20, 21
Ros, Jim, R 25
Rosa, slave, M 22
Rose, James, R 25
Rosello, Juan or Juan de Rusello, K 14
Ross, Francis J., R 26
Rouse, James, R 27
Rovira, Francis/Francisco, M 12, 22; P 31; R 21
Row, Seton Wedderburn, p. lxv
Rua, Filo E. de la, p. xi
Rua, Juan de la, R 28
Ruiz, John, R 29
Rushing, John G., R 30
Russell, Juan, P 19
Russell, Samuel, R 8

Saavedra, Ruperto, L 13
Saavedra, Tomas, P 30
Sabate/Sabates/Sabote, Paul/Pablo, Jr., p. xxviii; M 28a; O 11
Sabate/Sabote, Paul/Pablo, Sr., L 9
St. Maxent, Francisco Maximilian de, p. lxiii; P 50
Salom, John/Juan, M 45; P 53
Sams, Marianna, P 29
Samson, James, P 16
Sanchez, Antonio Abad, M 12
Sanchez, Bernardino, M 10, 12, 32; N 7
Sanchez, Bernardo, K 10, 18; M 12; R 26
Sanchez, Francisco Pasqual, K 15; M 18, 19, 20, 21, 34; P 35
Sanchez, Francis Philip, R 25 K 15

Sanchez, Francisco Xavier, K 15; M 30, 44, 45
Sanchez, Joaquin, L 9
Sanchez, John/Juan Manuel, K 15
Sanchez, Jose, P 35
**Sanchez, Jose M., P 20, 35**
Sanchez, Joseph/Jose S., p. xliii; M 6, 12, 33, 53
Sanchez, Maria Andrea, M 12
Sanchez, Maria de la O, M 12
Sanchez, Maria Fermina, P 35
Sanchez, Maria Florancia, P 35
Sanchez, Nicolas, L 14; M 12
Sanchez, Ramon, M 12; P 35
Sanchez, Santiago, P 35
Sanchez, Simon, L 14
Sanchez, Venancio Hill, P 35
Santana, Augustin, R 24
Sawyers, James M., M 3, 16; P 55, 59, 64
Scarlett, R. L., p. iii
Scurry, David, P 66
Sebastian, Albert, M 4; P 14, 59; R 2
Segui, Benito, P 13
Segui, Bernardo, K 12, 13, 14; L 7; M 5, 12; P 57
Segui, Bernardo Jose, K 10; M 21, 30, 32; P 7, 10, 20
Segui, Bernardo Jose, Sr., p. xlv
Segui, Juan, P 13
Seton, Charles, O 7
Sibbald, Charles/Carlos, L 32; M 40 49
Sibbald, George, K 12
Sibbald, Jane, K 12; M 43
Sibley, James W., M 26
Sibley, John, M 43
Silcock, William, P 47
Simonton, John W., R 23
Simmons, W. H., pp. vii, viii
Sims, Charles, M 4
Slogens, Danier [Daniel?], M 39
Smith, -- Col., R 17
Smith, Waters, L 17; M 52, 53
Snyder, Solomon, L 15
Solane/Solano/Salina, Alexander, L 11, 13, 32; M 29
Solano, Bartholomew, P 11
Solano, Lorenzo, K 20
Solano, Philip/Felipe, M 18; P 8, 31

Solon, Juan, M 34
Solon, Miguel, M 34
Soto, Jose de, p. lxiii
Sowerby, Henry, P 17
Sparkman, Stephen, L 6
Stafford, Ellis, L 5, 6; N 6
Stallings, Ann, P 66
Stallings, Elias, P 66
Standley, Shadrich, L 29
Stearns, M. L., p. xii
Steele, William F., p. xxxvii
Stiles, --, Dr., P 66
Story, James, N 4
Stout, John, M 17
Streeter, Squire, O 1
Strong, John B., L 18, 19, 21, 22; M 8, 38; P 40, 41, 42, 49, 51, 52
Suarrez, Antonio, K 20
Sumaras, Manual, M 58
Summerall, Joseph, L 22; P 40, 52, 66
Suwarres, Manuel, L 28
Suwarres, Sebastian, L 28
Swancy, Daniel see Sweeney
Swasey, Alexander G., p. xlv
Sweney/Swancy, Daniel, N 8; R 10
Sweney, Henry/Enrique, N 8

Taney, Roger B., L 12, 32; M 27
Tate/Tetes, John/Juan Eduardo, pp. xxiv, lxv
Taylor, George, M 32; P 27
Taylor, Robert, P 17
Teran, Francisco, L 1
Thomas, David, L 20; M 30; P 52, 53; R 8, 12, 14
Thompson, William, L 22
Tibbit, Augustus, M 30; P 53
Tingle, James S., p. vii; M 34, 38, 53; N 1, 10
Toms, Samuel, K 12
Tonyn, Patrick, pp. lvii, lxi; M 45; P 15, 18
Toole, Santiago, M 18
Torre, Manuel de la, L 9
Torres, Guillermo, R 9
Torres, Josefa, M 12
Torro, Juan Jose de, see Estrada y Torro
Townsend, John W., K 3, 14; M 12, 22, 32, 36, 53
Tracy, Charles C., L 11, 13, 32; M 29, 52

Travers, Juan, M 32; R 21
Travers, Thomas, L 9; M 52; O 11; P 25, 27
Travers, William/Guillermo, N 4; P 15, 16, 18
Triay, Francisco, M 9
Triay, John/Juan, M 9; P 2; R 24
Triay, Pedro, P 38
Tucker, Charles S., N 1
Turdas, Thomas, M 49
Turnbull, Andrew, pp. xvi, xvii; P 17
Turner, Edward, L 4; R 15

Ugarte, Jose Maria, L 9; M 21
Uptegrove, John, L 1
U. S. Boards of Commissioners, pp. i, iv, v, ix, xviii, xix, xxiv-xxvii, xxxiii, xxxv-xli, xliii-l, liv-lvii

Varnes, Isaac, K 3; M 12, 22, 32, 36, 53
Vattel, Emeric de, p. lviii
Vaughn, Daniel, L 32
Villalonga, Miguel, L 25
Viscoles, Charles, L 12

Walles, Joseph, P 5
Ward, G. W., p. xxxix
Ware, Nathaniel A., pp. xxxiv, xxxviii
Warrs, Jesse P., M 47
Washington, Henry, K 3, 14; L 1, 8; M 12, 32, 33, 36, 53; P 47
Washington, William, M 2, 10, 20; R 28, 29
Waterman, Eleiaza, L 31
Way, Andrew, p. lxv
Wells, Daniel, Jr., L 24; M 31; P 60
Wheeler, James, M 23
White, Enrique, pp. xxii, lxii, lxiii; K 1, 10, 12, 13, 14, 15, 18, 20, 21; L 1, 8, 10, 22, 23, 25, 27, 30, 31; M 8, 12, 13, 18, 20, 25, 28b, 29, 30, 32, 44; N 7, 9, 14; P 2, 4, 9, 22, 34, 37, 48, 65; R 14, 18, 21, 24, 25, 26
White, Joseph M., pp. xviii, xxxiv, xxxvi, xxxviii, lviii
Whitehead, John, L 15
Wickes, Bernard, K 24

Wickes, Isaac, K 12, 24; N 4, 7; O 9
Wiggens, Anna/Ana, M 41
Wiggens, Juan, P 29
Wildes, Nathaniel, K 13
Williams, Caroline Isabel/Esabel/Ysabel, see McHardy
Williams, John, R 4
Williams, William, R 4
Willis, George, R 3
Wilson, Emily L., p. viii
Wilson, Henry, P 45
Wilson, Joseph S., p. xii
Woods, Thomas T., p. lxv; K 8; L 5, 6, 32; P 60, 61
Wright, Henry, K 9

Ximines, Jose, K 21

Yeats, David, M 45; P 17
Yguiniz, Jose Antonio de, L 30
Yonge, Henry/Enrique A., K 13 M 41
Yonge, Phillip/Felipe Roberts, K 11, 23; L 11; M 41; P 31
Yonge, W. P., M 42
Youngblood, Jesse, N 6
Young, Richard M., pp. ix, xii, xiii
Yowell/Yumell, Joel F., L 23; M 7, 37, 38
Yshnardy, Miguel, P 25
Ysquierdo, Fermin, L 9
Yumell, Joel F., see Yowell
Yus, Joseph, see Hughes

Zamorano, Gonzalo, M 6
Zavalia/Zebalia, Jose de, K 3; M 38, 41; R 25
Zespedes/Cespedes, Vicente Manuel de, p. lxii
Zubizarreta, Jose de, K 10, 12, 13, 15, 18, 30; M 12, 22, 29; N 7; O 5; P 31; R 21
Zully, C., M 20
Zuniga, Mauricio, p. lxiii

INDEX TO PLACE NAMES
(Unless places are outside Florida the state has not been shown.
Page numbers refer to Introduction; other references to claims.)

Alachua [section], L 11; N 2
Alligator Point Punta del Cayman,
 K 3; P 13
Amelia/Amalia Island, K 14, 22;
 L 1, 20, 21; M 11, 18, 31, 33,
 39, 41; N 5; P 21
Amelia St., Fernandina, M 48
Anastasia Island, R 21
Aprecele Spring, M 27
Armstrong Branch, P 1
Arroyo Bog, R 11

Barra Chica, M 47; P 34
Barra Chica Creek, K 14
Bartaria Island, P 39
Battery in Fernandina, K 1
Bayou Mulatto, P 3, 44, 54
Bayou Taxar, P 46
Beauclere/Beauclark's Point, N 7;
 P 64
Bell's Creek, L 30
Bell's Old Field, L 30
Bell's Plantation, M 25
Bell's River, L 30, 31, 32
Big Bend, M 50
Big Creek, L 6
Big Hammock, M 7; P 26
Big Potsburgh Creek, R 8
Big/Long Lake, L 11
Big Spring, L 11, 13; R 23
Big Swamp, M 7
Biscayne Bay, L 16, 17
Bissett's/Bisset's/Biset's Place,
 M 26; see also Swamp and Plan-
 tation
Black Creek, L 11; P 62
Blide's Oil Field, M 53
Bluff of St. Johns River, see
 San Vicente Ferrer
Boggy Hammock, R 11
Borguet, Santo Domingo, M 20
Box's Plantation, M 11
Branchester, R 9

Brandy Branch, M 14
Buckler's Bluff, P 65
Buen Retiro, P 28, 34
Buen Suceso, see Good Fortune
 Plantation
Buena Vista, N 4; P 25, 26
Buena Vista on Anastasia Island,
 R 21
Bushnel/Bushnell's Sawmill, R 22

Cabbage Hammock, M 5
Cabbage Spot, L 21
Cabbage Swamp, M 28b, 29, 53
Cadiz, Spain, R 21
Camden Co., Ga., K 14; N 1, 2;
 M 7; R 1
Camden, S. C., K 3
Camino Real, see King's Road
Cano de Bell, M 23
Cano de la Escolta, see Creek
 of the Guard
Cape Florida, L 15, 17
Casacola Plantation, M 34
Casa Pula, P 57
Castle, P 35
Cedar Branch, M 40
Cedar Road of Roco, K 11
Cedar Swamp, R 6
Cedar Swamp Creek, N 4
Chachala, L 11; N 1, 2
Charleston, S. C., K 3; M 8, 19;
 N 1, 2, 4
Chocochate Road, M 20
Chocichatty/Chocochate, L 12
Clapboard Creek, R 30
Conicut River, M 10
Constitution Square, Fernandina,
 M 43
Cook/Cooke Plantation, K 10
Cowford, M 39; P 66; R 11
Creek of the Guard/Cano de la
 Escolta, R 21

Cuba, M 39; P 26
Cunningham Creek, M 22; P 22
Cuscawilla/Cuscavilla, L 11
Cypress Swamp, O 2

Damietta, O 9
Damas St., Fernandina, M 42
Darien, Ga., M 38
Deep Creek, P 11
De La Feria, see Tomoco River
Doctor's Branch or Creek, L 31, 32
Doctor's Lake, K 10, 11, 18; L 11; O 2; P 23, 51
Donsleck, see Dunn's Lake
Drayton/Dryton Island, K 12; R 7
Dudley/Dudles, R 8
Dunn's Creek, K 19; L 5, 7
Dunn's Lake, K 9; O 1; R 22
Durbin's Swamp, M 50; P 16
Dutch Island, M 7
Duval Co., M 29; P 66; R 1

East Florida, K 24; M 27; P 24, 66; R 1
Edward Turner's Plantation, R 15
Egan's Creek, K 22, 23
El Arroz, L 9
Encinal Grande, P 25
Escambia Bay, K 2; N 11, 12, 14; P 44; Q 1
Escambia River, K 4, 5; M 2, 4; N 11; P 64; R 28, 29

Fair River, p 35
Favorito Plantation, M 29
Feria del Camino Real, M 39, 44
Feria Plantation, M 44
Fernandina, K 1, 14, 20, 21, 22, 23; L 8, 31; M 7, 41, 42, 43, 48, 49, 53; P 25; R 20
Ferry of St. Nicholas, P 66
Flemming's Island, L 11
Florence McLean's Isla, see Hog Island
Florida, Province of, K 10; P 23; R 1
Flounder Creek, N 1, 3
Ft. George Island/St. George Island, K 14
France, P 28
Fuente del Alamo Plantation, see Laurel Spring

Fuerte de San Diego, M 12

Gate of St. Augustine, P 38
Georgia, State of, K 9; M 25; P 22, 23, 66; R 1
Gonzales Creek, P 27
Good Fortune Plantation/Buen Suceso, K 10
Goodham's/Goodman's Lake, P 67
Goodwin's Plantation, R 10
"Governor Grant"/"Gobernador Grand," /"Chimneys in Governor Grand", K 3; M 9, 23
Graham's Creek, L 23
Graham's Swamp/Pantano de Graham, M 18
Grand Bayou, L 26
Great Britain, K 10
Great Dunn's Creek, R 30
Greensborough, Georgia, P 22
Grotto Plantation, M 34
Guana Creek, K 3; M 9, 23, 24; O 11; P 13

Hagen's Creek, M 33
Halifax River, M 18; O 9; P 32; R 4
Havana/Habana, Cuba, K 20; L 9, 12; M 9, 18; N 1
Hickory Bluff, M 14
Hickory Grove, P 40
Higginbottom's Bluff, a part of Higginbottom Plantation, K 13, 16
Hillsborough River, M 26; N 1
Hog Island/Florence McLean's Isla, R 7
Holmes' Creek, M 37
Holmes' Plantation/Old Field/Savanico/Savanica, M 37
Hope Hill on St. Johns River, L 12
Hoswell see Mount Oswald
Hunny Branch Creek, P 10

Isla de San Jorge, see Island of St. George
Isle del Tigre see Tiger Island
Island of St. George/Isla de San Jorge, M 29
Indian/Is/Ys River, L 32; M 26, 28b, 29

Indian Road, K 11, 19
Ireland, M 17
Jacksonville, M 29; P 66
Johnston Creek, M 47
Jule Creek, P 27
Julington Creek, L 20, 22; P 16, 22, 40

King's Landing Creek/Wharf, L 9
King's Road/Camino Real, K 15; P 47
Kingsley Island, R 7

La Arbolada de los Morales, see Mulberry Grove
La Feria River, see Tomoka River
Laguna Larga, R 23
Lake City, L 32
Lake George, K 11; L 7, 11, 12 13; M 20; R 7
Lake Valdez, see Second Lake
Lamb's Old Field, L 1
Lane Plantation, L 2
Lane's Branch, see Six Mile Creek
Lang, L 3
Langford's Creek/Sanford Creek, O 4, 5, 6, 7
"Langley Bryan", M 40
Laurel Grove Creek, K 10
Laurel Spring Plantation, K 10 18
Lewis' Place, L 15
Liberty Hall Plantation, M 22
Little Bar, M 38
Little Dunn's Creek, R 30
Little Lake, M 20
Little Matanzas Bar, P 34, 37
Little Orange Grove, M 19, 20
Little St. Marys River, K 11, 13, 24; P 40
Live Oak Landing, K 8
Lofton's Bluff, P 40, 42
London, Eng., M 13, 32
Long Lake, see Big Lake
Long's Hammock, M 14

Macaris, M 59
McDougal's/McDugal's Plantation, M 26; N 1
McDougal's Swamp, M 26
McGirth's Creek (now known as Ortega River, but a branch of this river is known as McGirth's River or Creek), L 30; O 2

McQueen's Mills, R 6
Mangler Island, M 26
Mants/Mantas/Manats Island, see Stony Point Island
Marshall's Plantation, P 12
Martin's Island, M 25
Matanzas Bar, L 23

Matanzas Territory, P 29; R 7
Mester Men Plantation, L 9
Miami/Miame River, L 16, 17; M 29
Mickasuky Road, L 11
Mill/Miller/Milergue Creek, M 13; P 1
Mill's Ferry, N 6
Miss Nealey's Creek, L 24
Mitchel's Grove, M 56
Monroe Co., L 15
Monte de Laurel Colorado, R 11
Monte Hermosa, M 29
Montocar, R 22
Moral Grueso, see Mulberry Grove
Morgan's River, P 9
Moses Creek, P 7
Mosquito Lake, M 28b
Mosquito River, P 4
Mosquito South Lagoon, N 1
Mosquitoes, K 24; M 8, 26, 28a, 59; P 29, 33
Moultrie Creek, R 5
Mount Ford, M 55
Mount Oswald/Hoswell, P 32, 33
Mozell's/Mazell's Lake, M 14
Mulberry Grove/Moral Grueso/La Arbolada de los Morales, M 29, 30

Nassau Co., L 5, 24; O 7
Nassau River, L 18, 21, 23, 24; N 6; P 34
Nepomuceno Creek, K 18; P 23
New River, L 15
New Road, K 11
New Smyrna, p. xvi; N 4
New St., Fernandina, M 42
North Bay Creek, R 15
North Carolina, M 19
North/Yolomato/Tolamato River/ Creek, L 9, 32; M 6, 34, 36, 45, 53; N 9; O 11; P 12, 13
Nuestra Senora Guadulupe, see Royal and Military Hospital

Old Store, M 27
O'Neil Swamp, L 31
Orange Grove in the Swamp, K 19

Pablo Creek Road, see San Pablo
Pantano de Grahm, see Graham's Swamp
Pargue Plantation, R 12
Pasco de las Palmas, K 23
Payne's Savannah, N 1, 2
Pearson's/Pierson's Island, L 8
Pellicer's Creek, P 20
Pellicer's Plantation, P 20
Pelot's/Pilot's Island, L 8
Peno/Barreton, M 38
Pensacola Bay, N 12; P 50
Pensacola, City of, P 63
Perdida Bay, L 28
Pevett's/Pevet Swamp, R 25
Picolata, K 19; P 10; R 17
Plantage de Higginbottom, see Higginbottom's Plantation
Point Santa Esabela, R 14
Potsborough/Potsburgh Creek, R 6, 8, 13, 14
Punta del Cano del San Pablo, M 32
Punta del Cayman, see Alligator Point
Punta de Ysabel, R 9
Punta Negra, K 20; N 7

Quesada's Battery, M 39

Red Bay Hammock, R 11
Red Shoes Bluff, see Turvin's
Riverde, M 28b
Rolls Town/Rowle's Town, P 25
Rose's Bluff (or is it Bluff of Roses?), M 25, 53
Royal and Military Hospital/Nuestra Senora Guadulupe, R 4

St. Augustine, K 12; L 9, 27; M 6, 29, 34; N 9; O 11; P 1, 7, 17 33, 48; R 1, 18, 19, 24
St. Fernando St., Fernandina, M 48
St. Johns, in Duval Co., M 29
St. Johns Bluff, K 20, 21; R 6
St. Johns Co., M 40, 53; N 1; R 17
St. Johns River, K 9, 10, 12, 13, 19, 20, 21; L 4, 11, 12; M 5, 7, 11, 19, 20, 21, 23, 25, 27, 29, 40, 44; N 4, 7, 8; O 1; P 24, 26, 51, 65, 67; R 7, 8, 12, 13, 23, 30
St. John the Baptist/San Juan Bautista, L 19
St. Mary de Galves, Bay of, M 1, 57
St. Marys, Ga., L 30, 32; M 7
St. Marys River, K 7, 8, 13, 16; L 5, 18, 29, 31; M 14, 15, 20, 23, 25, 31, 33; N 6; O 7; P 41, 42, 61
St. Mary's River Bluff, L 5
St. Marys/Santa Maria District, M 50
St. Nicolas Battery/Port, M 39
St. Nicolas River, P 66; R 13
St. Sebastian River, L 25, 27; P 2, 27, 35; R 18, 24
St. Thomas/San Tomas, K 13
Salt Creek, L 9
Sandag's Bluff, K 16
Sanford Creek, see Langford's Creek
San Genaro's Plantation, M 9
San Jose Plantation, K 15
San Juan Bar, M 39
San Nicolas, K 9; P 35, 38
San Pablo Creek, M 11, 12; P 15, 17, 18
San Pablo Place, M 29
San Pablo Road, L 9
San Ramon Plantation, M 12
San/St. Diego, L 9; P 35
San Sebastian River, M 9
Santa Lucia, P 5
Santa Maria, see St. Marys
Santa Maria la Chica, L 3; M 55
Santa/St. Maria River, K 11; 20
Santa Teresa/Theresa, M 6
San Vincente de Ferrer, Port of K 20, 21; L 9; M 23, 32
Savanah, Ga., P 4
"Savanico"/"Savonica", M 37
Saw Mill Creek, K 11, 13, 17
Scambia River, see Escambia
Scotland, K 18
Second Lake/Lake Valdez, L 11
Seville, Spain, R 21
Ship Yard Creek, K 20
Ship Yards (tract), M 32

Six Mile Creek/Lane's Branch, L 4; M 47; P 1, 10, 47
Small Hope Place, M 13
Smith Creek, K 24; O 9; P 19
Smith Point, K 24
South Prong of Six Mile Creek, P 47
South Prong of Trout Creek, R 3
Springer's Branch, L 10
Spring Garden, L 11; R 4
Spring Garden Creek, M 19, 20
Spruce Creek, P 4
Stockade/Stockyeth, R 17
Stoney Point/Mantas Island, M 29
Strawberry/Strabare Hill, R 6, 10
Stuart's Swamp, M 28b
Sweet Spring Branch, L 6, 12
Sweetwater Creek, L 9

Talbot Island, K 14
Tallahassee, City of, N 14; P 44, 45, 63; R 29
Thompson's Branch, M 38
Tiger/Tyger Island, Isla del Tigre, M 35
Tolomoto River/Creek, see North River
Tomoka/Tomoca, M 28
Tomoka River, M 28a; P 4, 29, 33, 37, 38
Trader's Hill, M 31; P 40
Trout Creek, L 2, 4; R 1

Trout Creek Swamp, K 11
Tucker's Creek, L 8
Turkey Buzzard, M 7
Turnbull Plantation, P 30, 31, 32, 33
Turnbull Swamp, N 1; P 30
Turner's Swamp, P 60
Turvin's/Red Shoes Bluff, M 2, 4
Twelve-Mile Swamp, K 11, 13; M 50
Twenty-Mile House, M 50
Twenty-Mile Road, L 9
Two Brothers Creek, L 1
Tyger Hole, R 13

United States of America, M 18

Wagner's War, P 51
Walker's Swamp, K 8
Wanton's Old Field, R 17
Washington, D. C., L 11
Water Pond Creek, L 4
Weekiwa Creek, L 11
West Florida, K 3, 4, 5, 6; L 28
White Oak Creek, K 13
Wilder's Plantation, M 31
William's Place, R 4
Will's/Wilses Swamp, K 19; N 8

Yolemato/Yolomato Creek/River, see North River
Youngblood's Hammock, N 1
Ys River, see Indian River